Speaking Like a State

Founded in 1947 as a homeland for South Asia's Muslims, Pakistan has been beset by conflict throughout its existence. Alyssa Ayres' fascinating study examines Pakistan's troubled history by exploring the importance of culture to political legitimacy. As she explains, early leaders selected Urdu, the first language of a small percentage of Pakistanis, as the natural symbol of the nation's great cultural past. But due to its limited base, great efforts would be required to propagate Urdu and make it truly national. This paradox underscores the importance of cultural policies for national identity formation. In Pakistan's case, the process also fuelled resentments. By comparing Pakistan's experience with those of India and Indonesia, independent around the same time, the author analyzes how their national language policies led to very different outcomes. The lessons of these large multiethnic states offer insights for the understanding of culture, identity, and nationalism throughout the world. The book is aimed at scholars in the fields of history, political theory, and South Asian studies, as well as those interested in the history of culture and nationalism in one of the world's most complex, and challenging, countries.

Alyssa Ayres is Director for India and South Asia at McLarty Associates, Washington, DC. A cultural historian of modern South Asia, she has carried out research in India, Pakistan, and Indonesia. She has co-edited three books, including one forthcoming on power realignments between China, India, and the United States, as well as two volumes in Asia Society's *India Briefing* series. She received an AB *magna cum laude* from Harvard, and an MA and PhD from the University of Chicago.

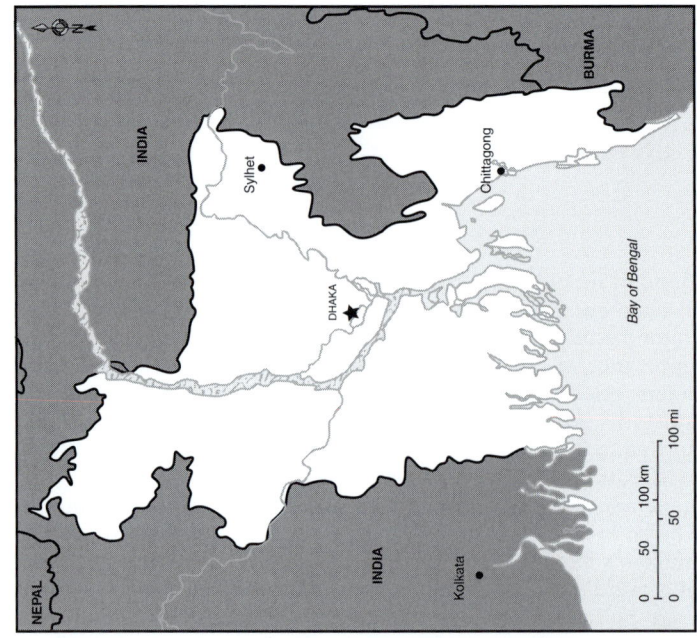
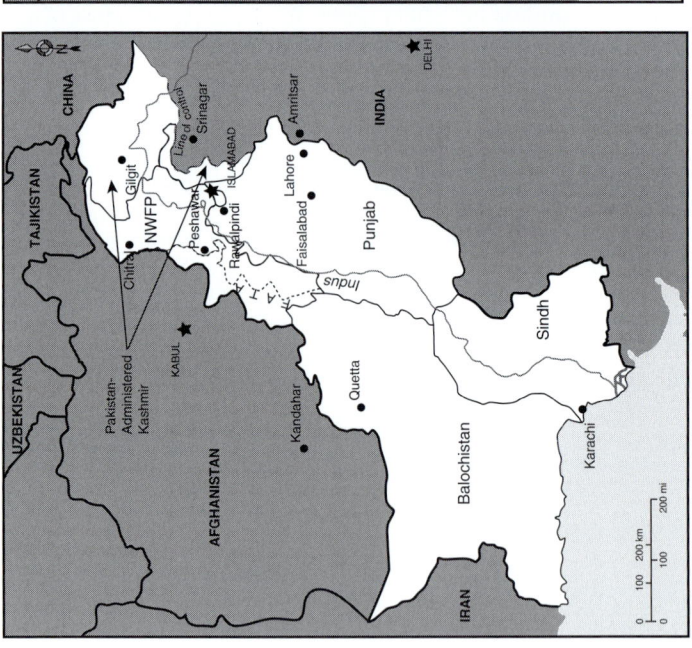

Map 1 (a) Basic map of Pakistan (b) Bangladesh, formerly East Pakistan/East Bengal province of Pakistan. Names and boundary representation are not necessarily authoritative.

Speaking Like a State
Language and Nationalism in Pakistan

Alyssa Ayres

CAMBRIDGE UNIVERSITY PRESS
Cambridge, New York, Melbourne, Madrid, Cape Town, Singapore,
São Paulo, Delhi

Cambridge University Press
The Edinburgh Building, Cambridge CB2 8RU, UK

Published in the United States of America by
Cambridge University Press, New York

www.cambridge.org
Information on this title: www.cambridge.org/9780521519311

© Alyssa Ayres 2009

This publication is in copyright. Subject to statutory exception
and to the provisions of relevant collective licensing agreements,
no reproduction of any part may take place without
the written permission of Cambridge University Press.

First published 2009

Printed in the United Kingdom at the University Press, Cambridge

A catalogue record for this publication is available from the British Library

ISBN 978-0-521-51931-1 hardback

Cambridge University Press has no responsibility for the persistence or
accuracy of URLs for external or third-party internet websites referred to
in this publication, and does not guarantee that any content on such
websites is, or will remain, accurate or appropriate.

Contents

	List of illustrations	*page* vi
	List of tables	viii
	Acknowledgments	ix
	Note on transliteration	xi
	Introduction	1
1	Articulating a new nation	16
2	Urdu and the nation	31
3	The nation and its margins	48
4	The case of Punjab, part I: elite efforts	67
5	The case of Punjab, part II: popular culture	87
6	History and local absence	105
7	Bringing back the local past	138
8	Speaking like a state: language planning	150
9	Religion, nation, language	171
10	Conclusion	188
	Bibliography	196
	Index	212

Illustrations

Figures

1	Cover image from the third edition of the pamphlet, "What Does the Pakistan National Movement Stand For?" (Cambridge: The Pakistan National Movement, 1942 [1933])	page 26
2	Cartoon: throne of education (from Saeed Ahmad Farani, *Punjābī Zabān Nahīn̲ Maregī*)	89
3	Cartoon: "This is the journey to the economic goal in the Islamic Republic of Pakistan?" (from Saeed Ahmad Farani, *Punjābī Zabān Nahīn̲ Maregī*)	90
4	Cartoon: Punjabi? Urdu, English inside? (from Saeed Ahmad Farani, *Punjābī Zabān Nahīn̲ Maregī*)	90
5	Cartoon: "Untitled" (from Saeed Ahmad Farani, *Punjābī Zabān Nahīn̲ Maregī*)	91
6	Film poster for *Maulā Jaṭ*	94
7	Film poster for *Maulā Jaṭ in London*	95
8	Pakistan in geological times (from Choudhary Rahmat Ali, *Pakistan: The Fatherland of the Pak Nation*)	107
9	Pakistan at the dawn of history (from Choudhary Rahmat Ali, *Pakistan: The Fatherland of the Pak Nation*)	108
10	Pakistan in the eighth century AD (from Choudhary Rahmat Ali, *Pakistan: The Fatherland of the Pak Nation*)	109
11	Pakistan in the eleventh century AD (from Choudhary Rahmat Ali, *Pakistan: The Fatherland of the Pak Nation*)	110
12	Pakistan in the thirteenth century AD (from Choudhary Rahmat Ali, *Pakistan: The Fatherland of the Pak Nation*)	111
13	Pakistan in AD 1318 (from Choudhary Rahmat Ali, *Pakistan: The Fatherland of the Pak Nation*)	112
14	Pakistan in AD 1398 (from Choudhary Rahmat Ali, *Pakistan: The Fatherland of the Pak Nation*)	113

15	Pakistan in AD 1525 (from Choudhary Rahmat Ali, *Pakistan: The Fatherland of the Pak Nation*)	114
16	Pakistan in AD 1605 (from Choudhary Rahmat Ali, *Pakistan: The Fatherland of the Pak Nation*)	115
17	Pakistan in AD 1700 (from Choudhary Rahmat Ali, *Pakistan: The Fatherland of the Pak Nation*)	116
18	Pakistan in AD 1751 (from Choudhary Rahmat Ali, *Pakistan: The Fatherland of the Pak Nation*)	117
19	Pakistan in AD 1780 (from Choudhary Rahmat Ali, *Pakistan: The Fatherland of the Pak Nation*)	118
20	Pakistan in AD 1795 (from Choudhary Rahmat Ali, *Pakistan: The Fatherland of the Pak Nation*)	119
21	Pakistan in AD 1933 (from Choudhary Rahmat Ali, *Pakistan: The Fatherland of the Pak Nation*)	120
22	The Pak Millat in 1940 (from Choudhary Rahmat Ali, *Pakistan: The Fatherland of the Pak Nation*)	121
23	The Pak Millat in 1942 (from Choudhary Rahmat Ali, *Pakistan: The Fatherland of the Pak Nation*)	122

Maps

1a	Basic map of Pakistan	*page* ii
1b	Bangladesh, formerly East Pakistan/East Bengal province of Pakistan	ii
2	Map of Pakistan and surrounding areas showing ethnic/linguistic boundaries	47
3	Map of Punjab Province of Pakistan	66
4a	India – before the linguistic states reorganization (state boundaries of 1950)	159
4b	India – after the linguistic states reorganization (states as of 2008)	159
5	Map of Indonesia showing ethnic/linguistic boundaries	170

Tables

1 The reach of Indonesian in Indonesia   *page* 182
2 Number of terms coined by subject area in Indonesian   183

Acknowledgments

No work is ever the product of a single individual, and I owe great debts to a very long list of people. This book's path was influenced by scholarly curiosities inflected by a desire for life outside the cloistered ivory tower. In the mid 1990s I interrupted my doctoral studies to serve first with the International Committee of the Red Cross, and then with the Asia Society in New York. That nagging sense of unfinished work led me to resume my academic program, which included a dissertation that grew into this book. Mentors from my time at the Asia Society encouraged me to make the leap, and I am deeply grateful to Nicholas Platt, Marshall M. Bouton, Robert W. Radtke, Vishakha N. Desai and Frank G. Wisner of the extended Society family for steering me in the right direction.

The University of Chicago incubated the ideas in this book, and supported me with many fellowships over the years. I thank Sheldon Pollock, Arjun Appadurai, and Carol A. Breckenridge for their reassurance and guidance as I returned to Chicago after six years away. Rapid changes in geopolitics meant that my original plan to carry out research in Pakistan was held up, along with my Fulbright-Hays fellowship, due to a security deterioration that remains the case today. Muzaffar Alam had the foresight to suggest a "Plan B," which fairly quickly became the primary line of inquiry. I could not have completed this work without his advice, nor the generosity and warmth of Rizwana Alam. Sumit Ganguly of Indiana University devoted more time to thoughtful critique of my chapters than I ever could have imagined. Ronald Grigor Suny offered many important suggestions to push this work toward greater accessibility for a broader readership, for which I am very grateful. But my greatest intellectual debt surely goes to Sheldon Pollock, who made sure I did not fall victim to numerous setbacks – and later encouraged me to keep pushing forward on the long path to making this a publishable book. A year-long residency at the Franke Institute for the Humanities allowed exclusive focus on research and writing during my final year, for which I thank Jim Chandler and Margot Browning. Thank you also to Jim Nye,

Sally Noble, Bronwen Bledsoe, Tom Thuerer, Elena Bashir, and Chika Kinoshita for all their wisdom and help.

In Pakistan, feedback from Imran Ali at the Lahore University of Management Sciences, and Tariq Rahman at Quaid-i-Azam University proved very helpful early on. Thank you to Anwar and Nabila Khan in Lahore, and to Sughra Imam for her kindness in Islamabad back in 2002. Pakistan's chair of the national language authority, Fateh Muhammad Malik, spent hours discussing language and nation. In Jakarta, where I spent six weeks at the Center for Strategic and International Studies, I must express a special thanks to Hadi Soesastro and Clara Juwono of CSIS. I learned an enormous amount about Indonesia's experience with national language formation as the result of my time there. Anton Moeliono, former head of Indonesia's Pusat Bahasa, provided the kind of insights that only a scholar-practitioner could. Many thanks as well to John McGlynn, founder of the Lontar Foundation, for his unfailingly good advice over the years. Interviews with Harimurti Kridalaksana, Lucy Montolalu, Chaider Bamualim, and Melani Budianta were invaluable. And Uri Tadmor shared his knowledge of all manner of subjects with infectious enthusiasm.

As the material here made its way to publication, I received constructive criticism and comments on the ideas here in discussions, as well as on drafts and articles, all of which greatly improved this work. Thank you to Amarjit Chandan, Daniel W. Drezner, Saeed Ahmad Farani, Husain Haqqani, C. Raja Mohan, Philip Oldenburg, Safir Rammah, Alok Rai, Kazim Saeed, Sunil Sharma, E. Sridharan, and Ashley J. Tellis, as well as the thoughtful critique from five anonymous referees – three for the *Journal of Asian Studies*, where the material on Punjab was published in 2008, and the two Cambridge reviewers who vetted this book in manuscript. The usual disclaimer, of course, applies.

There could be no better house for this book than Cambridge, and I am deeply grateful to Senior Commissioning Editor Marigold Acland for seeing the merits of this work from the very beginning. Sarah Green kept everything together as we moved into production. Once in production, Jamie Hood of Out of House Publishing and Gail Welsh guided the manuscript to its completion. Several extraordinary people read the book in page proof, and I will be forever grateful to R. Nicholas Burns, Bruce Riedel, Vishakha N. Desai, and Marshall M. Bouton for committing time they did not have to do so.

The nearly eight years over which this book was researched, written, revised numerous times, and ultimately published required enormous self-discipline. It would not have been possible for me to maintain this focus without my parents, who stepped in to help when I needed it. Last but not least, I thank Sadanand Dhume for his encouragement and support not just in life, but also on the page.

Note on transliteration

Urdu poses a number of transliteration problems. It contains sounds particular to Indic languages, such as a series of retroflex consonants and a differentiation between aspirated and unaspirated consonants. A font with diacritics used for Indic languages might be a good base. However, Urdu is written in a modified Arabic script, which introduces many additional distinct characters into the orthography. Many of these letters are not pronounced with any degree of distinction; the Urdu *zal*, *ze*, *zwad*, and *zoi* all sound the same, though to an Arabic speaker the four letters are very much distinct.

No font easily allows the transliteration of all the distinct Indic sounds as well as Perso-Arabic letters. In Pakistan, new experiments with romanization of Urdu are far less precise than the Library of Congress and Annual of Urdu Studies systems. So, for ease of reading, this book utilizes a hybrid scheme based on pronunciation, somewhere in between that of the Library of Congress romanization and the romanized Urdu variations in widespread use on the Internet. Words that appear more commonly in English, such as ulema, are not marked.

Vowels   a ā   i ī   u ū   e ai   o au
Consonants

be	b	*dāl*	d	*swād*	s	*gāf*	g
pe	p	*ḍāl*	ḍ	*zwād*	z	*lām*	l
te	t	*zāl*	z	*toi*	t	*mīm*	m
ṭe	ṭ	*re*	r	*zoi*	z	*nūn*	n / ṇ
se	s	*ṛe*	ṛ	*'ain*	'	*vao*	v / w
jīm	j	*ze*	z	*ghain*	gh	*he*	h
ce	c	*zhe*	zh	*fe*	f	*docashmī-he*	h
he	h	*sīn*	s	*qāf*	q	*ye*	y
khe	kh	*shīn*	sh	*kāf*	k	*hamza*	'

Notes:
1 Aspirated consonants are indicated with an "h." Thus *ghar* = house, *acchā* = good.

xi

2 Retroflex sounds, as depicted above, are differentiated by a dot below the letter.
3 The velar fricatives from Arabic (g̲hain and k̲he) are indicated with a subscript line.
4 Izāfat is indicated with -e- . Thus *jang-e-āzādī* and *tahrīk-e-pākistān*.
5 The v/w of conjunction is written *o*.
6 Doubled letters are written twice. Thus *qisse*.

Introduction

What is a nation? We are no closer to a parsimonious answer than was Ernest Renan in 1882 – but the nation has not weakened for lack of verbal concision. If anything, its power has grown, measured by the sheer number of nations and national claims that now swell our world.

One might expect the nation's hold to wane in our changed global landscape, one characterized by rapid increases in the circulation of people, images, and information across national boundaries. For even if we do not know quite what a nation *is*, we do know what it *does*: the nation, after all, claims and organizes political sovereignty – statehood – over discrete territory. Yet the erosion of sovereignty, the dramatic growth of migration, and the increasing ability of individuals to communicate across wide spaces on a scale never previously experienced has not dampened the appeal of the nation in any measurable way. In spite of globalization – some argue as a result of it – we find that the local impulses inherent to nationalism perdure.

The growth and spread of nationalism, as many scholars have explicated, operates through a political logic of cultural difference, one which at its endpoint posits that different peoples have a right to rule themselves. During the twentieth century, this basic assumption structured the emergence of new nation-states resulting from the decolonization wave, the boundaries of which – often created artificially – contained dizzying cultural diversity. If the successes of nationalism offered a more just world to those who had been imperial subjects, their corollary epistemology would naturalize the idea that nation-states by definition lay claim to a unique and unified culture and history – giving rise to the challenge of integration as a major issue for culturally diverse populations united by citizenship in newly formed states.

But the subsequent decades did not uniformly result in the "integrative revolution" for which many had hoped. By the last two decades of the twentieth century, instances of internal – rather than international – conflict had come to the fore. Moreover, in places where debates about national culture had long been settled, new migrations and circulations of ideas are reopening these very issues. In the United States, a renewed argument about immigration focuses on the southern border. In this latest version of an old American debate, the perceived unwillingness of Spanish speakers to "learn English" and assimilate into the Anglo-Protestant national culture is, in some tellings, the new threat to national unity.[1] In Germany, Turkish immigrants – many of whom are German citizens – are perceived to threaten German national culture due to religion (Islam) and insufficient assimilation of German culture. In the UK, it is Urdu, Bengali, or Punjabi-speaking immigrants who occupy this role. Migrations are not the sole catalyst for the resurgence of these debates: continued demands from autochthonous language communities in places such as Peru (Quechua), Spain (Basque, Catalan, Galicia), France (Alsatian, Languedoc, the languages of Oc), and Belgium (where the French–Flemish divide has recently intensified) also signal some ruptures at the edges of the culture–nation link.

Changed political boundaries and the emergence of new countries during the 1990s spurred widespread language and cultural policy changes in the former Soviet Union and the Balkans. The collapse of the Soviet Union and the end of the federation known as Yugoslavia seemed to confirm, in the fervor with which the new states implemented language laws to assert the historical continuity of their country's existence, that cultural difference ultimately cannot be contained within the political boundaries of the nation-state. As if to underscore this new conclusion, the Serbo-Croatian language – like the former constituent states of Yugoslavia – split apart, the hyphen no longer politically or culturally useful.

Each of these contexts serves to illustrate how language retains a strong hold as an emblem of national life and, more to the point, how changing ideas about the nation seem to require language change. Probing these two conclusions further, however, reveals a logical paradox. By any measure, and in any historical account, territories claimed as constitutive homes of today's national languages are the result of state practices: language laws, state education institutions, and media campaigns. Again using Western European examples – for it is Western Europe that has served as the assumed standard for much of social theorizing – a great deal of work was required to make Frenchmen of France's peasants, or to institutionalize what we know as Italian even in the territories we have long known as Italy. Eugene Weber's carefully documented history, for example, notes that French was a "foreign language" for half of France's citizens well into the early twentieth century; at its moment of

---

[1] Samuel P. Huntington, *Who Are We? The Challenges to America's National Identity* (New York: Simon and Schuster, 2004).

nationhood, Italian was spoken by 2.5 percent of the population.[2] Against history, the assumption that political formations should be (and are) culturally homogenous becomes a more difficult proposition to maintain, yet it is the foundation stone of nationalist discourse. Seen from this perspective, this newest phase of public discussion serves to reopen perhaps the oldest and most contentious debate of the modern world of nation-states: the cultural basis of national identity. And as we know from even recent history, this is the stuff of both patriotism and violence alike.

Language plays a central role in creating boundaries of belonging that shape, or rather are shaped by, choices of national identity. Despite the fact that language is a very pliant facet of one's social self, widespread and indeed formalized linkage of language with ethnicity has created our current world of nation-states. Earlier forms of political organization, such as empire, were able to contain linguistic and cultural diversity without fearing that the "center" would not hold. But in a world propelled by nationalism, the cultural distinctiveness of the nation proves its right to existence. The shift is not without consequences.

At its broadest, this book explores the contradictory roles that language plays in the creation of national identity in modernity. Throughout the world, debates about national identity inevitably revolve around the politics of culture, in which language serves as a cause, a solution, a muse for the national self, and a technology of the state. Each of these roles underscores the complicated work, and the myriad assumptions, expected of and loaded onto language. Yet all too often the historical process through which languages emerge with "national" status are effaced. Admitting the modern nature of this fundamental building block of national existence would undermine claims to antiquity, for nation-states lay claim to a foundational national culture that somehow, and invariably, should be seen as age-old, unique on earth, imbued with a particular spirit, and heir to a special history – often in sharp contrast to the more discursive understandings offered by academic historians.[3]

This book investigates the language–culture–nation linkage through a paradigmatic and important case, Pakistan. Pakistan's internal faultlines have been the subject of recent international attention, most particularly the growth of radical Islamic extremism and its threat to Pakistani civic life. The dominance of Pakistan's military and the country's struggle

---

[2] Eugene Weber, *Peasants into Frenchmen* (Stanford: Stanford University Press, 1976), 70. On Italian: Tullio de Mauro, *Storia linguistica dell'Italia unita* (Bari: Laterza, 1963), 41, cited in E. J. Hobsbawm, *Nations and Nationalism Since 1780* (Cambridge: Cambridge University Press, 1992 [1990]), 38.

[3] See Ronald Grigor Suny, "Constructing Primordialisms: Old Histories for New Nations," *Journal of Modern History* 73 (December 2001).

to regain civilian authority marks the other major international concern. This book focuses on the question of Pakistan's cultural identity, emblematized through language, which remains a source of conflict and internal competition. As such, this work contributes to the growing body of historiography on nationalism and the nation, a great part of which has centered on the experiences of Western Europe, with cases from Eastern Europe and the former Soviet Union a more recent addition. Drawing upon Pakistan's cultural history – with comparative reference to India and Indonesia – the study investigates how these three major postcolonial states conceptualized, defined, and legislated their national cultures. These three largest states to emerge from colonial rule, accounting for some one-quarter of humanity, pursued very different policies in the pursuit of national identity formation. The outcomes of those different decisions offer lessons about how ideologies of language impact public policy, and how policies of culture-making impact public life. The global growth in civil, rather than international, conflicts at the end of the twentieth century offers many examples of conflicts over culture; one of the goals of the research undertaken here was to offer a detailed narrative exploring why certain language policy choices in Asia resulted in such different outcomes, perhaps providing lessons for the future. In this sense, this work marks an effort to engage in historiographical scholarship that can have relevance to public policy decisions.

The puzzling history of language and nationalism in Pakistan forms the center of the inquiry. The first modern nation-state conceived and founded on the basis of religion – preceding Israel by a year – Pakistan was created from Muslim-majority territories partitioned out of India by the departing British in 1947. Overnight, Pakistan became the largest Muslim country in the world. Yet despite the Pakistan Movement's arguments that South Asian Muslims formed a coherent and unique civilization, a nation deserving its own territory, conflict began nearly immediately and centered on demands for cultural/linguistic pluralism. These demands, later reinforced by problems of economic and political power-sharing, formed a central complaint of Pakistan's Bengali-speaking East Wing, which in 1971 seceded from Pakistan to form Bangladesh. It was another first: in this case, the first successful secession from a postcolonial state. The country created, in the words of vanguard Muslim nationalist Mohammad Iqbal, as a homeland for "Muslim society, with its remarkable homogeneity and inner unity,"[4]

---

[4] Speech given at the 1930 All-India Muslim League meeting. Syed Sharifuddin Pirzada, ed., *Foundations of Pakistan: All-India Muslim League Documents: 1906–1947*, vol. II, 1924–1947 (Karachi: Ferozesons, 1970), 154.

split apart not twenty-four years later – as if disproving the earlier argument of civilizational coherence.

The cultural-linguistic challenges within the remaining Pakistan, reduced by half, continued. In the province of Sindh, of course, language conflict has remained unresolved since 1947, becoming bloodier during the 1990s. The Northwest Frontier Province, amidst its other troubles linked to the terrible conflict in Afghanistan, has repeatedly sought greater linguistic recognition and cultural autonomy for its Pashtun population. These linguistic demands have presented themselves in opposition to the dominant Punjabi majority in the country. Yet from the 1980s forward, gaining momentum particularly in the early part of the twenty-first century, a language movement within central Punjab – one quite distinct from the Siraki language movement of southern Punjab – has similarly begun to argue for official recognition of the Punjabi language and its cultural and literary history. The emergence of this movement from within the putative ethnic hegemon of the country raises additional questions about the theoretical relationship of language and nationalism, not the least of which lies in the strange paradox of a regional cultural, economic and political power harboring apparently unsatisfied cultural entrepreneurs within. Reframed in the language of cultural history, the case of Pakistan readily reveals the disjuncture between the nation-form and its demands for a unified cultural past and present, against the lived reality of a people yet "unproduced" through the nation.

Pakistan's experience with the Urdu language is a good place to examine how polity and the nation are structured through national culture. This first nation-state founded on the basis of religion, at the cost of more than a million lives and the displacement of between twelve and eighteen million people, has offered its citizens rather less than a secure and prosperous homeland for all. Language conflict has resulted in dissent, secession, and in the case of East Bengal/Bangladesh, genocide – underscoring the gnawing question posed by Ayesha Jalal in 1985: how did a Pakistan come about which fit the interests of most Muslims so poorly?[5]

Despite decades of language, education, and media policies designed to produce the people as Pakistani, one important recurring theme of virtually all analyses of the country is the question of subnational or regional identity movements. (As if to reiterate this point, a recent volume on Pakistan bears the subtitle *"Nationalism Without a Nation?"*)[6]

---

[5] Ayesha Jalal, *The Sole Spokesman* (Cambridge: Cambridge University Press, 1985), 4.
[6] Christophe Jaffrelot, ed., *Pakistan: Nationalism without a Nation?* (New Delhi; London, and New York: Manohar Publishers and Zed Books Ltd., 2002).

These analyses have long concerned themselves with "centrifugal" forces, a metaphor that, by suggesting a spinning outwards, reifies the notion of a totalizing national consciousness as necessary for the nation-state. In a state for which the battle for consciousness has always been between the "provinces" versus the "center," the question of course arises as to where national consciousness can be located. For decades the answer has been Punjab. Yet the above-mentioned linguistic and cultural revivalism gaining ground within Punjab, the Punjabiyat movement, suggests a sort of insufficiency of the bid to forge a nation per the demands of the form, with a coherent national language, culture, and history. In other words, there appear to be limitations of the national imagination, and those limitations are articulated in terms of language and identity – the building blocks of linguistic revivals, but now percolating throughout the center as well as the provinces.

In exploring these questions, this book tells two stories. The first is about the politics of making a nation against a backdrop in which that nation has been assumed to exist already. Pakistan's story is emblematic, and provides a vantage point from which to understand the central role that the creation of a "national culture" plays, and how language is central to that creation. This story is driven by a desire to think about why language has been such a contested site of conflict in Pakistan's history – for there is no question that it has – but has remained a less than central focus in academic analyses of Pakistan, occupying a mere footnote to ideas about ethnic identity which assume innate and fixed boundaries of ethnicity. This book explores the ways in which the state project to forge a Pakistani ethnicity through the cultural heritage of the Urdu language created antipathies where it sought unity.

The second story, which emerges from the first, takes the case of Pakistan as a point of departure to think more carefully about what role language plays in nationalism, in creating a sense of national belonging – indeed, in the articulation of the nation in the most literal of all senses. Our most powerful theories of nationalism rest on an assumption of language's centrality to communicative practices that form consciousness. I will question that assumption, suggesting that in fact the evidence here suggests that the idea of the national language flows from an idea of national consciousness rather than the reverse. That being the case, we can also investigate aspects of why certain national language projects have been more successful than others, and how language ideology – an important concept in linguistic anthropology – plays a powerful role in that determination, one underexplored in comparison with its political impact. I share James Scott's assessment that the high-modernist impulses of the twentieth century – the imperative to shape, mold, and "improve the human condition" by changing what existed naturally – produced state practices of simplification, which in many cases resulted in catastrophic outcomes.[7] Yet a comparative assessment of language policy in India, Indonesia, and Pakistan reveals some surprising lessons about how and when state simplifications, at least of language, can actually work. Only through probing comparatively can we identify the relevant lessons from history that may help shape a better future.

The nation, nationalism, and language

Perhaps no tension in the articulation of the nation is greater than this paradox: the widespread idea of language as some kind of proxy for particular racial and/or national belonging, in stark contrast – as much of this book explores – with complicated histories of language standardization and propagation required to "produce the people" in various nation-states. Benedict Anderson has remarked on this paradox with respect to the "Russifying policy orientation" of official nationalism in the Soviet Union, by which he meant the domination of Russia as the normative cultural basis for the Soviet Union.[8] The cultural logic of the nation, as has been shown by numerous historians, collapses polity into a form of sovereignty requiring an authorized culture.[9] As Ronald Grigor Suny has observed, "In the discourse of the nation, culture is the source of political power. The right to rule belongs to the people/nation that is imagined as coherent, bounded, and conscious of its position as the foundation of the state's legitimacy."[10] But legitimacy, and that authorized culture of the nation, is something which must be produced. Language occupies a central role in this discourse, though one not always foregrounded.

Scholars point to German philosopher Johann Gottfried Herder (1744–1803) as the intellectual inspiration for the notion that language

---

[7] James C. Scott, *Seeing Like a State* (New Haven: Yale University Press, 1998).
[8] Benedict Anderson, *Imagined Communities* (London, New York: Verso, 1991), 113.
[9] Etienne Balibar, "The Nation Form: History and Ideology," in *Race, Nation, Class: Ambiguous Identities*, ed. Balibar and Wallerstein (London and New York: Verso, 1991 [1988]); Partha Chatterjee, *The Nation and its Fragments* (Princeton: Princeton University Press, 1993); Prasenjit Duara, *Rescuing History from the Nation* (Chicago: University of Chicago Press, 1995); Antonio Gramsci, *Selections from Cultural Writings*, ed. Forgacs and Nowell-Smith, trans. Boelhower (Cambridge: Harvard University Press, 1985); E. J. Hobsbawm and Terence Ranger, eds., *The Invention of Tradition* (Cambridge: Cambridge University Press, 1983). For a comparison of the vernacular millennium in South Asia with that of Western Europe, see Sheldon Pollock, *The Language of the Gods in the World of Men* (Berkeley: University of California Press, 2006).
[10] Suny, "Constructing Primordialisms," 881.

and nationality, or language and race, are mutually bound like a sort of double-helix.[11] For Herder, "national genius" was located in poetry, literature, and folk songs – the products of the people, but not understood as produced *by* people as we today understand the contingent and constructed nature of identity. Rather, for Herder, the environment itself had agency instead of the people; he located "national genius" in the actual territorial soil, believing that "Climates and Nations are universally marked in it [national mythologies]."[12] Herder's sense of the bounded limits on national culture, derived from the particularities of the environment, was coupled with his idea that "all these tribes of men … have not invented, but *inherited*" their own mythology.[13] This concept is an important one, implying an unchanging and autarkic sense of nation in which the work of cultural production and reproduction takes place independent of the people imbued within it. We can see as well Herder's emphasis on the pure spirit of oral traditions as somehow "truer" to the ground, an unpolluted manifestation of national culture.

More than two centuries later, we find such ideas expressed in this way wildly naïve, even absurd; two generations of critical scholarship have rejected pure notions of a "culture concept" as a discrete, bounded entity. "Herderian" as an adjective implies today – at least in the academic world – a theoretically uninformed position unable to recognize the idea of national identity as an artifact of social construction, or indeed misrecognizing the internal variances and power relations within cultures for some coherent whole. While the careful work of scholars from several disciplines has illuminated the ways people both in contemporary and historic contexts have long practiced human sociality through multiple languages – notable cases being the Columbian Vaupes Indians, navigating some three to ten languages as part of everyday life, or closer to the study here, South Asia as a "linguistic region"[14] – the rigidity with which Herderian assumptions of language and nation have been bound has remained unyielding at the popular level, seemingly globally.

[11] Richard Bauman and Charles L. Briggs, "Language Philosophy as Language Ideology: John Locke and Johann Gottfried Herder," in *Regimes of Language*, ed. Paul Kroskrity (Santa Fe: School of American Research, 2000). On language and the environment, see Johann Gottfried Herder, "National Genius and the Environment," in *Reflections on the Philosophy of the History of Mankind* (Chicago: University of Chicago Press, 1968 [1784]).
[12] Herder, "National Genius," 43.
[13] *Ibid.*, 44.
[14] Jean Jackson, "Language Identity of the Colombia Vaupes Indians," in *Explorations in the Ethnography of Speaking*, eds. Bauman and Sherzer (New York: Cambridge University Press, 1974). Charles A. Ferguson, "South Asia as a Sociolinguistic Area," in *Dimensions of Sociolinguistics in South Asia*, eds. Dimock, Kachru, and Krishnamurti (New Delhi, Bombay, and Calcutta: Oxford & IBH Publishing Co., 1992).

This affects public discourse, public policy, and of course public self-presentations as a result.

For our purposes, the nature in which nationalists as well as many theorists of nationalism have assumed this Herderian trope has served to foreclose the possibility of imagining the nation as a multilingual sociopolitical unit. If indeed the nation as a form and the idea of nationalism spread modularly, from Western Europe throughout the world (again following Anderson), the unproblematized corollary of such dissemination would be the modular spread of the idea that the nation must be monolingual – even, and notably, in the postcolonial states for which linguistic uniformity had never been a feature. Etienne Balibar, in "The Nation Form: History and Ideology," gestures toward the necessary, in fact *required*, role of language in effecting the production of what he terms "fictive ethnic identity" indispensible to the production of patriotism, a fictive ethnicity drawing upon a teleological narrative of the past which serves to render the present nation form as natural.[15] Though Balibar sees language as necessary but not sufficient to produce ethnicity, precisely because of its "paradoxical properties" of "plasticity" – by which he means that humans have the ability to acquire new languages – at the same time, he underscores that:

> not only that the national language should be recognized as the official language, but, much more fundamentally, that it should be able to appear as the very element of the life of a people.[16]

Hence the "national language" in the world of nation-states – the twentieth century marked the rise of a new idea that political formations necessarily have a language, and without one, the claim to nationhood would always remain incomplete. To press further on the language–polity linkage, this book places language, the national language, as the central subject of inquiry. It is no longer sufficient given what we know about the complicated processes of nation-formation to ignore or treat as epiphenomenal the work of language in that process of articulation. A central argument this book makes is that the production of the national language, like national history, is itself recursively imbricated in that which it is expected to evidence, namely, *nationality*.

But language is not simply a sort of template or filter one can apply or remove with equal malleability. Were that the case, language revivals themselves theoretically should not exist, for in the aftermath of large-scale state instituted language propagation, cultural "memory"

---

[15] Balibar, "The Nation-Form," 96.
[16] *Ibid.*, 98.

of languages without state patronage would be expected to disappear. As we know, however, human behavior does not work this way. Equally true is that while the human capacity to learn languages is theoretically infinite – thus rendering narrow ideas about nation qua language, *à la* Herder, mechanically not to mention historically inaccurate – at the same time it is quite clear that language and the politics of its place in modern polities have been central questions for many states, suggesting that some forms of attachment exert very powerful pulls. Social science has tended to treat such attachments as non-rational or, worse still, a mask for other types of more instrumental motivations. Yet the historical narratives in the pages which follow offer evidence that ideas about particular aesthetic spaces can prove to be powerful incentives.

A cursory survey of politics in the late twentieth century reveals a globally widespread phenomenon of new nation-states legitimizing polity through creating new national languages, sometimes quite abruptly. This move operates in the direction of what I will call a "language paradox," where the national genius of the people is located in a language, and then the state undertakes to develop that language for modern national use. If this sounds circular, it is intentionally so, for nothing is more circular than the logic of creating the very thing posited as that which differentiates it. In the process, this state interventionism participates in processes of ethnogenesis by virtue of the new variable it introduces in concepts of cultural legitimacy. I elaborate on this concept in Chapters 4 and 5 by taking a closer look at cultural legitimacy and symbolic capital, with a particular focus on the case of Punjab.

The salient lesson of this phenomenon lies in the evidencing a modality of attachment to the *idea* of a national language with perhaps greater primacy than the attachment to any language itself, resulting in exercises of "language development" in order to forge a modern form of communication from local oral language forms, or even dormant languages of scripture. The most prominent examples are of course the resuscitation of Hebrew to become the official language of Israel, the "spoken Sanskrit" movement in India, and more recently the many linguistic revivals in the states created by the dissolution of the Soviet Union. Bhavna Dave's work on Kazakhstan and David Laitin's work, particularly on Estonia, best illustrate this phenomenon as it affected numerous new states in Eastern Europe and Central Asia during the 1990s.[17]

---

[17] Bhavna Dave, "Politics of Language Revival: National Identity and State Building in Kazakhstan" (PhD dissertation, Syracuse University, 1996); David D. Laitin, *Identity in Formation* (Ithaca: Cornell University Press, 1998). On spoken Sanskrit, see Adi Hastings, "Signifying Sanskrit in Hindu Revivalist and Nationalist Discourse"

Discussions of language politics have primarily employed two theoretical principles as *explanans*: primordialism and instrumentalism. In the 1950s, the concept of primordialism, argued most saliently by Edward Shils and Clifford Geertz, posited deep attachments to "primary groups." Geertz also argued that these attachments presented challenges of integration for the new states emerging from decolonization.[18] Somehow in the intervening decades this concept of primordialism has lost analytical nuance and emerged as the straw man against which constructivist models of self, history, and of course nation delineate the constantly changing process of nationalist production of these modes. Yet scholars have more recently asked questions about how what we know to be constructed could appear to adherents as longstanding historic forms.[19] What is true for invented traditions like parades and national commemorations is also true for language practices. With respect to the premodern era in South Asia, particularly relevant, historian Sheldon Pollock has suggested that "To study vernacularization is to study not the emergence into history of primeval and natural communities and cultures, but rather the historical inauguration of their naturalization."[20] Similarly, Ronald Grigor Suny's recent intervention, coining the term "constructed primordialisms," allows us to capture the simultaneous production of cultural/national forms which are at once new yet present themselves as age-old.[21] Informed by these approaches, much of this book focuses on the dynamics of state-instituted primordial culture and the responses articulated by other communities as they attempt to embroider their own naturalized senses of culture onto the national cloth.

The second theoretical position often invoked in discussions of language politics is that of instrumentalism. This concept is widespread and now a central tenet of the political-science literature on language politics. In brief, instrumentalism posits that political elites employ certain symbols around which to gather mass political strength. Instrumentalism speaks of the manipulation of symbols, for instance

(paper presented at the Semiotics: Culture in Context workshop, University of Chicago, 2002).

[18] Clifford Geertz, "The Integrative Revolution: Primordial Sentiments and Civil Politics in the New States," in *The Interpretation of Cultures* (New York: Basic Books, 1973); Edward Shils, "Primordial, Personal, Sacred and Civil Ties," *British Journal of Sociology* 8, no. 2 (1957).

[19] Perhaps the most cited such work is Hobsbawm and Ranger, *The Invention of Tradition*.

[20] Sheldon Pollock, "India in the Vernacular Millenium: Literary Culture and Polity, 1000–1500," *Daedalus* 127, no. 3 (1998): 42.

[21] Suny, "Constructing Primordialisms."

language, history, or religious practices, as means to the political ends of consolidating power.²² The instrumental use of cultural symbols also undergirds rational choice approaches to political strategizing behavior, a method of analysis focused on the individual actor. For the historian, the instrumentalist explanation appears to circulate within a specific and bounded band of space–time, raising the issue of how particular symbols may come to be constituted as important or valuable in the first place. While by no means denying that actors indeed, and perhaps often, make demands focused on instrumental ends – and the history of Pakistan's ethnic politics is replete with examples – one of the perplexing aspects of the Punjabi-language revivalism discussed here lies in its apparent lack of instrumentalist motivations, though it bears the shape and exhibits the behavior of classic nationalist movements. Because this case emerges from a region of Pakistan that has been widely assessed as holding all forms of political, economic, and even military power in the country, it allows us to question the reasons for the emergence of this movement to begin with. Language movements nearly always involve a subordinate group (indeed, the Bengalis, though numerically a majority, were not in control of national power) acting against a central authority and seeking to gain power, so the ability to analyze the contribution of non-instrumental motivations to this process has been limited. The case of Punjab offers an analytic counterfactual opportunity to do so. Thus it allows us to go beyond understandings of language politics as proxies for other kinds of motivations, and instead permits a different kind of purchase on the relationship of language to history, self, and affect – the kind of purchase Walker Connor called for by challenging scholars to "probe the nature of the nationalist's appeal."²³

I thus want to go beyond Herderian ideas to examine this peculiar but very revealing case to discuss what the meaning of attachment to language might actually mean. I am not positing a primordial notion of attachment in the sense of something perenially fixed. But deep-rooted practices forged over time, many suddenly marginalized through the logic of the nation-form in the twentieth century, have a way of demanding reinclusion. It is here, in this space, that we see appeals to language,

---

²² See the Brass-Robinson debate of the late 1970s: Paul R. Brass, "Elite Groups, Symbol Manipulation and Ethnic Identity Among the Muslims of South Asia," in *Political Identity in South Asia*, ed. Taylor and Yapp, *Collected Papers on South Asia* (London: Curzon Press, 1979). See also Paul R. Brass, *Language, Religion and Politics in North India* (Cambridge: Cambridge University Press, 1974), 119–274. The revised edition of *Separatism Among Indian Muslims* notes the role of ideology and the power of belief in that process: Francis Robinson, *Separatism Among Indian Muslims*, 2nd edn (New Delhi: Oxford University Press, 1993), xiv–xxv.
²³ Walker Connor, *Ethnonationalism: the Quest for Understanding* (Princeton: Princeton University Press, 1994).

nation, community, and heroism in a recuperative mode. Through these interlinked narrative explorations, this book explores how perhaps the most malleable of all forms of social being, language, can simultaneously acquire the artifice of primordialism. Pakistan's historical context has embedded its particular history of ideas about nation, community, and language within a matrix that includes a deep pre-Islamic civilizational heritage, a sense of membership in a global Islamic community with its special history, a more recent history of subordination to British colonial authority, and of course the troubled postcolonial present, the subject of this work.

Organization of the work

This book explores the perplexing questions of language and nationalism through several different and complementary lenses. Pakistan is a central point of departure for each of these. Chapter 1 situates questions of language and nation in South Asia as part of a longer history of ideological formations including the Hindi–Urdu controversy in colonial South Asia, the emergence of the Pakistan Movement alongside the Indian independence struggle, and the birth of Pakistan as the first country founded on the basis of religion. This context helps us better understand the subsequent sixty-plus years of struggle over national subjectivity in the new Pakistan. To be sure, this struggle has taken place across several divides – Islam and secularism, sectarianism, civil versus military authority, for example – but the work here takes a language-centered approach precisely because it remains understudied, despite its obvious importance and despite the centrality with which the Pakistani state has valorized language as an inextricable part of "nation-building."

Chapter 1 traces the linkages of ideas about cultural and ethnic difference defined on the basis of religion, but articulated as something inherently civilizational with the Two Nations Theory. The idea that South Asian Muslims form a separate *nation* became a powerful trope, ultimately receiving political endorsement with the Pakistan Movement and the eventual creation of Pakistan in 1947. How this religious nationalism came to have so close an identification with one single language, and that too one without a scriptural role in Islam, would determine and indeed undermine the politics of the country it created.

Chapters 2 and 3 provide an overview of the politics of language policy over the course of Pakistan's short life. Such an overview illustrates graphically how national efforts to produce the people as Pakistani assumed that only through an incorporation of all into a unitary Urdu-speaking nation-state could the country recognize itself as a nation. The overview disrupts or bifurcates that linear history by showing how, virtually from inception, the model subject projected by the nation-state was contested from all corners.[24]

The chapters focused on the case of Punjab, 4 and 5, examine in greater detail the gradual growth of the Punjabiyat language movement, located primarily in Lahore. This movement, emerging from the very heart of the region considered the "hegemon" within Pakistan – Punjab – provides evidence for rethinking our models of nationalism, as well as the how and why of its growing appeal. From Karl Deutsch's model of social communication to the literacy and print-text centered theories of Benedict Anderson and Ernest Gellner, the role of language in the articulation of the nation has been a central, if unproblematized, fulcrum doing the theoretical heavy lifting. In the case of Punjab, however, this region-cum-ethnicity has witnessed a slowly increasing language revival movement aiming to forge a written literary culture from a language that (in Pakistan, at least) has had a limited print-textual existence in the country. Second, the Punjabiyat movement places a great deal of emphasis on aesthetic rather than economic-instrumental considerations, suggesting that we ought to take seriously the idea that culture or aesthetic values may not be epiphenomenal developments. This intriguing case points to the importance of symbolic capital, an argument developed extensively in the chapter.

Chapter 6 revisits what has become a headline controversy in contemporary Pakistan: nationalist historiography and the state. The relationship between Pakistan's Islamically-imagined past, one which has excised the pre-Islamic history of the country's territory, has been linked from the very beginning with the Urdu language. By examining the content of education policy planning documents from independence through 2003, the chapter clarifies that the Islamization of national history was an explicit focus of state planning from the very beginning, not an abruptly innovated later feature instituted by General Zia ul-Haq (1977–88). Chapter 7 explores the complaint that the Urdu language overtly dominates nationalist historiography, pushing a variety of heroes and literatures of the regions which comprise Pakistan to the peripheries of national consciousness. The chapter focuses on newer efforts of some Pakistanis "writing back," as it were, authoring new historical narratives that demand the inclusion of Punjabi or Sindhi heroes – as constitutive of the state even if that means including a past before the coming of Islam

---

[24] On the question of the assumed unified subjectivity of the nation, see especially "Bifurcating Linear Histories in China and India" in Duara, *Rescuing History from the Nation*, 51–82.

and indeed before the coming of Urdu as well. Re-centering history on the regions permits access to different pasts, recovered through the use of regional language sources which exhibit different narratives of ethnicity and even of heroism.

Chapter 8 moves laterally from the question of national consciousness and the national language to look at the disjuncture between ideas of language and polity under empire and then in the modern world of nation-states, then examining India's postcolonial national language formation. India began its independent existence with national language plans very similar to Pakistan's – focused on the necessity of one language, and fearful of disunity in plurality. Yet by the mid-1960s India decided to respond to language agitations by greater devolution of power and with greater recognition of the regional languages in roles of official state authority. The result has been a virtual elimination of language conflict in this dizzyingly multilingual country.

Chapter 9 then turns to a comparison with Indonesia, the country that bears the greatest structural similarity with Pakistan. Indonesia, too, pursued a single-language policy at the national level, yet language has never been the source of conflict. This comparison permits conclusions about the nature of language and the nation, partially hinted at in the previous chapters, but more fully elucidated through the comparison. First, the perceived necessity of retrofitting new national populations with new languages to make them "national" stands as a common feature. This suggests that we ought to reconceptualize the linkage between nation and language not as one in which the latter gives rise to the former, but rather that the nation-form itself seeks to produce a common language to evidence its own existence. This recursive proposal better captures the otherwise peculiar nature of the language paradox phenomenon, social engineering to accomplish the propagation of a language which is somehow represented as embodying the nation despite its limited reach. This proposal also allows us to think more carefully about the relative success or failure of national language projects. The comparison particularly between Indonesia and Pakistan illustrates a fundamental divergence in language ideology, which I believe explains the comparative enthusiasm with which Bahasa Indonesia spread throughout the archipelago, without conflict, against Pakistan's more bitter experience with Urdu. The comparative lessons of national language creation point to ways to think about modernity and how nations craft sustainable legitimacy – questions that concern scholars. But because these processes are articulated as well as realized by politicians and policymakers, who have direct stakes in the outcomes, the comparative lessons elucidated here as well have practical merit.

1 Articulating a new nation

> This language didn't just give birth to the Pakistan Movement – it caused it to flourish, and advanced it forward. This language was the language of the War of Independence on the one hand, and on the other hand it was the medium through which science and literature were expressed.
> Dr. Jamil Jalibi, *Qaumī Zabān* (1989)

> In his presidential address the "Father of Urdu," expressing regret over Urdu's lack of status in Pakistan, said that neither Jinnah nor Iqbal had made Pakistan: rather, Urdu made Pakistan. The real reason for the opposition between Hindus and Muslims was the Urdu language. The whole Two-Nations Theory and all of the discord was only because of Urdu. For this reason, Pakistan has a great obligation to Urdu.
> Item from journal *Qaumī Zabān*, February 16, 1961

Urdu's emergence as the national language of Pakistan was neither obvious nor natural. That it became so marks the triumph of a particular understanding of the nation as a territory, a people, and a language in the singular. The choice of one language as the national language for this large territory squared neither with the broader administrative history of language under the British, nor with that of the Mughal or Sikh empires, nor with the longer histories of cosmopolitan and vernacular language use in the subcontinent.[1] The year of independence, 1947, thus marked the beginning not only of a new political formation – a homeland founded on the basis of religion – but also of a new belief about the linguistic medium of a unitary culture in a large bounded territorial homeland. On this basis, Urdu was presented as a spiritual muse by the heads of state of this new Pakistan. Indeed, the claim that the Urdu language gave birth to Pakistan, and that the Pakistani nation owed it a great obligation, appears rather strange in retrospect. Given what we know about the difficult and contentious language politics that beleaguered the new

---

[1] For language under the Mughals, see Muzaffar Alam, *The Languages of Political Islam in India* (Chicago: University of Chicago Press, 2004). For language in the subcontinent through 1500, see Pollock, *Language of the Gods*.

country, these assertions made by two highly esteemed scholars of Urdu literature and history invite further investigation.

The discord and opposition between Hindus and Muslims to which Maulvi Abdul Haq – the "Father of Urdu" quoted above – referred drew upon narratives of the past and of religious community that had their roots in a nineteenth-century language controversy in northern India. Many scholars have argued that the progressive differentiation of Hindu and Muslim communities was the result of colonial intervention rather than due to a sharp and inherent sense of difference.[2] This insight extends as well to the identification of linguistic difference during the same period. Indeed, the historical record here underscores the contention of linguistic anthropologists Susan Gal and Judith Irvine that ideologies have the capability to construct boundaries of languages from what had previously been fluid interactions.[3] Given the powerful linkage of language to religion and nation, a conceptual linkage with roots in the nineteenth century, some of the analysis in this book will draw upon theoretical ideas of linguistic anthropology. This branch of the discipline helps us to articulate the beliefs structuring behaviors about language, or what are called *language ideologies*.[4] Attention to the ideologies of language as they construct and deconstruct boundaries of group identities in Pakistan yields some critical insights into the subject of conflict and contestation for Pakistan's entire existence. For our purposes, the relevant language ideology was one that bonded language with religious community such that one became overtly identified with the other: Muslim Urdu and Hindu Hindi.

Fort William College and the Hindi–Urdu controversy

The presumption that Urdu was the obvious national language of the region's Muslims was the outcome of two intertwined phenomena: the geographical base of the Muslim League's primary support, and the

---

[2] See Gyanendra Pandey, *The Construction of Communalism in Colonial North India* (Delhi: Oxford University Press, 1990).

[3] Susan Gal and Judith T. Irvine, "The Boundaries of Languages and Disciplines: How Ideologies Construct Difference," *Social Research* 62, no. 1 (1995).

[4] Susan Gal, "Language and Political Economy," *Annual Review of Anthropology* 18 (1989); Gal and Irvine, "Boundaries of Languages;" Judith T. Irvine and Susan Gal, "Language Ideology and Linguistic Difference," in *Regimes of Language*, ed. Kroskrity (Santa Fe: School of American Research Press, 2000); Michael Silverstein, "Language Structure and Linguistic Ideology," in *The Elements: A Parasession on Linguistic Units and Levels*, ed. Clyne (Chicago: Chicago Linguistic Society, 1979); Kathryn Woolard, "Introduction: Language Ideology as a Field of Inquiry," in *Language Ideologies: Practice and Theory*, ed. Schieffelin, Woolard, and Kroskrity (New York: Oxford University Press, 1998).

pre-history of what became known as the "Hindi–Urdu controversy." Until 1946 the primary support for the Muslim League's Pakistan demand was located in the provinces now in northern India in which Muslims were a minority. The contentious Hindi–Urdu controversy that took place in the second half of the nineteenth century was located in precisely this territory, where a salient political issue for Muslims was the "protection" of Urdu.[5] Although Muslims in the vast expanse of British India and the various princely states obviously spoke a wide variety of other languages, with the political core centered on the Muslim minority provinces, ideas about who and what constituted Islamic India collapsed the cultural imagination onto the historical and cultural traditions of that particular region in northern India (as opposed to the northwest, or the Bengali east) to the exclusion of everywhere else.

But why did Urdu need "protection," and from what or whom? How did language protection acquire a veneer of religion? Scholars have written in depth about this language controversy, which paved the way for a growing consensus that linked language and religion into the just-so slogans, "Hindi-Hindu-Hindustan" in opposition to "Urdu-Muslim-(Pakistan)."[6] Given the factual conundrum that neither Hindi nor Urdu, at least in the forms they would assume by the twentieth century, had any particular role in sacred religious texts, this opposition appears all the more perplexing in retrospect. In effect, these two languages became the bearers of religion first, then nation by proxy.

Identifying Urdu's origins constitutes an exercise in intellectual circuitousness given the many ways it has been described, conceptualized, and canonized. Although written in a modified Arabic script, the legacy

---

[5] The best history of the political fortunes of Jinnah, the Muslim League, and the Pakistan demand is Jalal, *Sole Spokesman*.

[6] The social and literary histories of Hindi, Urdu, and their schismogenesis are now voluminous. On Hindi and Urdu before the nation, see Vasudha Dalmia, *The Nationalization of Hindu Traditions* (New Delhi: Oxford University Press, 1997); Christopher R. King, *One Language, Two Scripts* (Bombay: Oxford University Press, 1994); the *Literary Cultures in History* volume, ed. Sheldon Pollock (Berkeley: University of California Press, 2003); Pandey, *Construction of Communalism*, 201–32; Amrit Rai, *A House Divided* (Delhi: Oxford University Press, 1984); Brass, *Language, Religion and Politics in North India*, 119–81; Shamsur Rahman Faruqi, *Early Urdu Literary Culture and History* (Delhi: Oxford University Press, 2001); Ayesha Jalal, *Self and Sovereignty* (London and New York: Routledge, 2000), 102–38; Robinson, *Separatism among Indian Muslims* (1974), 33–132. On Hindi and Urdu after the nation, see especially Aijaz Ahmad, "Some Reflections on Urdu," *Seminar* 359 (July 1989); Aijaz Ahmad, "In the Mirror of Urdu," in *Lineages of the Present* (Delhi: Tulika Press, 1993 [1996]); Philip Oldenburg, "'A Place Insufficiently Imagined': Language, Belief, and the Pakistan Crisis of 1971," *Journal of Asian Studies* 44, no. 4 (August 1985); Tariq Rahman, "The Urdu-English Controversy in Pakistan," *Modern Asian Studies* 31, no. 1 (February 1997); Alok Rai, *Hindi Nationalism* (New Delhi: Orient Longman, 2000). Tariq Rahman's sociolinguistic work on language in Pakistan is so prolific that I will not cite all of his writings here, as the following chapter makes extensive use of his scholarship.

of Persian's regional influence through the Central Asian rulers of north India, Urdu's grammar is nearly identical to that of Hindi, India's official language and one written in the Devanagari (Sanskrit) script.[7] The name "Urdu" is itself a short form of "Zabān-e-Urdū-e-Muʿalla," or "Language of the Exalted (Military) Camp" – attesting to the belief that the language's origins lie in the interaction of Turkish and Persian-speaking military troops with indigenous Indian soldiers in the Mughal employ.[8] Indeed, ordinary speakers occasionally refer to Urdu as a *lashkarī zabān*, or "army language," which seems to reinforce this origin narrative at a popular level. Recently, however, noted scholar Shamsur Rahman Faruqi has argued that the name "Urdu" came into existence only at the end of the eighteenth century, the very tail end of the historical period which supposedly produced the language.[9] Faruqi's explanation is that the word "Urdu" instead referred to Shahjahanabad, and that the actual birth of Urdu as a literary language stemmed from literary production of Sufis in the Deccan and in Gujarat.[10] But as Faruqi notes as well, what we call Urdu today could – at any point from perhaps the late sixteenth through nineteenth centuries – have been called, variously, Hindvī, Hindī, Dihlavī, Gujrī, Dakanī, Rekhtah, "Moors" (a British coinage[11]), Hindoostanic, Hindoostanee, and Industans.[12] Muzaffar Alam has noted a similar fluidity in language naming in Mughal-period Persian texts, which by referring to the "Hindvi" could actually indicate Telugu, Marāthi, Dakani – perhaps anything other than Persian.[13] Clearly there was a question of boundaries at work here, or rather a lack thereof.

Such a promiscuous history of naming forces us to ask: if Urdu was not Hindi, but at one time it was, then what was Hindi, how could it be distinct from Urdu, and how could each language be the proxy for religious community? This question, as Alok Rai observes, in fact can never be adequately answered:

> Even the simplest questions beget further controversy, but no clarification. Thus, consider the following elementary queries: are Hindi and Urdu two names of the same language, or are they two different languages? Does Urdu

---

[7] On Indian Persian, or *sabk-i Hindi*, see Muzaffar Alam, "The Culture and Politics of Persian in Pre-Colonial Hindustan," in *Literary Cultures in History*, ed. Pollock; Muzaffar Alam, "The Pursuit of Persian: Language in Mughal Politics," *Modern Asian Studies* 32, no. 2 (1998).
[8] David Lelyveld, "Zubān-e-Urdū-e-Muʿalla and the Idol of Linguistic Origins," *Annual of Urdu Studies* 9 (1994).
[9] Faruqi, *Early Urdu Literary Culture and History*, 60–2.
[10] See "Chapter Five: A True Beginning in the North" in *ibid.*, 109–26.
[11] See Henry Yule and A. C. Burnell, *Hobson-Jobson*, reprint edn (London: Routledge and Kegan Paul, 1996 [1886]), 584.
[12] See Faruqi, *Early Urdu Literary Culture and History*, 22.
[13] See Alam, "Culture and Politics of Persian," 157.

become Hindi if it is written in the Nagari script? Is Hindi Hindu? Is Urdu Muslim, even though Muslims in distant Malabar have been known to claim it as their mother tongue? The only reasonable, *and maddening*, answer to all these questions is, well, yes and no. In respect of neither Hindi nor Urdu can one give an unambiguous answer: one has to go into the historical detail to explain how/ why it isn't; and then, in the space of a few decades, why it is.[14]

As Rai suggests, the devil is in the details of history. Much of this is perhaps unknowable to the degree of precision we may wish to have, or at least the kind of precision that would map onto our twenty-first century categories of analysis. What we do know is that the arrival of British colonizers, early missionaries as well as later East India Company officials, began a new chapter in the identification of language boundaries in north India. In the very same way that Company men sought to codify a contemporary Hindu law from ancient Sanskrit texts, on the assumption that there must be a Hindu law and those legal traditions would obviously be located in Hindu texts, the process of writing grammars for the languages they found in India would be inflected by ideologies of language and race, and a belief in the necessity of different races having different languages. And a belief that Hindus and Muslims were different races.

Of course, recognition of *some* kind of difference manifested in language – be it religious or aesthetic, or even a response to an Iran-centered Persianate regional world – was at work prior to British colonization, if the now-mythical story of famed poet Valī's trip to Delhi is any guide. Valī was advised to purge his Hindvi language of the indigenous idiom in favor of a purer Persian – and after he began to do so, his poetry took Delhi "by storm."[15] Yet even Valī's Persianization exercise was not the same, most certainly without the large-scale political impact, as the identification of language as the bearer of religion, for which we must briefly revisit a colonial epistemology, one propagated via the East India Company's Fort William College.[16]

Language becomes the bearer of religion

In 1800 the East India Company founded Fort William College in Calcutta, a school created first to train its officers in the local languages so they could function in their new administrative roles, but which would

---

[14] Rai, *Hindi Nationalism*, 4. Emphasis in original.
[15] See Chapter 6, "Valī," in Faruqi, *Early Urdu Literary Culture and History*, 129–42. Amrit Rai dates the separation of Hindi and Urdu to this moment: see Rai, *A House Divided*.
[16] The following account, substantially collapsing a much more discursive and lengthy process, is drawn from Dalmia, *Nationalization of Hindu Traditions*, 161–221; King, *One Language, Two Scripts*; Rai, *Hindi Nationalism*, 65–92.

later embark upon a program of educating Indians for employment as well.[17] The College had professors to teach law, Greek, Latin, English, Persian, and Arabic; the Indian language offerings were first Hindustani and Sanskrit. Hindustani, presented in the Arabic script, was taught by the author of the first grammar of Hindustani and an English–Hindustani dictionary, Professor John Gilchrist. When the College hired a Gujarati Brahmin instructor to teach "Bhākā" (in the Nagari script) in 1802, according to Dalmia "the foundation was laid for Hindi as the language of the Hindus." The instructor, Lallūjīlāl, authored a number of texts that formed the beginnings of modern standard Hindi, with its Sanskritic vocabulary purged of Perso-Arabic influence.[18]

Missionaries employed this new Hindi to translate their own texts to spread the Word to Hindus, and as well in writing school textbooks for their expanding missionary education activities among India's vast population. When the colonial government began to support local primary education in vernacular languages, in their need for school textbooks they drew upon missionaries' work. As Dalmia notes, "the texts remained, for all their simplicity, Sanskrit-oriented. It was an explicitly Hindu culture which … formed the frame of reference."[19] The only problem remaining was that Indians themselves were not yet aware that their own language was impure, and that it needed remedial attention. As late as 1846, the principal of Benaras College implored his students to use their *own* language, the language of their culture. To this request he was told:

> We do not clearly understand what you Europeans mean by the term Hindi, for there are hundreds of dialects all in our opinion equally entitled to the name … If the purity of Hindi is to consist in its exclusion of Musalman words, we shall require to study Persian and Arabic in order to ascertain which of the words we are in the habit of using every day, is Arabic or Persian and which is Hindi. With our present knowledge we can tell that a word is Sanskrit or not Sanskrit, but if not Sanskrit it may be English or Portuguese instead of Hindi for anything we can tell.[20]

In 1837 the British passed a resolution replacing the court language, Persian, with local vernaculars. This would lead to its replacement by Bengali and Oriya in Bengal, and Hindustani in the Arabic script in

---

[17] The colonial production, revision, and misuse of local knowledge is by now well documented. See Bernard S. Cohn, "The Command of Language and the Language of Command," in *Subaltern Studies IV*, ed. Ranajit Guha (Delhi: Oxford University Press, 1985).
[18] Dalmia, *Nationalization of Hindu Traditions*, 166.
[19] Ibid., 173.
[20] See Ballantyne account in *ibid.*, 174–5; King, *One Language, Two Scripts*, 90; Rai, *Hindi Nationalism*, 66.

the Northwest Provinces. (The Punjab region was not yet part of the British Empire as it remained under Sikh dominion until 1849.) While Hindustani enjoyed official state patronage, a consciousness of Hindi as a separate language, and indeed one with a completely different script, was gradually increasing. Hindi-language publications in Devanagri were expanding quickly, with far greater circulation numbers than Urdu, and a new current of thought began to emerge, one that sought parity for Hindi against the patronage already afforded Hindustani/Urdu. Benaras and Allahabad, for example, became the centers of a new Hindi publishing movement. Through the creation of this new literary sphere, Hindi proponents began to establish a standard language with a literary canon, laying claim to a pre-Islamic heritage through a purified language, employing explicitly Hindu themes, and a landscape valorizing sites important to Hindus. As Dalmia puts it, "Hindi as a language and literature, then, restricted the meaning of Hindu, even as it claimed to inscribe the autobiography of Hindustan as a nation."[21]

Advocacy for Hindi in the Nagari script continued to grow, and the demands became political. Hindi proponents petitioned the colonial authorities for the equal privilege to use Nagari-script Hindi in the courts, and as well for the right to a Hindi-language primary education. Pamphleteering for Hindi's right to participate in the official spheres of public life allied the language with the masses – the Hindu masses – and forged a discourse at once about religion and the spread of democracy, through language. Urdu was figured as a foreign imposition, an alien script with alien words that came from alien invaders. As Hindi became a more potent sociopolitical force, Urdu speakers felt themselves under attack. Urdu then became a language in need of "defending," a language represented by its partisan proponents as a core aspect of Muslim life itself. The emergence of "Urdu defense associations" in the region illustrates this sense of embattlement.[22]

Thus the Hindi–Urdu controversy in north India, in conjunction with movements for religious reformation within Hinduism and Islam slightly predating and continuing during the same period, participated in a process of schismogenesis, which at its endpoints would result in the complete association of Urdu with Islam and Hindi with Hinduism.[23] As we saw above, prior to this period there was fluidity of these boundaries;[24]

---

[21] Dalmia, *Nationalization of Hindu Traditions*, 337.
[22] C. A. Bayly, *The Local Roots of Indian Politics* (Oxford: Clarendon Press, 1975).
[23] "Schismogenesis" here in Bateson's usage of "progressive differentiation." Gregory Bateson, *Steps to an Ecology of Mind* (New York: Ballentine Books, 1972), 61–72.
[24] Muzaffar Alam addresses this problem of post-facto historical separatism. See Alam, *The Languages of Political Islam in India*.

writers experimented with using both scripts, with incorporating vocabulary from Sanskritic, Persian, English, even Portuguese sources, all illustrating that the idea of Hindi–Urdu as separate languages, and even that different scripts meant linguistic difference, was well a work-in-progress rather than a natural form of existence.[25] Following this period of reformation and codification, however, such fluidity would become almost unimaginable. Today's languages have diverged from one another beyond all recognition.

One result of the prominent role occupied by language in the contemporary social imagination was that protecting the Urdu language came to stand in for protecting Muslim interests writ large. Institutionally, the families and organizations founded to protect Urdu led to a next-generation successor in the Muslim League.[26] While defending Urdu may have been an important concern for residents of the Muslim minority provinces, no one ever suggested that it rose to a similar level of primacy in the Muslim majority territories which would eventually form Pakistan. Indeed, East Bengal had its beloved Bengali; Sindh had Sindhi; the Northwest Frontier Province had Pashto, and of course Punjab had Punjabi and what was then known as Multani, now called Siraiki. Within Punjab, as a result of an unusual social configuration, the Punjabi language existed in three scripts: Gurmukhi as a sacred language of the Sikh religion, but as well in Arabic script form as a language of Sufi verse and regional romance tales, and in a Devanagari form as well.[27] But by the eve of Pakistan's birth, the elision of Urdu-Muslim-Pakistan was complete, and yet highly compromised.

Articulating a new nation

We have seen how the late nineteenth-century experience with colonial administration resulted in a cultural economy that divided Hindus and Muslims, perceived as having separate languages each, into an oppositional and competitive stance. In the first half of the twentieth century, the opposition was replicated in the two movements for independence from the British. The two parallel movements differed greatly in their

---

[25] See Christopher Shackle and Rupert Snell, *Hindi and Urdu Since 1800: A Common Reader* (London: School of Oriental and African Studies, 1990).

[26] Bayly notes that in Allahabad, ten of thirteen patrons of the Muslim League in 1912 were sons of the members of earlier Urdu defense associations. Bayly, *Local Roots of Indian Politics*, 222.

[27] Similarly, Harjot Oberoi has argued that the hardening of religious boundaries of Sikhism was a late nineteenth-century development. See Harjot Oberoi, *The Construction of Religious Boundaries* (Chicago: The University of Chicago Press, 1994).

conceptions of nationalism, polity, minority rights, and who laid claim to representing the subcontinent's Muslims. The result was Partition.

The Indian National Congress, the party of Gandhi and Nehru, was a mass social movement advocating Indian self-rule and demanding that the British quit India. It claimed to represent the voices of all Indians. Indeed, the Congress enjoyed a tremendous grassroots following, and it explicitly included India's significant Muslim minority, then 20 percent of the population. At the same time, many argued that the existence of a Hindu-majoritarian wing of the party compromised its ability to claim complete neutrality on the matter of religion. Mohammad Ali Jinnah's Muslim League sought to be the Muslim voice, also demanding independence from colonial authority but arguing that the interests and basic rights of Muslims could not be assured without some clearly articulated political autonomy, for in any dispensation, Muslims could be outvoted by Hindus nearly four to one. The Muslim League advanced the "Two Nations Theory," the concept that Hindus and Muslims belonged to two separate nations which could never satisfactorily live side-by-side. Yet the Muslim League was not the sole voice of the subcontinent's Muslims, and its claim to represent Muslim interests was not borne out by voting patterns until the year before Partition. The Muslim League was least appealing to the very territories, the Muslim-majority areas in the northwest and east, which it hoped to incorporate for the envisioned Pakistan.

In Punjab, a northern Indian state claimed by the Pakistan movement as the central territorial building block, both the Congress and the Muslim League faced a regional power, the Unionist Party, in competition for mass support. The Unionist Party was a coalition of Hindu, Muslim, and Sikh landed interests, and was not in favor of Partition, which would tear the province of Punjab apart. Again, in Bengal the Muslim League did not command the allegiances of all the province's Muslims, many of whom cast their lot with Fazlul Haq's Krishak Praja Party in eastern Bengal. In the Northwest Frontier Province, the Khudai Khidmatgars, led by Khan Abdul Ghaffar Khan, advocated an independent Pukhtunistan (land of the Pashtuns), and thus saw their interests as not well represented by either the Congress or the Muslim League. It would not be until 1946, the year prior to Partition, that the Muslim League would make even a respectable electoral showing in the Muslim seats for the central legislature in these territories, and thus lay claim to representing the desires of the subcontinent's Muslims. Before 1945–6, the Muslim League and its calls for a separate national territory were extremely limited in their appeal. So the Pakistan demand was itself a contingent outcome, one which resulted from careful politicking prior to 1947 and which was emphatically not the declared demand of all the subcontinent's Muslims. The contentious nature of this history is hard to remember sixty years on, but it underscores the limits of the nation projected by the Pakistan Movement even before its legal form came into being.[28]

Even the word "Pakistan" itself prefigured the tensions which would emerge in the new country. The concept of an Indian Muslim state, albeit unnamed, offered by Iqbal in his 1930 address to the All-India Muslim League[29] would be given a shape and a name three years later in the writings of a young Cambridge University student, Choudhary Rahmat Ali. In a 1933 pamphlet, "Now or Never," replicated in various related pamphlets released periodically until the end of 1946, Rahmat Ali called for a homeland for Muslims, named for and carved from **P**unjab, **A**fghania, **K**ashmir, **S**indh, and Baluchis**TAN**. This English-language acronym – bringing together the names of the provinces comprising today's Pakistan, though significantly including Kashmir and omitting Bengal – imagined a nation composed of pieces assembled like a puzzle (see Figure 1).

Rahmat Ali's prolific, even manic territorial designs envisioned not just Pakistan but a Bang-i-Islam, a Haideristan, a Faruqistan, a Siddiqistan, Usmanistan, later a Maplistan in South India, all to be carved out of the subcontinent of India, which he renamed the "Continent of Dinia" (recalling the Arabic word *dīn*, "religion") to thereby save Muslims from the "menace of Indianism." Of these offerings, only Pakistan came to fruition, although the 1971 creation of Bangladesh suggests the prescience of "Bang-i-Islam" as well.[30] Despite their frenzied quality, Rahmat Ali's various pamphlets and his Pakistan proposal seemed to codify in a readily digestible form what a separate Muslim nation in India could mean. By 1938 – only five years after its coinage, nearly a decade before the country would come into existence, and two years before the Lahore Resolution endorsing the pursuit of a Pakistan – the word "Pakistan" had already made its way into the *Encyclopedia of Islam* published in

---

[28] For the detailed history of Jinnah's Muslim League and how the Pakistan demand was eventually secured, see Jalal, *Sole Spokesman*. On the Unionists, see Ian Talbot, *Khizr Tiwana* (Oxford and Karachi: Oxford University Press, 2002). On NWFP, see Stephen Rittenberg, *Ethnicity, Nationalism, and the Pakhtuns* (Durham: Carolina Academic Press, 1988).

[29] With the publication of the three-volume *Foundations of Pakistan* series, Iqbal's address – delivered in English – can be read in its entirety. See "All-India Muslim League, Twenty-First Session, Allahabad, December 29–30, 1930" in Pirzada, ed., *Foundations of Pakistan, Vol. II*, 153–70.

[30] See Choudhary Rahmat Ali, "What Does the Pakistan National Movement Stand For?" (Cambridge: Pakistan National Movement, 1942 [1933]).

Figure 1 Cover image from third edition of pamphlet, "What Does the Pakistan National Movement Stand For?"

Leiden, defined in part as "the land of the Pāks. The word *Pāk* ... stands for all that is noble and sacred in life for a Muslim."[31]

The *Encyclopedia* entry accurately understood that the word Pakistan meant much more than just an acronym. The other dimension of this coinage hinged on the meanings of "pāk" and "-stān." "Pāk" is an adjective, present in Islamicate languages of Northern India via Persian, and it denotes purity, virtue, even holiness. Its antonym, *nāpāk*, means dirty or defiled. The second half of the new country's name, -*stān*, is a suffix that forms "place of" or "land of," like Afghanistan and Tajikistan – the land of the Afghans, the land of the Tajiks, or the land of the Pāks. Yet in one of the great etymological ironies of history, both morphemes have

---

[31] *Encyclopedia of Islam* (supplement) (Leiden: Brill, 1938), 174.

Sanskrit cognates. The "pāk" of Persian is cognate with the Sanskrit "pāvaka," and the "stān" of Persian is cognate with the Sanskrit "sthān." That the very word meant to signal purification and separation from Hindu India should be itself linked to a common origin would seem to overtly undermine the two-nation theory.[32]

Given the connotation of "pāk" and "stān," respectively, "Pakistan" was far more than just the acronym presented by Rahmat Ali. It was a lexeme for population unmixing, a cleansing, that the land itself would have to undergo to become pure and pāk. (Jinnah, at least in 1943, sought to downplay this association, but nonetheless adopted the name which unavoidably carries the connotation.)[33] Moreover, this concept of national purity, at least insofar as the Pakistan Movement represented it, was very closely linked to the Urdu language as the authorized language of South Asian Islam. A perusal of the All-India Muslim League annual meeting documents, for example, reveals that during the period 1930–46 – from the time of Iqbal's first articulation of a separate but unnamed Muslim nation within India – through the eve of Partition, the only language which was ever the subject of a League resolution acknowledging its importance to Islam is Urdu. This, despite the wide variety of Muslim literary traditions in regional languages in use in the Muslim majority provinces. The 1943 annual gathering at Karachi appears to be the only such meeting that explicitly noted the cultural diversity of the land, engaging presentations of poetry in Urdu, Sindhi, Punjabi, and even a "poem demanding the establishment of Pakistan" delivered in Pashto by Maulana Khan Mir Hilali of Peshawar.[34] This linkage of religion to nation to language revealed an overt language ideology as a neatly logical proposition: [*If* Muslim *then* language = Urdu]. The logical contrapositive, [*If* language ≠ Urdu, *then* **not** Muslim] would structure the politics of language and culture in Pakistan over the subsequent decades. But this concept would negate the idea of the nation as an amalgamation of many parts.

Nationalism: boundaries, borders, and language

Conflict stemming from issues of language began with the creation of Pakistan in 1947, and the chapters which follow explore the lineaments of those conflicts and their implications for our thinking about

---

[32] See John T. Platts, *A Dictionary of Urdu, Classical Hindi, and English* (Lahore: Sang-e-Meel, 1994 [1911]), 219, 637.
[33] Jinnah's April 1943 presidential address to the Muslim League attempted to backtrack from the notion of cleansing by insisting that the name Pakistan was "foisted" by the Hindu and British press. See Pirzada, ed., *Foundations of Pakistan, Vol. II*, 425.
[34] See *ibid.*, 462.

the nation-form and nationalism. The history of these cultural conflicts reveals the limits of nation-building even in a context in which the idea of a cohesive Muslim nation, a "civilization of 100 million" had been widely discussed *by Muslims* as an entity assumed to exist already. The history of these conflicts also reveals the pervasiveness of mental structures that reproduce one type of opposition – the Hindu versus Muslim socioreligious division – onto other relationships which on the face of it may not have otherwise been perceived in the same way. These divisive, "dichotomizing oppositions," in the words of Susan Gal, can recreate themselves recursively, in the manner of fractals – which replicate their forms on "ever-smaller social units."[35] This process changes the perceptions, interactions, and symbolic relationships among all social actors involved.

In Pakistan, the overt linkage of the Urdu language with the Islamic faith led to a presumption on the part of the Muslim League leadership that Urdu would naturally serve as the national language for this new country. Those who objected, or sought an alternative, were stigmatized as "anti-Pakistan" fifth columns. Other languages of the territories of Pakistan would be denigrated as "too Hindu" or insufficiently civilized. The history of these language conflicts, and the difficulties crafting a national cultural ideology of pluralism suggests several questions that demand exploration, not the least of which is: why only one national language? As can be readily seen in the debates leading up to Partition, everyone knew that the proposed territory of the new Muslim homeland was comprised of several regions with a number of well-developed literary traditions in languages other than Urdu. The importance placed on the idea of one language as central to the Pakistan national project leads to important observations on nationalism and the process of its spread beyond Western Europe. Equally important is the divergence of this process from earlier political forms in South Asia characterized by multilinguality, as has been argued recently by Sheldon Pollock for premodern India.[36]

Beyond the cases delineated in the chapter which follows, a further challenge to the constructed primordialism of Pakistan's national language project has emerged from within the very heart of what has long been considered the "ethnic hegemon" of Pakistan, Punjab. This development raises questions for the way we think about nationalism and its mechanics in theoretical terms, for the case does not fit the by now well-established models of regional mobilization against a center.

---

[35] Susan Gal, "Bartok's Funeral," *American Ethnologist* 18, no. 3 (August 1991): 446.
[36] Pollock, *Language of the Gods*.

The case displays further evidence of the replication of one set of oppositions across another, however poorly they fit. It also, however, suggests limitations on pure constructivism, for in the effort to craft a seemingly old but emphatically new Punjabi literary culture and history, we see the imprint of the partly successful, partly failed effort to forge a Pakistani Urdu national project.

It is difficult to understand, without thinking of these symbolic relations as recursive processes, why such cultural antipathies would have emerged within a newly created country premised on the unity of Islam. That Muslims can be of many cultures would appear to be self-evident, but the oppositional syllogism so crucial to the political mobilization of the Hindi–Urdu controversy and the politics of the Pakistan Movement leading to Partition would continue to replicate itself in cultural spaces in the new Pakistan, and with ever-more-narrow arenas of focus.

Thinking of the history of language policy and nation-building in Pakistan in this way will allow us to see that the categories of ethnicity, culture, language, and identity are shaped by discursive engagements, defined by the boundaries of separation or differentiation rather than some clearly identifiable ethnic substance. In this sense, this book's historical narratives follow the anthropological literature, pioneered with Fredrik Barth's *Ethnic Groups and Boundaries*, which focuses on the zones of contestation and the boundaries between groups as centrally constituting conceptions of group identity rather than merely the particulars contained by them.[37] For the project of nationalism is, at its core, an effort to formalize, through the creation of political boundaries, the canonization of a culture and its claims to authority. As Katherine Verdery has put it,

> If we see culture (as many anthropologists now do) not as a zone of shared meanings but as a zone of *disagreement* and *contest*, what happens to the idea of ethnicity as shared culture? It necessarily becomes the study of culture as politics ... a view of ethnicity as tied to social ideologies, particularly to ideologies of nationalism, which specific social groups construct around notions of "culture" and "origin."[38]

From this perspective, the subsequent sixty-plus years of conflict over language, culture, center–province relations – whatever the term – can be explored as processes of reshaping, of *rethinking* the boundaries that

---

[37] Fredrik Barth, *Ethnic Groups and Boundaries* (Boston: Little, Brown, 1969); Hans Vermeulen and Cora Govers, eds., *The Anthropology of Ethnicity: Beyond 'Ethnic Groups and Boundaries'* (Amsterdam: Het Spinhuis, 1994).
[38] Katherine Verdery, "Ethnicity, Nationalism, and State-making," in *The Anthropology of Ethnicity*, ed. Vermeulen and Govers (1994), 42.

define what it would mean socially and politically to be Pakistani. These discursive interactions have produced, over time, a number of counter-intuitive developments – new interpretations of culture and origin, new propositions of cultural pluralism, and new limitations on the idea of the nation. Language has played an outsized role in the national quest for a culture that can truly be "national," as the following chapters show, and this work explores how those links have been as constitutive as the quest for Islam's proper role for the state project. Indeed, the collapse of language, religion, and nation into one indivisible form, projected as the nation, offers an opportunity to explore the limits of a case in which the presentation of national identity has appeared obvious and natural yet historically false and artificial all at the same time.

2 Urdu and the nation

> In the demand for Pakistan, Urdu was most thoughtlessly declared to be the language of a "separate Muslim nation," so now it is also paying the price for the creation of the "homeland."
>
> Qurratulain Hyder, "Chapter 66. Letter from Karachi," *River of Fire*

The late Qurratulain Hyder published her epic novel *Āg kā daryā* ("River of Fire") in 1957, a decade after Partition.[1] Considered a masterwork of Urdu fiction, the novel covers a time period from the fourth century BC through Partition's aftermath, with four interlinked characters spanning cycles of rebirth throughout millennia, and across the severed political fates of the two countries created in 1947.

At the time the novel appeared in Urdu, a number of significant language conflicts had already emerged in Pakistan, occasioning the narrator's observation that the language was "paying the price" for the emphasis on the national importance of Urdu for the creation and existence of the Muslim homeland. Indeed, the strange and troubled disjuncture between the *idea* of the Urdu language as emblematic of the nation and the *reality* in the then-new country is demonstrated by the ill-fated cases of Karachi's first film, *Hamārī Zabān*, and the creation of a new song genre for the nation. The film *Hamārī Zabān* ("Our Language"), an effort to eulogize Urdu and its national importance, was released in 1955 only to sink ignominiously, as film historian Mushtaq Gazdar noted, for its "admonitory sequences" were not audience pleasers. A similar reception met the new musical genre created and disseminated by Radio Pakistan, one known as *Iqbāliat* because it fused the national poet's work with the *qawwālī* musical idiom.[2] The mere fact that it was felt necessary to make *Hamārī Zabān* and create the Iqbāliat genre, however, illustrates both the shallowness of Urdu's

---

[1] The 1998 translation – source for the epigraph above – is Hyder's own.
[2] Regula Qureshi, "Recorded Sound and Religious Music," in *Media and the Transformation of Religion in South Asia*, ed. Babb and Wadley (Philadelphia: University of Pennsylvania Press, 1995), 152–3.

roots, as well as the power of language ideologies in determining national language choice.

Statistics collected in Pakistan's early days underscored the limited reach of the Urdu language in the territories which formed the country, even following the mass migration of Muslims from lands which remained in India: according to the 1951 Census, some 7.2 million overall, of which 5.7 million were from areas of northern India where Urdu was a common language. Even so, in gross percentage terms the results of the 1951 Census illustrated Urdu's limitations as a national language. In the words of the Census author, E. H. Slade himself:

95 per cent of the inhabitants of Pakistan have claimed one or other of the following 5 chief languages as their Mother-tongue, namely *Bengali, Punjabi, Pushtu, Sindhi* and *Urdu*. 98 percent of the inhabitants of East Bengal have *Bengali* as their Mother-tongue and they represent 55 percent of the total population of Pakistan. *Punjabi* is the Mother-tongue of 28 percent of the total inhabitants of Pakistan, *Sindhi* 5.3 per cent, *Pushtu* 6.6 and *Urdu* 3.3 percent.[3]

Given Urdu's prominence as a language of administration, and more particularly as a language of high culture and formal literacy, its appropriateness as a link language was heralded in the early days of Pakistan as an explanation for why it, rather than any of the other languages with much larger demographic bases, should occupy the role of national language. But again, even when enumerating the percentage of Pakistanis speaking Urdu as a first language as well as "additional language," the total *in West Pakistan alone* was a slim 14.7 percent. Numerically this number was dwarfed nationally by Bengali as well as Punjabi, with aggregate speakers of 54.6 and 28.4 percent respectively. In practical terms, this led to the continued primacy of English as the medium of government and higher education.[4]

The assumption of Urdu's necessity rested, of course, to some extent on the administrative and documentary uses of the language, which in this land of very low literacy levels (18.9 per cent overall in 1951) still accounted for an overwhelming presence of the country's periodicals.[5] In addition, despite Bengali's overwhelming dominance as a spoken language in statistical terms (albeit limited to East Pakistan), as a language of literacy in Pakistan, its adherents numbered only 5,948,120 – compared to 2,360,063 for Urdu and 1,953,221 for English. In short, those

---

[3] Data on migrants from E. H. Slade, "Census of Pakistan, 1951" (Government of Pakistan, 1951), 30. Quote from Slade, "Census of Pakistan, 1951," 68.
[4] Charles H. Kennedy, *Bureaucracy in Pakistan* (Karachi: Oxford University Press, 1987), 183–4.
[5] Urdu speakers in West Pakistan from Slade, "Census of Pakistan, 1951," 68. Urdu in periodicals from Slade, "Census of Pakistan, 1951," 78.

who learned to read and write were, if not in Bengali, likely to learn those skills in Urdu or English. This represented only a tiny fraction of the country's estimated population of some 73.8 million in 1951, leading to a situation that directly privileged the English- and Urdu-speaking elites in the country who formed the governing class after Partition. To encourage Pakistanis to accept the idea of Urdu as the appropriate language to embody the new national culture, necessary to forge national cohesion, Pakistani leaders emphasized Urdu's centrality to the nation.[6]

But the limited enthusiasm citizens of the new country accorded efforts like *Hamārī Zabān* and the Iqbāliat genre points to the limitations of these efforts of symbolic domination. The poor fit between the imagined country and its reality has been the subject of a number of scholarly and popular monographs, each of which have contributed to our understandings of the problems inherent in the way the country was "insufficiently imagined," to use the signally appropriate words of Salman Rushdie in *Shame*.[7] This insufficiency took two forms. At the administrative level, it was as if focused attention had not been given to the very real questions of communication, resource allocation, and status implied in the creation of a national culture, particularly with the challenges of illiteracy, very large populations with distinct language traditions, not to mention the hurdle of the country's two territories separated by India. But at the conceptual level, the level from which all else flows, this insufficiency took the form of an inability to envision how a Muslim nation could also be multiethnic, could be anything other than the inheritor of the north Indian Islamic culture associated with the literary and cultural traditions of Urdu. Although the two categories in and of themselves would not appear to be mutually exclusive, the national hierarchization obtaining – as a result of the deeply embedded language ideology which structured the national imagination of Pakistan's creation – privileged one above all others, leading to political and policy choices that contributed to the country's internal crises, rather than forged national unity.

A brief recap of Pakistan's political history will situate the narratives of this and the subsequent chapter, both of which are centrally concerned with the relationship between culture and the state, and the politics of

---

[6] Table 8.A of Slade, "Census of Pakistan, 1951," 8-6,8-7.
[7] See Ian Talbot, *Pakistan: A Modern History* (Lahore: Vanguard Books, 1999); Owen Bennett Jones, *Pakistan: Eye of the Storm* (New Haven: Yale University Press, 2002); and Mary Anne Weaver, *Pakistan: In the Shadow of Jihad and Afghanistan* (New York: Farar, Straus and Giroux, 2002). On the conundrum of the nation versus the state of Pakistan, see Stephen P. Cohen, *The Idea of Pakistan* (Washington, DC: Brookings Institution Press, 2004).

culture that shape the nation at its so-called margins. Pakistan, by any measure, has led a difficult sixty years of independence, more than half of which has been under military dictators. Strong political centralization and an over-reliance on the military as a means to "hold" the country together further exacerbated the national emphasis successive rulers placed on the necessity of creating a singular national Islamic culture, with Urdu as the centerpiece.[8]

After achieving independence in 1947, Mohammad Ali Jinnah served as the country's governor-general until his untimely death in 1948. His death, and the lack of a deeper cohort of political leadership, led to a troubled first decade, characterized in part by the country's failed efforts to draft a constitution to govern itself, a problem which has continued to plague Pakistan even today.[9] General Ayub Khan, later Field Marshal, carried out the country's first coup in 1958. He held power for eleven years, only to hand over the reins to another general, Yahya Khan, who ruled from 1969 through 1971 and presided over the bloody war in East Pakistan, ultimately losing half the country when it seceded. A brief period of democratic leadership under Zulfiqar Ali Bhutto (1972–7) offered a populist interlude in which one "region" (Sindh) received greater cultural patronage than it had in the past. Bhutto allowed greater cultural expression to the regions, and it was also during his administration that cultural heritage institutions like Lok Virsa and the Panjabi Adabi Board were founded. However, it was also Bhutto who refused to recognize a clear Bengali political victory in the parliamentary elections of 1971, sparking events that culminated in war and the secession of half the country. Three years later, it was also Bhutto who quelled an armed rebellion in Baluchistan by deploying the army in the province for three years. This past makes it difficult to evaluate Bhutto's leadership unequivocally positively.

But Bhutto was a true democrat compared with what came next. General Zia ul-Haq seized power from Bhutto in a coup, and then hanged him in a televised execution. Zia stayed for eleven years until his death in a still-unexplained plane crash in 1988. General Zia's goals dovetailed with global events catalyzed first by the geoeconomic changes in the Gulf, which affected the country's national imagination from the 1970s forward. Gulf oil wealth created new economic and ideological

[8] For an excellent overview of the process of "developing" and propagating Urdu, see Tariq Rahman, *Language, Ideology and Power* (Karachi: Oxford University Press, 2002), 263–87. His sociolinguistic research provides the basis for much of the analysis in this chapter.
[9] On political leadership, see especially Khalid Bin Sayeed, *Pakistan: The Formative Phase, 1857–1948*, 2nd edn (London: Oxford University Press, 1968).

connections with Pakistan; millions of Pakistanis became guest workers in the region, remitting capital to their families back home, while moving in the other direction Gulf countries (particularly Saudi Arabia and the UAE) began programs and foundations for religious proselytization. Pakistan, seeing itself as the vanguard of the Islamic world, began to pursue a foreign policy to locate itself as a strategic member of the Middle East and Central Asia, thus further orienting its frame of reference to its Islamic western borders rather than toward India to the east.[10]

Then, the 1979 Soviet invasion of Afghanistan ushered in a decade of covert operations to funnel cash and arms to Islamic radicals willing to fight back godless Communists, creating new Islamist "most favored lords" in the process. The ill after-effects of this partnership continue to reverberate today, particularly in the growth of radical Islam and Islamist militias patronized by the country's intelligence agency.[11] What all this meant for Pakistan internally was a more forceful push on the state project to produce the people by further emphasizing the idea of the state as Islamic, with a concentration on the austere Deoband tradition patronized by Zia and reinforced by Saudi Wahhabism. In Pakistan, the Islamization push quite aggressively imagined its ultimate product to be a cultural, linguistic, and indeed behavioral sphere of uniformity epitomized by an idea of "Urdu culture" as the sine qua non of South Asian Islam.[12]

Thus the long decade of the 1990s was the only time that Pakistan experienced some form of sustained civilian leadership, albeit in a round-robin, chaotic fashion. The late Benazir Bhutto, daughter of Zulfiqar, alternated power with Nawaz Sharif in three-year cycles until 1999. The 1990s were a decade, as explored in the chapters focused on Punjab, in which a greater expressive freedom for the country's diverse language and cultural traditions was allowed to surface. It was during the 1990s that the contemporary debates on the problem of historiography in Pakistan came to the foreground, for example. But it was also during the 1990s that a dramatic increase in sectarian violence took place, and law and order utterly collapsed in the commercial capital of Karachi. In 1999 General Pervez Musharraf deposed Nawaz Sharif

---

[10] Marvin Weinbaum and Gautam Sen, "Pakistan Enters the Middle East," *Orbis* 22, no. 3 (Fall 1978).
[11] See Steve Coll, *Ghost Wars* (New York: Penguin, 2004).
[12] Ahmad, "Some Reflections on Urdu;" K. K. Aziz, *The Murder of History in Pakistan* (Lahore: Vanguard, 1993); Ayesha Jalal, "Conjuring Pakistan: History as Official Imagining," *International Journal of Middle East Studies* 27, no. 1 (February 1995); A. H. Nayyar and Ahmed Salim, *The Subtle Subversion* (Islamabad: Sustainable Development Policy Institute, 2002); Sibte Hasan, *The Battle of Ideas in Pakistan* (Karachi: Pakistan Publishing House, 1986).

in a bloodless coup, seized power, and reconstituted the army's ruling authority in the country, as well as assisted radical Islam's rise to political power. The civilian leadership elected in February 2008 continues to debate the nature of its role, the place of the military, and what should be done about the growing Talibanization that now threatens the country well beyond the Tribal Areas.

This brief overview should serve to illustrate the political tumult that has characterized Pakistan since its birth. Whether the country was under civilian or military rule, one common thread has been the insistence with which central leaders, and central institutions, have indulged religious leaders, in some cases some of the most illiberal Islamists available. In sharp contrast to a popular understanding in the West of a country "caught" between a secular or moderate Muslim leadership and a bubbling cauldron of Islamist activists, increasingly analysts agree that Pakistan's leaders have coopted Islamism in order to capture and retain control of the discourse of legitimacy.[13] As the previous chapter emphasized, the discourse of legitimacy in Pakistan's specific terms has carried with it the implication that Urdu, and its literary-historical complex, should have the natural central role in the country's cultural life. Taking that decision as a given – for Tariq Rahman has ably chronicled the story of Urdu in Pakistan – this book examines the resulting faultlines. The chapter begins with the curious status of English and Arabic, two prestige languages playing critical roles in Pakistan. It then turns to the critical case of Bengali, the language movement that fueled the first successful secession in a postcolonial state. The chapter which follows, "The nation and its margins," considers the language movements of Sindhi, Siraiki, Pashto, and Balochi. The counterintuitive case of Punjab, of course, is considered separately in Chapters 4 and 5.

English in the registers of power

As a former British colony, Pakistan at independence inherited state institutions of administration and education which used English as their language. The elite Government College, the civil services, the courts, and the country's leadership conducted business through English. Discussions of implementing a national language were, in this sense, focused not merely on various regional languages in use in the territories which became Pakistan, but of course as well with the colonial

---

[13] Hassan Abbas, *Pakistan's Drift into Extremism* (Armonk, NY: M.E. Sharpe, 2004); Husain Haqqani, *Pakistan: Between Mosque and Military* (Washington: Carnegie Endowment for International Peace, 2005); Seyyed Vali Reza Nasr, *Islamic Leviathan* (New York: Oxford University Press, 2001).

prestige language. We can see this dilemma of symbolic capital in the public addresses made by Mohammad Ali Jinnah: his emphatic public addresses, including those asserting that, "Urdu is the language of Pakistan and no other," were all made in English.

Thus English-language use marks a cycle of privilege: those who speak it as a first language or speak it well as a second language have had the opportunity to attend either expensive and exclusive English-medium private schools, or made the cut to attend the officer and/or civil service academies. Those who graduate from these elite schools often move into ruling elite, whose children later attend the same schools and repeat the cycle. The current state of English is the same as it was in 1947 despite a series of commission reports and recommendations to remedy and provide either greater opportunities for English learning for all (an Ayub-era initiative), or to limit the sphere of English and extend Urdu for all.

As with many postcolonial countries, Pakistani leaders viewed English in the early days as a temporary obstacle, one which would eventually be replaced by Urdu. During the First Education Conference in Karachi in 1947, the chairman Fazlur Rahman remarked regarding English that "We should not throw away a language which give us so easy access to all the secrets of western science and culture."[14] Toward the goal of promoting Urdu while not limiting Pakistan's progress, specific institutions were established primarily in the Punjab to coin a scientific and legal vocabulary in Urdu, thus facilitating scientific advancement. In particular, Punjab's governor created the Official Language Committee (Majlis-e-Zaban-e-Daftari) in 1949. Its sole function was to coin new Urdu vocabulary. In addition, schools were ordered to change their language medium from English to Urdu, and the courts, the legislature, and government offices were supposed to conduct their business in Urdu. Of these official spheres, the only office which actually functioned in Urdu was the Official Language Committee.[15]

While the first meeting of the Advisory Board of Education in 1948 was in general agreement that Urdu should become the medium of instruction at the secondary and university levels, it reached no decision regarding the exclusive English medium schools and academies.

---

[14] See Pakistan Educational Conference, *Proceedings of The Pakistan Educational Conference, Held at Karachi, From 27th November to 1st December 1947*, reprint edn (Islamabad: Government of Pakistan, Ministry of the Interior (Education Division), 1983 [1947]) and M. Geijbels, "Urdu and the Pakistani National Language Issue," in *The Rise and Development of Urdu and the Importance of Regional Languages in Pakistan*, ed. Geijbels and Addleton (Rawalpindi: Christian Study Centre), 19.

[15] Tariq Rahman, *The History of the Urdu-English Controversy*, vol. 311, *Silsilah-e-matbu'āt-e-Muqtādirah-e-Qaumī Zabān* (Islamabad: National Language Authority (Government of Pakistan), 1996), 54.

By deferring decision, the English schools would only multiply and that too at the government's expense. It was as if two monologues took place rather than a dialogue: the training ground for the ruling class remained English, while the new institutions for propagating Urdu were busily working away. English remained dominant by the time of Ayub's ascendance to power, and his own emphasis on modernity and progress would only reinforce English at the upper levels. The Hamood ur-Rahman Education report, released in 1966, expressed regret that Karachi and Punjab universities permitted the BA examination in Urdu medium, and that the University of Sindh allowed the same in Sindhi. The report would have preferred English.

During Yahya Khan's era, Nur Khan's *Proposals for a New Educational Policy* recommended that Bengali be the medium of instruction in East Pakistan and Urdu in West; the document also had a phase-in plan which set 1974 as the target date for these languages to be used by provincial governments, and at the center by 1975. The Nur Khan plan would phase out English, precisely because it perpetuated a "caste-like distinction between those who feel at ease ... in English and those who do not." The proposal was contested, and when it was published publicly a year later as *New Education Policy 1970*, it delegated the issue of phasing out English to a commission scheduled to be established in 1972. Pakistan, however, collapsed into civil war before then, and when Bhutto came to power in 1972 he did not act upon the Nur Khan report. Zulfiqar Ali Bhutto's government declared Urdu the national language of Pakistan – enshrined in article 251 of the 1973 Constitution – and added a phase-in clause such that "a period of 15 years ... for the replacement of English by Urdu." This particular amendment has yet to see full implementation.[16]

General Zia's goal of Islamizing the nation to integration led to his desire for Urdu to resound throughout the nation. To accomplish this, he "pass[ed] an order that Urdu would be the medium of instruction in all schools from 'class 1 or KG as the case may be from 1979.'" However, pressure from the English schools, and not the regional language movements, ultimately resulted in Zia's withdrawl of the order in 1987. English schools remained, and proliferated.[17]

Throughout the many democratic governments since 1988, each has proclaimed its intention to establish Urdu fully as Pakistan's national

---

[16] Both quotations from *ibid.*, 62.
[17] Geijbels, "Urdu and the Pakistani National Language Issue," 21; Tariq Rahman, "Language Policy in Pakistan," *Ethnic Studies Report* 14, no. 1 (1996): 88. See also Mukhtar Zaman, *Thoughts on National Language Policy*, trans. Syed Faizi (Islamabad: National Language Authority/Muqtadira-e-Qaumi Zaban, 1985), 13.

language, with the eventual goal of replacing English. This has not come to fruition. With the rise of global English, a further mushrooming of private English-medium schools has taken place, especially in Pakistan's major cities. Parents, even those without disposable income, are demonstrating their willingness to sacrifice in order to provide their children with an education that they believe will enhance employment prospects. Parents of children attending schools operated by the Aga Khan Rural Support Program in the Northern Areas of Pakistan, for example (a region about which there is little in the way of official statistical information) staged a grassroots "revolt" of sorts during the mid-1990s and demanded that English be the medium of education.[18]

Arabic and the Islamic nation

The creation of Pakistan as a Muslim homeland would suggest a significant role for the Arabic language, as classical Arabic is the language of the Quran and is the religiously sanctioned prestige language for Islam. Though Arabic language policies in Pakistan have their beginnings with Ayub Khan, it is a curious footnote of history that the Aga Khan, head of the Ismaili Shi`a Muslim community, suggested Arabic as the state language in 1951 – as an alternative to the contentious Urdu versus Bengali debate at the time.[19] There have been no contentious conflicts over Arabic; rather, its role in the symbolic economy has, over time, produced profound change in Pakistan.

General Ayub Khan was the first Pakistani leader to advocate the institution of Arabic language teaching as part of national planning. His Commission on National Education made two recommendations, one which never came to pass and one which created the first step toward integrating and normalizing private Islamic schools, or *madrasa* (*madārīs* in plural form). Where his impulse toward modernization caused him to give English and Urdu primacy over all other languages – he recommended romanization of all the scripts of Pakistani languages – he sought to affect the curricula of the private Islamic *madārīs* as well by proposing "greater integration of English into their teaching. Modern Arabic literature (as opposed to premodern treatises) were [*sic*] additionally advised as a means to 'introduce the ulema to the modern world.'" This proposal was not implemented by the Islamic *ulema* running their own private schools; to date, Rahman reports that only 2.87 percent of *madrasa*-educated students are taught English at all. Ayub's educational

---

[18] Jonathan Mitchell, telephone interview, March 12, 2002.
[19] Rahman, "Language Policy in Pakistan," 88.

plan emphasized Urdu and English as the primary languages of Pakistan, but additionally recommended that Arabic be a secondary language of instruction along with English. This proposition paved the way for a perception that modernity, the nation, and links to the world would take place via English and Arabic – thus routinizing the idea of Arabic in state-run schools.[20]

It would be the Islamization programs of General Zia ul Haq which would again take up Arabic at the national level and promote its use. Zia's understanding of national cohesion was that Islam was the binding force of the Pakistani nation. He thus advocated the promotion of Arabic and Urdu as a means of overcoming the provincial and "centrifugal" forces which threatened to rip the nation further apart.

In 1982, faced with a shortage of trained secular teachers of Arabic, Zia conscripted the religious scholars (*ulema*) of the *madrasa* schools to come into the state schools specifically to teach Arabic. In 1984 and 1985, Zia implemented a new system known as "Iqra Centres," part of his literacy and mass education campaign. The Iqra Centres were centers for the teaching of Urdu but established within the premises of local mosques and *madāris*.[21] With these two steps – conscription of *mullahs* as Arabic teachers in the state schools along with the establishment of Urdu literacy programs in religious institutions – the imbrication of the Islamic educational system with state education programs began in earnest. Zia additionally instituted the use of Pakistani state-owned airwaves in 1984 as a powerful medium for his Islamiyat initiatives; the state began broadcasting news in Arabic on television.[22] This initiative continues to this day, though it is unclear whether ordinary Pakistanis actually understand the broadcast. The Arabic news broadcasts are supplemented by daytime nationwide broadcasts of Arabic language learning and Quranic text learning. Though Arabic is the central language for these *madāris* for obvious religious reasons, it is not taught as a living language, nor as a medium for the students to communicate: it is for textual recitation and memorization. Students memorize the sounds of Arabic and learn their meanings via Urdu but never learn to generate their own sentences.[23] Arabic has not become associated with any notion of a bounded ethnic category in Pakistan, although its influence as a religious prestige language is being felt most dramatically in corpus

---

[20] Tariq Rahman, *Language, Education, and Culture* (Islamabad: Oxford University Press and Sustainable Development Policy Institute, 1999), 105, 110.
[21] *Ibid.*, 111.
[22] C. G. P. Rakisitis, "Centre-Province Relations in Pakistan Under President Zia," *Pacific Affairs* 61, no. 1 (Spring 1988): 80.
[23] Rahman, *Language, Education, and Culture*, 105.

planning and development of Urdu. In this sense it participates in the continued reification of the Urdu language as somehow a preferred bearer of religion, of Islam, in the subcontinent.

Bengal's trouble with Urdu

The Bengali language movement is the best known of the subnational conflicts Pakistan has faced. To be sure, language was only one of many grievances that led to East Pakistan's secession in 1971. Bengalis were under-represented in the bureaucracy and the military, and the federal structure of the Constituent Assembly did not allocate seats that reflected East Bengal's simple majority of the population. Both the quota system of representation in the federal bureaucracy, as well as the One-Unit administrative reform of 1954 (which grouped all the provinces of West Pakistan as one) were efforts to address these disparities.[24] And indeed, economic and political disparities were the subject of Bengalis' complaints. But the annual commemoration of the beginnings of Bangladeshi national consciousness centers not on bureaucratic under-representation or any other statist question, but on language. Bangladeshis remember their state's beginnings by celebrating *ekushe*, the Bengali word for "twenty-one," each February 21st, commemorating the day in 1952 that four Bengalis died protesting for the administrative use of Bengali. Though language alone was not the determinative factor in Bengali nationalism, its role as a first-order consideration in Bangladeshi historical consciousness has become undeniable.[25]

Public discourse surrounding the "language question" was particularly dramatic in the case of Bengali. Speeches made by Jinnah – in English, at Dhaka University – arguing the necessity of Urdu are to this day cited approvingly and quoted at length by official government publications, so the rhetoric lives on.[26] What is so astounding in retrospect is the vehemence with which Pakistan's top leadership – the Governor-General and the Prime Minister – dismissed East Bengal's demands to create a formal, official role for Bengali. That the language of 56 percent of Pakistan's population – and of nearly all of East Pakistan's – was not afforded a national role from the moment of independence underscores

---

[24] On the quota system in Pakistan's bureaucracy, see Kennedy, *Bureaucracy in Pakistan*, esp. 181–208.
[25] For a thorough examination of the ideological, political, and economic crises that converged in the secession of East Bengal and the birth of Bangladesh, see Rounaq Jahan, *Pakistan: Failure in National Integration* (Dhaka: Oxford University Press, 1973).
[26] See, for example, the introductory pages of Jalibi, *Qaumī Zabān* (Islamabad: Muqtadira Qaumi Zaban [National Langauge Authority], 1989).

42   Speaking Like a State

the deep significance the leadership had invested in Urdu. This symbolic hierarchy served to deny national importance for other languages in Pakistan, categorizing all of them despite widespread usage, as merely "regional," a process similar to what has been termed "national hierachization" in the former Soviet Union context.[27]

As early as October 1947, less than two months after the birth of Pakistan, a "Rashtra Bhasa Sangram Parishad" (State Language Committee of Action) was formed in East Pakistan to protest Bengali's omission from the new official forms, currency notes, stamps, and coins of the new Pakistan.[28] The first street demonstration took place on December 5, 1947, with another protest meeting at Dhaka University held the following day to object to the new Education Conference's recommendation that Urdu be the only state language of Pakistan.

In February 1948, students at Dhaka University demonstrated against Pakistan's insistence that Urdu be the only national language. Both Jinnah and then-Prime Minister Liaqat Ali responded with public addresses that explicitly laid out the imagined cultural contours of the nation. Then-Governor-General Jinnah delivered two important speeches in Dhaka so extraordinary for their content that they are worth quoting at length here:

But I want to tell you that in our midst there are people financed by foreign agencies who are intent on creating disruption. Their object is to disrupt and sabotage Pakistan. I want you to be on your guard; I want you to be vigilant and not to be taken in by attractive slogans and catchwords. They say that the Pakistan Government and the East Bengal Government are out to destroy your language. A bigger falsehood was never uttered by a man.[29]

[...]

Let me tell you in the clearest language that there is no truth that your normal life is going to be touched or disturbed so far as your Bengali language is concerned. But ultimately it is for you, the people of this province, to decide what shall be the language of your province. But let me make it very clear to you that the State Language of Pakistan is going to be Urdu and no other language. Any one who tries to mislead you is really the enemy of Pakistan. Without one State Language, no Nation can remain tied up solidly together and function. Look at the history of other countries. Therefore, so far as the State Language is concerned, Pakistan's language shall be Urdu.[30]

[27] The term appears in Ronald Grigor Suny, "Back and Beyond," *The American Historical Review* 107, no. 5 (December 2002): 874.
[28] Rafiqul Islam, "The Language Movement," in *Bangladesh: Volume One, History and Culture*, ed. Chakravarty and Narain (New Delhi: South Asian Publishers, 1986), 148.
[29] Mahomed Ali Jinnah, *Quaid-i-Azam Mahomed Ali Jinnah: Speeches As Governor-General of Pakistan 1947–1948* (Karachi: Pakistan Publications, 1976), 82.
[30] *Ibid.*, 86. Jinnah delivered his speech, "National Consolidation," on March 21, 1948 in Dhaka.

That was Jinnah's very first visit to East Bengal, a full seven months following independence. Though he apologized at the start of that speech for having so delayed a visit to the East Wing of the new country he governed, his tone and suspicions that the "language question" was in fact the work of an Indian fifth column did not suggest a spirit of cooperative equality in the construction of a new democratic nation-state, of which East Bengal comprised more than half the population.

Three days later, Jinnah went even further on the matter of language during his speech to the University of Dhaka's convocation:

Let me restate my views on the question of a State language for Pakistan. For official use in this province, the people of the province can choose any language they wish. This question will be decided solely in accordance with the wishes of the people of this province alone, as freely expressed through their accredited representatives at the appropriate time and after full and dispassionate consideration. There can, however, be only one lingua franca, that is, the language for inter-communication between the various provinces of the State, and that language should be Urdu and cannot be any other. The State language, therefore, must obviously be Urdu, a language that has been nurtured by a hundred million Muslims of this sub-continent, a language understood throughout the length and breadth of Pakistan and above all, a language which, more than any other provincial language, embodies the best that is in Islamic culture and Muslim tradition and is nearest to the language used in other Islamic countries.[31]

Prime Minister Liaqat Ali Khan similarly affirmed Urdu's necessary role, citing historical as well as religious basis:

Pakistan has been created because of the demand of a hundred million Muslims in this sub-continent and the language of a hundred million Muslims in Urdu ...[32] Pakistan is a Muslim state, and it must have its lingua franca, a language of the Muslim nation ... It is necessary for a nation to have one language and that language can only be Urdu and no other language.[33]

Of course, the idea that Bengali was not the language of an overwhelming number of those hundred million Muslims who had supported the demand for Pakistan is untenable. The first census of the new nation in 1951 revealed that only roughly 3 percent of all Pakistanis claimed Urdu as their first language, but 56 percent claimed Bengali. Any

---

[31] *Ibid.*, 90. "'Students' Role in Nation-Building,' Speech at the Dacca University Convocation on 24th March 1948."

[32] Constitutional Assembly of Pakistan Proceedings (1948: 17), cited in Rafiqul Islam, "The Bengali Language Movement and Emergence of Bangladesh," *Contributions to Asian Studies* XI (1977): 143.

[33] Ahmad, "In the Mirror of Urdu," 203, also cited in Tariq Rahman, *Language and Politics in Pakistan* (Karachi: Oxford University Press, 1996), 86. Original text of speech from Legislative Assembly Debates of Pakistan, February 25, 1948, 16 (per Rahman).

"dispassionate consideration" could just as easily have proffered Bengali, Sindhi, or Punjabi as the languages of "an overwhelming number" of the Muslims in Pakistan. In terms of sheer numbers, Bengali had a clear claim. In terms of ideological proximity to Islam, Sindhi has a higher proportion of Arabic words – as Aijaz Ahmad has pointed out – but it was never suggested by Pakistan's national leadership to be an intimate part of the national Muslim identity.[34]

If the idea was that Urdu was somehow primordially intertwined with Muslim consciousness, the converse seemed to be the case for Bengali, at least as far as West Pakistan was concerned: that it was, by virtue of its script and vocabulary, inherently un-Islamic.[35] Bengali does not use a modified Arabic script; it is written from the left to the right, and its very appearance was visibly "Indic" rather than "Persianate." Its vocabulary, scientific as well as literary, had been derived largely from Sanskrit. Those agitating for its implementation as a national language were under suspicion as agents of the Indian state – for what good Muslim would abjure Urdu for Bengali? Here we see an exclusionary language ideology, something quite different from the "fuzzy boundaries" of language of an earlier, premodern way of being in South Asia.[36]

Policy studies from this period recommended formalizing the Jinnah–Liaqat Ali view on Urdu's national role. The widely rejected report of the first Basic Principles Committee, convened to design a constitution and a form of governance for Pakistan, recommended in 1950 that Urdu should be the only state language.[37] Efforts to render Bengali more "Islamic" began with the creation in 1950 of re-education centers to teach Bengali through the Arabic script, and the creation of a Language Committee charged with stripping Bengali of its Sanskritic origins through a new script and a lexical purge.[38] Though this plan was never actually implemented, the discourse about the proper place of language and national (as opposed to regional) belonging was already well underway.

---

[34] Ahmad, "In the Mirror of Urdu," 203–4. See also Oldenburg, "'A Place Insufficiently Imagined'," 716.
[35] See especially Oldenburg, "'A Place Insufficiently Imagined'," 716.
[36] On the fuzziness of language boundaries, see Sudipta Kaviraj, "Writing, Speaking, Being: Language and the Historical Formation of Identities in India," in *Nationalstaat und Sprachkonflict in Süd-und Südostasien*, ed. Hellmann-Rajanayagam and Rothermund (Stuttgart: Franz Steiner Verlag, 1992). See also Sheldon Pollock, "Cosmopolitan and Vernacular in History," *Public Culture* 12, no. 3 (Fall 2000).
[37] Jahan, *Pakistan: Failure in National Integration*, 37.
[38] Rahman, *Language and Politics in Pakistan*, 89. Islam, "The Bengali Language Movement," 153; also see Rahman, "Language Policy in Pakistan," 88–9. East Bengal Language Committee Report (1949: 102–3), cited in Islam, "Bengali Language Movement," 146.

In January of 1952, Prime Minister Khwaja Nazimuddin reiterated in Dhaka that "Urdu will be the state language of Pakistan."[39] This public announcement ignited rioting and protest over the course of the next two months by students in Dhaka. Daily demonstrations resulted in a declaration of curfew, and on February 21 – *ekushe* – some students decided to defy this order. The riot that followed was a turning point; police opened fire on the protesters, killing four. The day was from that year forward memorialized as Language Day, and would emerge as the most powerful icon of East Bengal's desire and demand for Bengali to be recognized as national.

The first constitution, in 1956, declared Bengali a national language along with Urdu, but Bengalis felt that their language was still subordinate to Urdu, and indeed national public spaces such as currency and government signs did not use Bengali. Bengalis also felt that state-owned media overtly favored Urdu.[40] When General Ayub Khan declared martial law in October 1958, he proclaimed – in accordance with his modernist sensibility – in December 1958 that all languages of Pakistan ought to shift to using a roman script. This proposal replicated what Ataturk had done with Turkish, and indeed what Muslim majority Indonesia and Malaysia had done with Bahasa Indonesia/Melayu. Ayub's plan was never implemented.

The Constitution of 1962 reiterated Bengali's status as a national language along with Urdu, but without the political will in West Pakistan to make it so by mandating Urdu and Bengali for all citizens – or even for Bengalis in East Pakistan, the formal policy again remained an empty promise. Access to national power and administrative office, even in East Pakistan, for example, was enhanced solely by command of English and Urdu and not by Bengali. Further, despite Bengali's constitutional status as a national language, it continued to be viewed as a suspect "Hindu" language, particularly when used in forms of cultural expression not Islamic in origin. Monem Khan as Governor of East Bengal banned the songs of Nobel Laureate Rabindranath Tagore from being played on Radio Pakistan in 1966. He did this using the charge that Bengali was a "non-Muslim" language and a carrier of "cultural domination" by Calcutta – actions which took place under a constitution which nominally afforded Bengali national status. Khan's revival of the attack against the Bengali language served to consolidate Bengali opposition to the federal center.[41]

---

[39] Rahman, *Language and Politics in Pakistan*, 90.
[40] *Ibid.*, 96.
[41] Jahan, *Pakistan: Failure in National Integration*, 163.

By this point Bengali nationalism was fueled not just by language but by glaring economic and political disparities as well: Shaikh Mujibur Rahman's political program, Six Points, presented first in 1966, signaled the extent to which the Bengalis had moved away from the language issue and toward a political position of autonomy – focusing instead on issues of representation in the Constituent Assembly and demanding economic equity within the nation. None of the Six Points mentions language.[42] The Awami League swept the elections in December 1970, which should have allowed them to form the Pakistani government as the single largest party in the National Assembly. The Pakistan People's Party, led by Zulfiqar Ali Bhutto, had trouble accepting a government headed by a pro-Bengali party, and as it had received the second largest number of seats in the Assembly (and the majority within West Pakistan) began trying to negotiate a power-sharing arrangement. Shaikh Mujib declared the independence of Bangladesh on March 26, 1971, and was imprisoned for treason the following day. A civil war broke out which then grew to include India as well. Pakistan surrendered in December 1971, after months of violent atrocities, even genocide, in East Pakistan.[43] The outcome of this civil war was the birth of Bangladesh.

The case of Bengal provides the clearest evidence for the mental replication of dichotomizing oppositions discussed in Chapter 1, and how such replication can create unbridgeable boundaries of difference. We can see how the Hindi–Urdu controversy was replicated onto Bengali–Urdu – despite the fact that the Bengali speakers in this opposition were nearly entirely Muslim, fellow citizens of the new Pakistan, and not *against* Urdu, just seeking symbolic and legal parity for the Bengali language. But in the structural opposition inherited from the Hindi–Urdu controversy, the available category of opposition to Urdu implied anti-Muslim, leading to the transference of this opposition onto Bengal. One might be able to explain this away on the basis of Bengali's script, or its more Sanskritic vocabulary, as symbolically distinct. But Chapter 3, "The nation and its margins," examines the conflicts arising from language movements in the territories of West Pakistan, all of which employ an Arabic-derived script for their language, and which have much greater Arabic and Persian vocabulary influence in their lexicons. That the very same replication of this dichotomizing opposition occurred with numerous other languages in Pakistan shows the language ideology to be far more extensive.

[42] For the text of the Six Points and the Pakistani government's response to each, see "6 Points," *Pakistan Forum* 1, no. 4 (April–May 1971).
[43] The Hamood ur-Rahman report details the contempt that non-Bengali Pakistanis held for Bengalis (particularly Hindus).

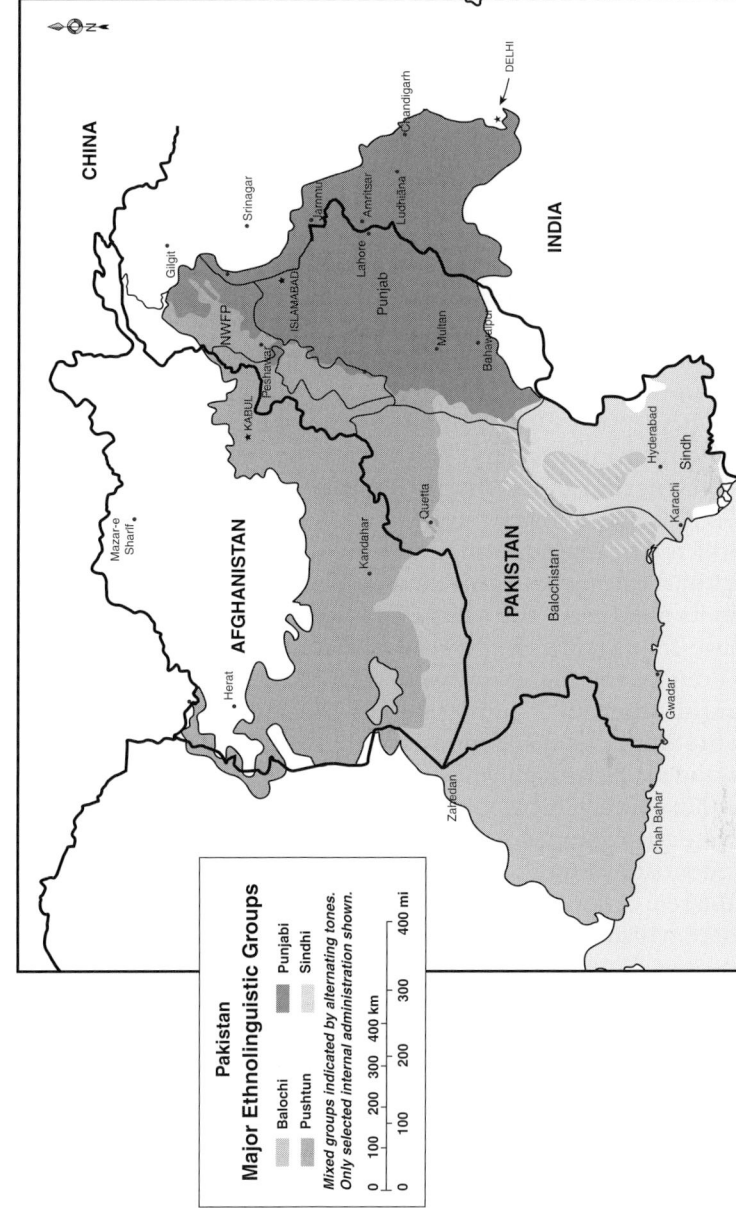

Map 2 Map of Pakistan and surrounding areas showing ethnic/linguistic groups. Names and boundary representation are not necessarily authoritative.

3 The nation and its margins

If East Pakistan, separated from its western wing by the vast space of India, had an attenuated relationship to the country's political center, that explanation fails for the regions in the territory that remains Pakistan today. As we saw in the previous chapter, much of the justification for the state's desire to remake the Bengali language revolved around the perception of its "un-Islamic" nature, whether due to its Sanskritic script or vocabulary, or prestige cultural traditions shared with Hindu Bengalis as well. By virtue of the fact that all the languages in the West Pakistan territory utilized an Arabic script, however, this charge could not be leveled. And yet several regions of Pakistan have felt similar cultural grievances. This chapter examines the problem of the nation and its margins in the territorial spaces where easy explanations of difference fail: Sindh, the Northwest Frontier, the Siraiki space of southern Punjab, and the sparsely populated large area of Balochistan. Sindhi, and the mohajir ("immigrant" or "settler") conflict, are examined first; the Sindhi–mohajir opposition illustrates the process of ethnogenesis taking place through language. The more limited but important case of Siraiki, another "new" ethnolinguistic category is also examined. I recapitulate the example of Pashto as a language suspected of channeling irredentism along the Pakistan–Afghanistan border, and briefly consider the role of language and cultural politics in Balochistan's long-running nationalism.

Sindh, Sindhi, and the emergence of the category "mohajir"

The question of language and identity in the province of Sindh has resulted not only in violent conflict in Pakistan, but also in the creation of two new categories of ethnicity, *mohājir* and Bihari.[1] From the

---

[1] On violence in Karachi, see Abbas Rashid and Farida Shaheed, "Pakistan: Ethno-Politics and Contending Elites," (Geneva: United Nations Research Institute on Social Development, 1993); Stanley J. Tambiah, "The Nation-State in Crisis and the Rise of

mid-1980s forward, this conflict took on extremely violent dimensions such that Karachi, Pakistan's largest and most important commercial city, became more noted for guerilla warfare than for its stock exchange. Transnational groups like the Muttahida Qaumi Movement (the "United Nations Movement," formerly the Mohajir Qaumi Movement, or "Mohajir National Movement") and the World Sindhi Congress battled each other and the nation-state of Pakistan from mobilized global networks that demanded separate homelands for mohajirs and Sindhis. For many reasons well beyond the scope of this study, the conflict in Karachi mobilized ethnic antipathies which grew to include Pathan versus Bihari, Sindhi versus Pathan, Sindhi versus Balochi, and Sindhi versus Punjabi – against a backdrop of sectarian conflict that pitted Pakistan's Shi`a Muslims against Sunni. This armed conflict, however, was rooted in earlier disagreements over the public role of language, which led gradually to a process of ethnogenesis. The history of this conflict centers on Sindhi and Urdu, with the Urdu-speaking mohajirs a major new category of identity created as a result.[2]

Sindhi, like Bengali, enjoyed regional hegemony throughout the British era (1843–1947). The British seized Sindh from the Talpur, a Baloch feudal family which ruled the region from 1782–1843. Sindhi was used regionally as an administrative as well as a literary language. Its forms of literary expression were honed through poetic and musical performance traditions closely associated with the practices of Sufi religious orders.[3] A Sindhi language movement emerged in the early twentieth century (1917–36) to lead the crusade for Sindh's administrative separation from the British territory known as the Bombay Presidency in 1936.[4] This institutionalization of a Sindhi "national consciousness"

Ethnonationalism," in *The Politics of Difference*, ed. Wilmsen and McAllister (Chicago: The University of Chicago Press, 1996). On ethnicity, politics, and violence in Sindh, see Oskar Verkaaik, *Migrants and Militants* (Princeton: Princeton University Press, 2004). For ethnolinguistic issues in Sindh, see Adeel Khan, *Politics of Identity: Ethnic Nationalism and the State in Pakistan* (New Delhi: Sage Publications India, 2005); Rahman, *Language and Politics in Pakistan*, Chapter 7; Rahman, *Language, Ideology and Power*, Chapter 10.

[2] "Mohajir" refers to settlers who came to (mainly) Karachi and Hyderabad from the United Provinces (now Uttar Pradesh) in India at the time of Partition. "Bihari" refers to refugees from East Pakistan who came to Karachi following the independence of Bangladesh.

[3] See Annemarie Schimmel, *Sindhi Literature*, vol. 8, Part 2, fasc. 4, *A History of Indian Literature* (Wiesbaden: Harrassowitz, 1974). Or Ali Asani, "At the Crossroads of Indic and Iranian Civilizations: Sindhi Literary Culture," in Literary Cultures in History, ed. Pollock (Berkeley: University of California Press, 2003); also Rahman, "Language Policy in Pakistan," 80.

[4] For Sindh's separation from the Bombay Presidency, see Allen Keith Jones, "Muslim Politics and the Growth of the Muslim League in Sind, 1935–1941" (PhD dissertation, Duke University, 1977), 31–53.

with language a primary organizational and administrative metaphor meant that this particular channel for expression was already in place even prior to Partition.

Partition brought abrupt and dramatic demographic changes to the subcontinent. Karachi and Hyderabad in particular saw an enormous influx of migrants from north India – the Urdu-speaking mohajirs – and from Punjab, Baluchistan, and NWFP as well. At the same time, Hindus, who had comprised 64 percent of the population of Sindh prior to Partition, left for India.[5] Homes and possessions left behind in Karachi and other urban centers (as well as agrarian lands in the Sindh interior) were claimed by mohajirs. The result of this influx was striking: in Karachi, mohajirs comprised 57.55 percent of the city by 1951; in Hyderabad, 66.08 percent; and in Sukkur, 54.08 percent.[6] These cities were literally cleaved in half, and then filled with strangers. Muslims to be sure, but strangers nonetheless.

With the dawn of Pakistan, Sindhis, just like Bengalis, were surprised to find that their language had been stripped of its formal official role and would be subservient to Urdu in the national cultural hierarchy. This unwelcome development was exacerbated by the inherent advantage in the competition for bureaucratic employment gained by the newcomer mohajirs, whose mother tongue was the national language. Sindhi and Urdu both use a modified Arabic script, but Sindhi has a number of additional letters representing implosive sounds that do not exist in Urdu. The two languages are largely not mutually intelligible. As with Bengali and Urdu, the Sindhi–Urdu language conflict has taken place in the realms of administrative authority: government offices, signage, and university language policy.

A crucial moment in the incipient Sindhi–Urdu tensions occurred early in Pakistan's life: on July 23, 1948, the provincial government of Sindh had offered Karachi to the federal government for use as the new capital of Pakistan; the federal government headed by Jinnah accepted, then decided to "separate" Karachi from Sindh and reconstitute it as a federal territory. The chief minister of Sindh objected to the "separation" of Karachi, only to be dismissed by the federal government on grounds of maladministration and corruption, making Karachi's absorption by the federal government possible.[7] Urdu was already in public

---

[5] Yu. V. Gankovskiy, "Ethnic Composition of the Population of West Pakistan," in *Pakistan: History and Economy*, ed. D'Yakov (Washington, DC: U.S. Joint Publications Research Service, 1961 [1959]), 22.

[6] Tariq Rahman, "The Sindhi Language Movement and the Politics of Sind," *Ethnic Studies Report* 14, no. 1 (1996): 103.

[7] Allen McGrath, *The Destruction of Pakistan's Democracy* (Karachi: Oxford University Press, 1998), 47.

use, first as cosmopolitan lingua franca, then further due to the influx of mohajirs and then, as well, due to its having become the federally mandated national language. But most importantly, the economic and cultural capital of Sindh was perceived as having been hijacked by the Pakistani state to the detriment of Sindhis. This government Urdu policy and reclamation of Karachi created a catch-22 for Sindhis in their own territory: they would have to learn a "foreign" language in order to be competitive for stable government jobs, but the newly arrived "foreigners" didn't have to learn Sindhi to go about their daily lives in urban Sindh, which is where most of them lived. It was as if Karachi suddenly acquired extraterritorial status, with diplomatic immunity for mohajirs alone. There was no compelling reason for mohajirs to integrate with Sindh or Sindhis, and Sindhis perceived this situation as discriminatory against their language.[8]

When Karachi vanished from Sindh's administrative orbit, the University of Sindh – only just established in 1946 – was forced to move to Hyderabad, the second largest city in Sindh, and the University of Karachi took the physical place of the University of Sindh. Urdu was declared the medium of instruction at the University of Karachi. Further, virtually all accounts of this conflict invoke the issue of a mohajir "cultural arrogance" as a further catalyst of the tensions – a sign of the national hierarchization problematic that in so many cases leads to resentment and conflict. And as the primary areas of mohajir settlements were in the two major cities – Karachi and Hyderabad – that notion of a "cultural arrogance" was compounded by urban cosmopolitan contempt for the rustic rural Sindh.[9] Finally, since mohajirs had undergone so much – had left their homes back in India – to help create Pakistan, they "saw [themselves] as the standard bearer of the Pakistan 'idea'."[10] From their perspective, it must have been quite unthinkable that Pakistan would not employ Urdu as the national language. Later on, mohajirs would actually counter-mobilize against the Sindhi objection to Urdu and mohajir hegemony in urban Sindh.

When the One Unit proposal first arose in 1954, Sindhis opposed it intensely, perceiving it as an effort by the center to swallow up Sindhi identity. Here again we can see the tension between the idea of a pure Pakistani nation versus the idea of an amalgamation of parts. Indeed, as a result of the One Unit, Sindhi lost its status as a regional language

---

[8] Gankovskiy, "Ethnic Composition of the Population of West Pakistan," 22.
[9] For example, Rahman, *Language and Politics in Pakistan*, 103. Tariq Rahman, "Language, Politics and Power in Pakistan: The Case of Sindh and Sindhi," *Ethnic Studies Report* 17, no. 1 (1999): 31–2; Rashid and Shaheed, "Ethno-Politics and Contending Elites," 14.
[10] Rashid and Shaheed, "Ethno-Politics and Contending Elites," 14.

since the legally reconstituted "region" was now the large One Unit. The Sindhi Adabi Sangat (Sindhi Literary Society) demanded that Sindhi be declared an official language for Sindh.[11] In an effort to preserve Sindhi culture and language, the then-governor of Sindh had the Sindh legislature endow a Sind Cultural Advancement Board with funds for a library, gallery, and literature development. Martial law in 1958 continued the One Unit, and Ayub's Education Commission report of 1959 recommended that Urdu and Bengali should be the national languages. The report, published in 1961, noted that only in Sindh was the language of instruction past Class 6 the regional language, Sindhi, in some schools, and it called for the introduction of Urdu medium throughout. Again, Sindhis viewed it as intrusive and unacceptable.

Demonstrations in protest of the new policy – including a Sindhi Day on November 9, 1962 – managed to take place despite the ordinances against public gathering under martial law, and Ayub scaled back the efforts.[12] The laissez-faire approach to Sindhi did not mean, however, that Sindhi would be endorsed by Ayub's regime. To the contrary: the number of Sindhi-medium schools decreased; signs on official government buildings replaced Sindhi with Urdu; writers in Urdu were given patronage whereas Sindhi writers were not; and Sindhi language radio broadcasts were decreased. These subtle efforts at the implementation level had demonstrable impact on usage of Sindhi language in the public sphere. During these years under Ayub and the One Unit, Sindhi was dropped as a medium of education in Sindh. It was also during these years that the leading figure of Sindhi nationalism, G. M. Sayed, founded the Sind Adabi Board (Sindh Literary Board) in 1967. G. M. Sayed spent the last thirty-plus years of his life under house arrest, deemed anti-national as the leader of the Jiye Sindh Mahaz, a Sindhi nationalist organization.[13]

When General Yahya Khan's new education policy – the report of Air Marshall Nur Khan – was published in 1969, it made the logical recommendation for Urdu use in the West Wing and Bengali in the East Wing. In Sindh, this policy was perceived as an insult and a displacement of their language by Urdu. Sindhi nationalist youth movements

---

[11] Rahman, "Language Policy in Pakistan," 81.
[12] Rahman, "Language, Politics and Power in Pakistan: The Case of Sindh and Sindhi," 34. Rahman, "The Sindhi Language Movement and the Politics of Sind," 105.
[13] On broadcasts, see Rahman, "The Sindhi Language Movement and the Politics of Sind," 105–6. On medium of education, see Theodore P. Wright, Jr., "Center-Periphery Relations and Ethnic Conflict in Pakistan: Sindhis, Muhajirs, and Punjabis," *Comparative Politics* 23, no. 3 (April 1991): 302. On G. M. Syed, see Wright, "Sindhis, Muhajirs, and Punjabis," 304.

reacted with a list of demands for retaining Sindhi. Like the Bengali language movement, the Sindhi language movement gained its strength from students, and the worst language-related conflagrations took place in the context of the university.

In August 1970, the University of Sindh (now based in Hyderabad) declared Sindhi as its language of administration. It had officially implemented Urdu in keeping with national policy only in 1965. Sindhi nationalism had gained in popularity and additional voices joined the fray to express support for Sindhi – the Sindhi Adabi Sangat and a group of 108 writers among others. The Urdu press, in a reprise of the fifth-column accusations against Bengali youth, denounced Sindhi supporters as "leftists, anti-Islamic … anti-Pakistan dissidents." Still, in response to this demand, the Hyderabad Board of Intermediate and Secondary Education recommended that Sindhi be adopted as an official language, in addition to which Sindhi should be compulsory as a subject for students whose first language was Urdu. It was the mohajirs' turn to protest. Both mohajir and Sindhi nationalists then carried out protests against the perceived incursions of each others' languages. The protests lasted throughout January and the army was eventually called in to Karachi by the end of January 1971.[14]

By 1972 Pakistan had lost its East Wing and Zulfiqar Ali Bhutto – himself Sindhi – was in power at the center. The Sindh Legislative Assembly began considering the Sindhi language bill in July, which mandated that Sindhi and Urdu both be required subjects from classes 4–12, and Sindhi a required subject from grade 4 onward in Urdu medium schools. The bill also included a provision for Sindhi to be used in all governmental departments. On July 8, 1972, the Urdu daily, *Jang*, featured a headline drawn from the poet Rais Amrohvi, declaring the "death of Urdu:" "Urdū kā janāza hai, zara dhūm se nikle" ("This is Urdu's funeral procession … let it go out with fanfare"). Mohajirs vehemently opposed this bill, and the language riots which resulted were the worst in Pakistan's history. Mohajirs attacked not just Sindhi people, but the representation of Sindhi language as well by burning the Department of Sindhi at the University of Karachi. Bhutto intervened from the center with a new policy that claimed to ensure economic parity for speakers of both languages: "a proclamation to the effect that for twelve years jobs would not be denied for lack of knowledge of Sindhi or Urdu." In practice, however, Sindhis remain at a disadvantage because

---

[14] See Rahman, "Language, Politics and Power in Pakistan: The Case of Sindh and Sindhi," 36; Rahman, "The Sindhi Language Movement and the Politics of Sind," 107–8.

it was impossible for the government to mandate the use of Sindhi by the Urdu speakers.[15]

With General Zia ul-Haq's regime and his emphasis on Islam as a national unifier, and with Urdu as a salient means to achieve that unity, the mohajir cause was implicitly endorsed. Zia's harsh rule silenced any opposition. But the Movement for the Restoration of Democracy – a panregional Leftist alliance, led by the Pakistan Peoples' Party – found a sympathetic base with rural peasant Sindhi nationalists.[16] In the fall of 1983 riots took place in rural Sindh that targeted the Urdu-language public signs and government offices such as post offices and police stations – again focused upon the linguistic representations of authority.[17] It was at this time that Altaf Hussain emerged as a student leader and founder of the MQM.[18] Regardless of the social mechanisms through which Hussain gained political strength – a great deal of press speculation has emphasized his support by the ISI – for our purposes the important element lies in the availability of the category of mohajir as a mobilizing construct.[19] "Mohajir" became a fully ethnicized category and an ethnopolitical group commanding significant loyalty thirty-seven years after anyone actually migrated to Pakistan. The younger members of the MQM had not "migrated" at all, but were marked as such by virtue of language, and in a double-reversal of the relationship of dominant versus subordinate, sought to rectify what they saw as injustice against the language that the national state hoped all Pakistani citizens would adopt.

In the late 1980s extreme violence took hold, particularly in urban Sindh, ushering in a phase when Karachi and Hyderabad would see mass killings of mohajirs and then Sindhis in return. Beginning in 1988, mohajir–Sindhi killings took place on a scale of hundreds – a vastly greater scale than the four students killed in Dhaka in 1952, for example.[20] On September 30, 1988, Sindhi nationalists (said to be

---

[15] Adeel Khan, "Pakistan's Sindhi Ethnic Nationalism: Migration, Marginalization, and the Threat of 'Indianization'," *Asian Survey* 42, no. 2 (March/April 2002): 222; Rahman, *Language and Politics in Pakistan*, 125, 105.

[16] According to the 1981 Census figures, Sindhi is spoken by 52.4 percent of total households in the province, but if Karachi is removed from the count, Sindhi's share jumps to more than 70 percent – suggesting dramatic rural homogeneity. See Jonathan S. Addleton, "The Importance of Regional Languages in Pakistan," in *The Rise and Development of Urdu*, ed. Geijbels and Addleton (Murree: Christian Study Centre, 198-?), 65.

[17] Rakisitis, "Centre-Province Relations," 80.

[18] Wright, "Sindhis, Muhajirs, and Punjabis," 305.

[19] Khan, "Pakistan's Sindhi Nationalism," 226–8; Rashid and Shaheed, "Ethno-Politics and Contending Elites," 21.

[20] See Stanley J. Tambiah, *Leveling Crowds* (Berkeley: University of California Press, 1996), esp. 173–83. The paraphrasing which follows is based on Tambiah's research.

over a dozen) opened fire on people in Hyderabad, killing "over 250 persons, mainly Muhajirs." The following day "about 60 people, mostly Sindhis, were killed in an apparent 'backlash by Muhajir militants in Karachi.'"[21] A December 1988 agreement, signed by the PPP and the MQM only temporarily halted the violence. By July 1989 mohajir activists at University of Karachi were shot. A year later, what was called a "massacre" in Hyderabad – 250 reported injured and sixty dead on May 27, 1990 – appears to been linked, according to Tambiah, to Mohajir protests against a special exam admission quote for Sindhi students.[22] Despite periodic "crackdowns" against Sindhi and Mohajir militant groups, by 1994 Karachi witnessed 1,113 deaths due to snipers, and by 1995 that figure had risen to 2,095.[23]

Though these grim statistics reflect much more than language conflict, for the intervening decades brought with them the Afghan War and an influx of small arms that have made life far more violent throughout Pakistan, the salient point is that the production of group identities which originally centered on language grew more violent, more defined, and more irremediable over time, another paradox of schismogenesis against the idea of a cohesive Muslim nation. By the 1990s, the radical Sindhi movements were calling for a partition and a "Sindhu Desh" while the radicalized MQM calls for the same in the form of a "Mohajirstan."

That the very people whose families had left India to forge the first nation-state in modern history created on the basis of religion should be calling for another separate homeland on the basis of a linguistically-defined identity once again illustrates the perplexing conceptual presence of recursive oppositions. Sindhi *looks like* Urdu, yet the fact that Sindhi speakers sought to maintain a level of symbolic capital for their language in the new Pakistan resulted in accusations, just as with the Urdu–Hindi controversy, that it was anti-Islamic, anti-Pakistan – a veiled accusation of being too Indian, just as with Bengali.

Siraiki

In comparison with the large-scale conflicts linked to Bengali, Sindhi, and Urdu–Mohajir movements, the Siraiki movement is little-known.[24]

---

[21] Both quotations from *Herald* (Karachi) cited in *ibid.*, 173.
[22] *Ibid.*, 175.
[23] Khan, "Pakistan's Sindhi Nationalism," 228.
[24] There is very little journalistic writing on Siraiki, and limited academic work as well. Christopher Shackle and Tariq Rahman, therefore, stand out for their carefully researched work. See Rahman, *Language and Politics in Pakistan*; Tariq Rahman, "The Siraiki Movement in Pakistan," *Language Problems and Language Planning* 19, no. 1 (Spring 1995); Christopher Shackle, "Siraiki: A Language Movement in Pakistan,"

Even the idea and the name "Siraiki" are relatively recent phenomena; in perhaps the first scholarly survey of the Siraiki movement in Pakistan, Christopher Shackle noted the "quite recent introduction of the term on a general scale in its homeland," illustrating the degree to which notions of ethnicity and self-definition are relational processes and the creation of new notions of borders and difference.[25] Prior to the 1960s, the language denoted by "Siraiki" was referred to as "Multani" or "Bhawalpuri" dialects of Punjabi, or in the taxonomy of the Grierson's colonial-era *Linguistic Survey of India*, a western Punjabi ("Lahnda") dialect. Only with the emergence of Pakistan and a sense of deprival against the backdrop of greater Punjab and the nation has the idea of a distinct "nationality" of southern Punjab gained a currency and a name. This has allowed the movement to make claims about the boundaries of difference which define it and its local history, both against the dominance of the national Urdu *as well as* against the perceived hegemony of an Urdu-speaking Punjabi province that fails to recognize Siraiki's unique heritage.

A Siraiki speaker claimed that they can learn to speak any language in the world, but others cannot learn Siraiki because its sounds are difficult. But Punjabi speakers often dismiss Siraiki's claim to language status, saying that Siraiki speakers think they are speaking a special language but it sounds "just like Punjabi." Grammatically, Siraiki is similar to Punjabi, and as Christopher Shackle points out, its vocabulary is also closer to Punjabi. Its distinguishing features are voiced aspirates (which have disappeared from Punjabi, converted into unvoiced unaspirates of the same series, with a rising tone) as well as a series of implosives, which do not exist in Punjabi but do exist in Sindhi.[26] It is spoken primarily in the districts of Bhawalpur, Multan, and Rahim Yar Khan, though there are speakers in Sargodha, Dera Ghazi Khan, Muzaffargarh, Jhang, Dera Ismail Khan, Jacobabad, Sukkur, Khairpur, and even Kachhi in Baluchistan. The Siraiki language has no firm boundaries delineating regions of its use, so estimates of its native speaker population range from the 9 percent reported in the census of 1981 to the high of 45 percent of the entire Punjab, an estimate one Siraiki ethnonationalist gave me. This diffuse presence throughout districts in all four provinces has perhaps limited its ability to mobilize, and the areas with the greatest degree of language consciousness are those which comprise the more concentrated Siraiki heartland of Bhawalpur-Multan.

Modern Asian Studies 11, no. 3 (July 1977). Owen Bennett Jones devotes two pages to "Seraiki."
[25] Shackle, "Siraiki," 379.
[26] *Ibid.*, 389.

Though the origins of the word "Siraiki" are contested, Shackle sees it most plausibly as deriving from the Sindhi word for "north" (*siro*) and thus used to describe "the language of immigrants from the north, particularly the Baloch tribes who acquired the language on their migration south."[27] The areas of greatest Siraiki speaker concentration are thus the southern part of Punjab, overlapping into the north of Sindh. The movement's claim to literary and cultural uniqueness lie in the mystical hymn tradition of the Sufi *pīr* Khwaja Ghulam Farid (1845–1901). Both Shackle and Rahman date the origins of Siraiki linguistic and national consciousness to the activities of a lawyer, Riaz Anwar, who founded a biennial fair to commemorate Khwaja Ghulam Farid in 1960–1.[28] These fairs took place throughout the 1960s.

Dovetailing with the Siraiki movement's claims to cultural and linguistic distinction are issues of governance and administration that emerged only when the new Pakistani nation-state came into being. A Bhawalpur province movement – taking Siraiki as important evidence of a separate culture – arose along with the Anti-One Unit Front as early as 1956: as the Anti-One Unit Front sought redivision of the One Unit along linguistic lines, the Bhawalpur movement demanded a Siraiki area as compensation for having lost its identity as a separate princely state after accession to Pakistan. This may have come to pass in 1957, when the West Wing was slated for break-up into provinces once again, but Ayub Khan's declaration of martial law in 1958 ensured that the West Wing remained One Unit until General Yahya Khan's decision to restore the provinces eleven years later.[29]

At this time, Bhawalpur state was headed for amalgamation with Punjab, a position it had never previously occupied, and the political demand for Bhawalpur province led by a political party, the Bhawalpur Mutaheda Mahaz (BMM, "Bhawalpur United Front") began protests and demonstrations. As with the Bengali and Sindhi language movements, police took a violently repressive tack and opened fire during an April 24, 1970, procession. Two protesters were killed, and a number wounded. This creation of martyrs did not escalate violence but rather provided impetus for political action via the electoral candidacies of members of the BMM, many of whom contested as independents or as members of other parties but recognizably BMM members. The December 1970 election, which resulted in Zulfiqar Ali Bhutto and his PPP assuming power, saw the success of BMM candidates elected

[27] *Ibid.*, 388.
[28] Shackle dates the fair's origins to 1961, whereas Rahman gives 1960 as the inaugural year. Rahman, *Language and Politics in Pakistan*, 180; Shackle, "Siraiki," 393.
[29] Rahman, "The Siraiki Movement in Pakistan," 9.

to the national and provincial assemblies instead. However, the Mahaz members elected apparently did not continue vigorous agitations for a Bhawalpur province, and the party fragmented by 1972.[30]

Paradoxically, the BMM conducted all its discussions and published its literature in Urdu; the actual implementation of the Siraiki language was not a primary issue. Yet it created a mobilized political identity which segued directly into the literary-language movement that began to demand greater recognition. Twenty-three Siraiki organizations held a Siraiki Literary Conference in Multan in 1975. With the acknowledgment by the government that Siraiki was a separate language in the 1981 Census, it at least raised its stature. The 1981 Census gave Siraiki activists a statistical arsenal with which to reinvigorate their claims for a separate Siraiki province, a "Siraikistan," to be carved out of the center of Pakistan, for they were able to demonstrate that several key districts had a preponderance of Siraiki speakers. The map of this Siraikistan indeed covers more than half of what is present-day Punjab.

The Siraiki Lok Sanjh, created in 1985, seeks recognition of Siraiki by demanding the use of Siraiki for official documents of the region, and reserved ethnicity-based seats for voting. This Sanjh is not a political party, but it has a clear linguistic and political agenda.[31] Contemporary Siraiki-identity movements (Siraiki Qaumi Movement, the Sanjh, Siraiki National Party, Pakistan Siraiki Party – an offshoot of the PPP) demand primarily socioeconomic redressal of grievances, which include complaints about the federal government allocating land to non-Siraikis from Siraiki areas, the settlement of "Biharis" into Siraiki land, the re-inclusion of Siraiki on the Census as a language, and more radio and TV programming in the language.[32] The Siraiki National Party continues to push its claims for further division of provinces in Pakistan on a linguistic basis, with the Siraikistan area to form a separate province.[33] This push is perceived by Punjabi nationalists as an effort to weaken Punjabi, as can be seen in the pro-Punjabi polemic published in 1992 by Chaudhry Nazir Kahut. An entire chapter of his nationalist text is devoted to Siraiki as threat to Punjabi, "The Partition of Punjab and the Horrifying Siraiki Conspiracy to Destroy the Punjabi Language."[34] For Punjabi nationalists, the idea that Siraikis want to carve out their own demarcated arena of political and cultural dominance is seen as a threat

[30] *Ibid.*
[31] *Ibid.*, 12.
[32] *Ibid.*, 19.
[33] Abdul Majid Kanjoo, Conference presentation, Sustainable Development Policy Institute (March 11, 2002).
[34] See Chaudhry Nazir Kahut, *Āo, Panjābī Ko Qatl Karen* [Come, Let's Kill Punjabi] (Karachi: Waris Shah Publications, 1992), Part 3.

to the effort to achieve recognition for Punjabi in the national context. The effect has been to doubly marginalize the Siraiki cause, for they see themselves not as allies of Punjab, but as a victim struggling against *Punjabi* domination.

Pashto and Pashtunistan

I have been a Pakhtun for thousands of years, a Muslim for 1300 years, and a Pakistani for 40 years. (Wali Khan, on his various identities)[35]

Pashto, a member of the Iranian language family, is the primary language spoken in the Northwest Frontier Province. It is the language of the Pashtuns (var. Pakhtuns, Pathans), who live on both sides of the Durrand Line. The line, drawn in 1893, separated what was the then-Indian subcontinent from Afghanistan and has been an undercurrent of dispute between Pakistan and Afghanistan since 1947. Drawn by the British, the line separates a broader geography of Pashtun territory and has split them into different nation-states, but many Pashtuns claim allegiance to a broader Pashtun nation. Pakistan has repeatedly sought to discourage the use of Pashto for fear that it would contribute to the consolidation of a Pathan identity and strengthen the ever-present irredentist claim across the boundaries of the Durrand Line.

One of the first signs that national coherence might be a problem in the newly formed Pakistan appeared in NWFP. Khan Abdul Ghaffar Khan, often called the "Frontier Gandhi," had not initially supported Jinnah's Muslim League in the call for Partition and the creation of Pakistan because he was instead in favor of a Pakhtunistan – an autonomous land for the Pathans – rather than a Pakistan in any form. In pursuit of this goal of Pakhtunistan for decades, Ghaffar Khan had founded the magazine *Pakhtun* in 1928 which promoted the use of Pashto language and literature. Post-Partition, Ghaffar Khan's National Congress party, one known to have sympathies with the Indian National Congress, was in power in the NWFP assembly and led by Ghaffar Khan's brother Dr. Khan Sahib.[36] Jinnah perceived Dr. Khan Sahib and his brother as a threat to national cohesion, and dismissed the assembly not one week after Pakistan came into existence. Jinnah then invited their political opponent Abdul Qaiyum Khan to form a government. Qaiyum Khan was not able to secure a majority to form an assembly until January

---

[35] This is a very well known quote, bordering on the apocryphal and often misattributed to anonymous Baloch tribesmen. Cited here in Akbar S. Ahmed, "The Politics of Ethnicity in Pakistani Society," *Asian Affairs* 21, no. 1 (February 1990): 25.

[36] Tariq Rahman, "The Pashto Language and Identity-formation in Pakistan," *Contemporary South Asia* 4, no. 2 (1995): 151–70.

1948, some five months later, but the security of Qaiyum Khan's allegiance to Jinnah and the idea of Pakistan was apparently preferable to an elected leader of a majority interested in promoting Pashtun identity and an independent Pakhtunistan.

The Pakistani government perceived Pashto, and those who supported Pukhtunkhwa or Pukhtunistan, to be anti-national elements. Efforts to promote Pashto even at the literary level were monitored by the police. The new Legislative Assembly of the NWFP, led by Abdul Qaiyum Khan, moved a resolution in 1950 designed to prove their allegiance to the Pakistan nation by making Urdu the language of the courts. The same NWFP government, however, also created a Pashto Academy in Peshawar in 1955 to placate Pathan nationalists.[37]

With the creation of the One Unit, Ghaffar Khan emerged again in strong opposition and as a member of the Anti-One Unit Front, an alliance of various regional nationalists opposed to the erasure of their cultural identity and administrative autonomy which the One Unit merge implied. The National Awami Party remained a vocal Pashto language supporter during both Ayub and Yahya Khan's tenures, though since they were not in power, they could not legislate for it. When the National Awami Party finally came to power in 1972, in a coalition with the Jamiat-e-Ulema-i-Islam, they dropped the demand. Rahman attributes this shift to their desire to stay in power and prove their loyalty to the center, a likely scenario since Bhutto had just dismissed the NAP government in Baluchistan and imposed martial law. The NAP in NWFP surely sought to avoid the same fate, though Bhutto ultimately banned the party in 1973.

Political and linguistic agitation seemed to ebb away in NWFP, with only the use of Pashto in the legislative assembly a contested issue. Though the official language of the Assembly was Urdu, many members of the NAP chose to deliver their remarks in Pashto. During one session in 1972, the debate grew to the point where the opposition members of the PPP (Bhutto's party) staged a walkout.[38] Yet this represents quite a de-escalation when compared with Ghaffar Khan's call for a separate Pakhtun nation. Some have attributed this calming to a gradual integration of NWFP's population "into the state structure and market economy" of Pakistan. Additionally, with the outbreak of the Afghan war, some two million Afghan refugees poured into camps primarily in NWFP and "the nationalist demand for Pakhtunistan, i.e. an autonomous state

---

[37] On the courts, see *ibid*.: 161. On the academy, see Rahman, "Language Policy in Pakistan," 82.

[38] Rahman, "The Pashto Language and Identity-formation in Pakistan," 164.

comprising Pakhtuns on both sides of the Pakistan Afghanistan border ... finally collapsed."[39] One result of the collapse of the Pakhtunistan demand was that Zia's regime – one suspicious of all regional languages and one insistent upon the use of Urdu – allowed the introduction of Pashto as a medium at the primary school level in 1984.[40]

The Northwest Frontier Province has experienced difficult and increasing violence that resulted from the Afghan War and its aftermath, much of which lies beyond the scope of this study on nationalism in Pakistan. Notably, geopolitical events of the past decade have refocused attention to the strong ethnic linkages among the Pashtuns of the Pakistan–Afghanistan border region, including the role of Pashtun tribalism in the rise of the Taliban. More recently, the complex relationship of Pashtun tribes in Pakistan's Federally Administered Tribal Areas to their kinsmen in southern Afghanistan (and the continued existence of impenetrable safehavens in FATA's remote mountains) has brought negative scrutiny to the area, all of it revolving around the links between Pashtun tribes, al-Qaeda, and terrorism. Understandably, with headlines like these, little attention has been given to questions of cultural nationalism and ethnicity. For a brief period in the late 1990s it appeared that the appeal of Pashtun nationalism was gaining ground once again: in 1997, the province's Awami National Party (the successor to the National Awami Party) demanded that the province be renamed to "Pakhtunkhwa," but the National Assembly rejected this demand in January of 1998.

Furthermore, General Musharraf's period of government, from his 1999 bloodless coup to the national and provincial assembly elections of 2002 and beyond, introduced Islamist political parties to new positions of political power – all of which served to further mute the local appeal of Pashtun demands. Indeed, for the first half of the 2000s, Islamist parties controlled the provincial assembly in NWFP; the provincial assembly's undertakings were focused on implementing Islamic law, or Sharia, in the province. With the elections of 2008, voters booted the Islamists from power and returned the Awami National Party to control of the province. The ANP's manifesto explicitly prioritizes the state's renaming as "Pakhtunkhwa," and emphasizes Pashto-language education.[41] These developments are too new to be considered here, but the return of the ethnic agenda to this province illustrates its perduring presence even in the face of myriad others.

[39] Rashid and Shaheed, "Ethno-Politics and Contending Elites," 12.
[40] Rahman, "Language Policy in Pakistan," 87.
[41] See http://anp.org.pk/manifesto.shtml

Balochi

The conflicts in Balochistan throughout most of Pakistan's history appear unlinked to language policy and are more directly related to economic deprivation and a perceived inequity in resource allocation from the federal government. If focusing only on language conflict, Balochistan's narrative is short and not particularly notable. Yet the broader history of conflict in Balochistan has been extensive. It is the only province in Pakistan, for example, which has suffered the extended presence of Army troops for four years, from 1973–7. The Shah of Iran actively assisted Pakistan in repressing the Balochi uprising, fearing of course for Iran's security should the Balochi nationalist movement encompass the Balochis in Iran's Sistan-wa-Balochistan. In the past half-decade, Baloch nationalists have revived the simmering conflict, occasionally bombing energy and transportation infrastructure that connects Balochistan with other parts of Pakistan, and which for them emblemizes the Pakistani state's efforts to extract their natural resources without adequate compensation.

Balochistan is a large territory, comprising 45 percent of Pakistan's land. It is bounded to the north by Afghanistan and to the west by Iran. Territorial lines of demarcation have partitioned larger Pathan tribal areas into Afghanistan and Pakistan, and similarly partitioned Balochi tribal areas into Iran and Pakistan. Balochistan did not ascend to equal status with the other provinces in Pakistan until the formation of the One Unit; it was an amalgamation of various princely states with numerous languages spoken among them, the most widely used being Pashto, Balochi, and Brahui, a Dravidian language isolate. Pathan versus Baloch conflicts have been prevalent in the province, and extend the reach of the larger Pukhtunkhwa conflict with Pakistan.

Because Balochistan is so ethnically and linguistically diverse, the province used Urdu as a link language internally. Using Urdu as the official language was a decision made by the noted Balochi nationalist Ghaus Baksh Bizenjo, a decision which some observers thought was designed to ward off Pashto or Brahui ascendancy in the province. Curiously, elements of Balochi nationalism are now beginning to rise and are finding some expression of independence through language. During Benazir Bhutto's first term in office, Nawab Akbar Bugti, the late Balochi nationalist, became chief minister.[42] He took up the cause of disseminating the Balochi language more widely, demanding more radio time and championing Baloch identity through culture and

---

[42] Bugti was killed in an Army operation to end a showdown with the Baloch during the summer of 2006. The cave in which he was hiding was bombed.

literature, steps which reinforce the role of language in creating a strong sense of ethnic identity.[43] The budding language movement would see a few years of success when the Balochistan Mother Tongue Use bill (No. 8 of 1990), passed. This bill, a product of Benazir Bhutto's government, mandated the use of Balochi, Brahvi, and Pashto in governmental non-elitist schools. Of note is that the bill exempted elite English medium schools from the language policy. However, in 1992 with Nawaz Sharif in power at the center and a PML chief minister at the helm in Baluchistan, a decision, an amendment of sorts, was passed regarding the Mother Tongue Use bill, which decreed it "optional."[44] In practice, education in the mother tongues ceased altogether in Balochistan; no further textbooks were produced and teachers were no longer trained in the mother tongues.[45] The ongoing armed conflict in this province at present does not focus on cultural dimensions, however.

Conclusion

This chapter, and Chapter 2 before it, has sketched the politics of culture arising in the wake of decisions about language and its role in the modern nation-state made by the government of Pakistan. While bound tightly with the belief that a people should have one and only one official language, the Pakistan nation-state has struggled with trying to reconcile the ideology of the national language, Urdu, as South Asia's most Islamic language, with regional claims to other language traditions. Sites of conflict have invariably been those of modern administration: schools, signage, legislative assemblies, and the census – the administrative zones of the state which Clifford Geertz identified some fifty years ago as the sites of "parapolitical warfare."[46]

The dichotomizing opposition process that accorded principal symbolic value to Urdu culture and language rendered regional, rather than equally national, the language traditions other than Urdu in use in the territories which became Pakistan. This structural hierarchy at first glance appears to replicate a core–periphery relationship, on the model of Russia and its peripheries in the former Soviet Union, and indeed analyses of Pakistan's center–province relations treat it precisely in this way. Yet this model does not fully account for the territorial dislocation inherent in the national project. Certainly Urdu was a cosmopolitan

---

[43] Addleton, *ibid.*, p.41.
[44] Tariq Rahman, "Language Policy in Pakistan," p.88.
[45] Tariq Rahman, *Language and Politics in Pakistan* (Karachi: Oxford University Press, 1996), p.168–9.
[46] Geertz, "Integrative Revolution," 274–6.

language in the sense that it was in use in urban centers in South Asia, and in the Punjab region Urdu had a strong presence as a language of formal and literary communication – even if it was not most residents' first language. But so, Urdu was much more widespread as a first language in the territories that did *not* form Pakistan. Thus the center of the cultural basis for this new nation was displaced, creating a national legitimating discourse departing from the modern Westphalian standard where culture, polity, and territory achieve an isomorphic fit. From this perspective, Pakistan's problems with center–province relations can be seen as territorially-rooted efforts to "bring back" this displaced national center – and indeed, the emergence of a language-culture consciousness from within Punjab, long identified as the core of Pakistan, points to the need to better understand the working of this displacement on cultural consciousness.

Of the tendencies in the language conflicts surveyed briefly here, one trend is invariable: in the face of considerable economic incentives that one might suspect would limit the social benefits of loyalties to languages other than Urdu, the historical record shows that such loyalties have continued. Exclusionary language ideologies that reduced the Urdu language to an iconic role as the linguistic embodiment of the Pakistan demand had the net effect of branding partisans of other languages – regardless of the often deeply Islamic Sufi traditions of their specific literary histories – somehow bad Others, bad patriots as well as bad Muslims. This was most dramatic in the case of Bengali, where its Indic origins, Sanskritic vocabulary, and Indic script were targeted for "re-education" programs in an attempt to bring an entire language in line with what was believed more suitably Islamic. In this sense, Bengali was a true outlier in comparison with the languages of West Pakistan. Yet Sindhis, Punjabis (as will be explored in great detail in Chapter 4), and Pashtuns also suffered the accusation of insufficient patriotism, albeit less dramatically so, when they agitated for regional language use. In the cases of the mohajirs and the southern Punjabi Siraki-speakers, a process of ethnogenesis has taken place, telescoping backwards the speakers of a language into new ethnic categories in a sort of reverse Herderian process, where the people must be made to fit the language of a nation.

There are surely economic reasons that partially explain much of this history – Pakistan's exceptionally limited human development indicators tell one story about education and resources – but at the same time, the perduring categories of differentiation in Pakistani society on the basis of language bespeak the important place that language as a form of consciousness occupies in the country, in fact as a synecdoche for nation itself. The usage of this form of nation-identification can be seen in a typical news item from an English-language weekly analyzing results of the Sindh provincial assembly elections in 2003:

> None of the seven MQM ministers (including Mirpurkhas winner Shabbir Kaimi) speaks Sindhi. Its Culture and Minorities minister Yaqoob Ilyas Masih is Punjabi-speaking. Finance Advisor Aftab Shaikh is Urdu-speaking. Three of the eight remaining ministers are also non-Sindhi speaking. Marwat, Chaudhry Iftikhar and Syeda Malik are Punjabi-speaking.[47]

Chapter 4 begins this book's detailed examination of the Punjabiyat movement, a language movement that has not been the subject of sustained research interest. Punjab's sheer size allows it to dominate all of Pakistan's institutions. This has important implications for the national ideology as well as the national language, and should therefore be explored in greater detail. Most importantly, however, the unusual structural features of the Punjabiyat movement mark it as a case which does not fit our classic explanations of nationalism and indeed also suggests the clear limits of symbolic domination in contexts where the competitive market for cultural capital has left Punjabi with low status despite being the first language of approximately half the country's citizens. With nearly a century and a half of widespread Urdu language use in the Punjab, through colonial and now post-colonial language policies, the Punjabi language didn't die – it just moved to the peripheries of oral literary culture, a periphery from which its partisans now seek to rescue and restore it, and forge a written literary culture.

---

[47] Hasan Mansoor, "Winners and Losers in the Great Sindh Game," *The Friday Times*, January 10–16, 2003.

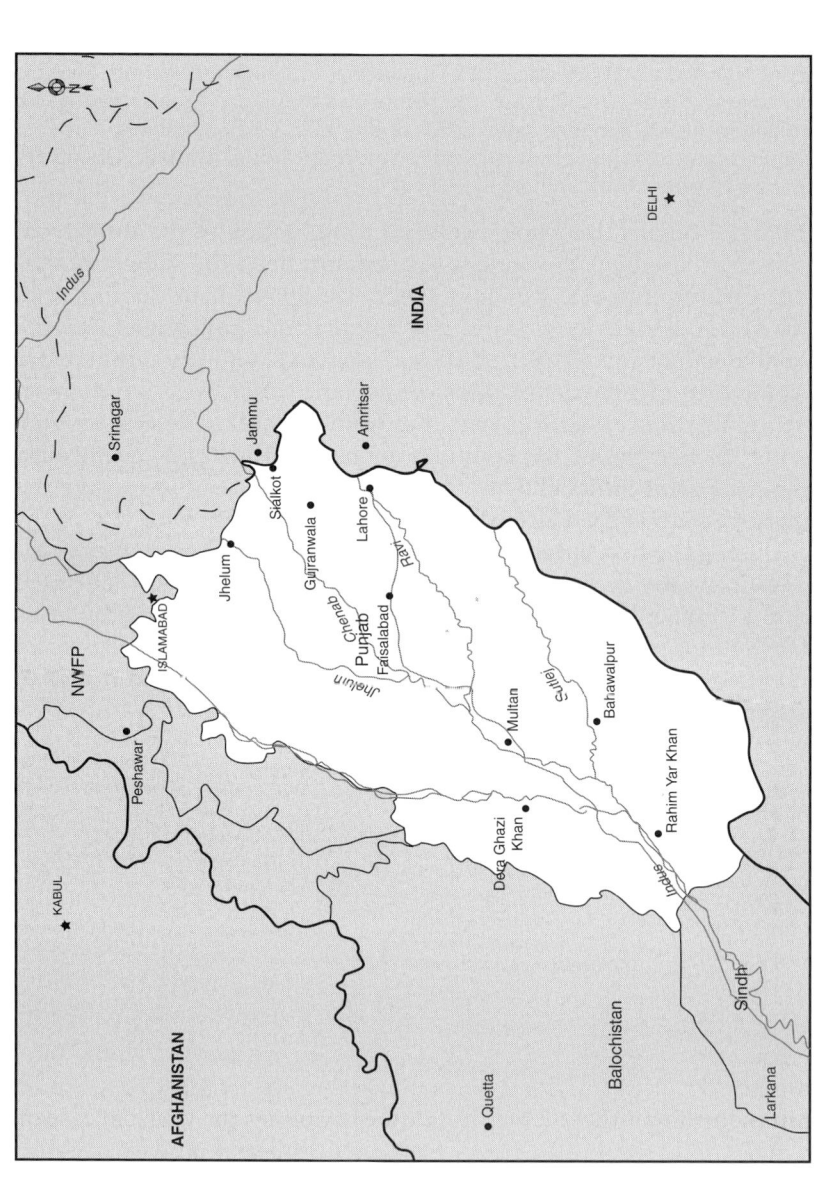

Map 3 Map of Punjab Province in Pakistan. Names and boundary representation are not necessarily authoritative.

4 The case of Punjab, part I: elite efforts

> Young Punjabi poets and writers are reinterpreting their own classical works and have reformulated the message of the mystic poetry of the great sufi poets of Punjab ... as the poetry of resistance against unbridled and unjust authority ... In so far as it is a step towards the rediscovery of the rational basis of the national identity, this movement is not anti-nationalist ... Yet to be a Punjabi is to be as much a Pakistani as Punjab is an integral part of Pakistan.
>   –Partial text, Article 18 of Writ Petition No. 3603 of 1978 in the Lahore High Court, Fakhar Zaman son of (Retd) Major Muhammad Zaman resident of 178-C Model Town, Lahore (Petitioner)

On April 9, 1996, the Lahore High Court reached a judgment on a case that had been pending for eighteen years. Four Punjabi-language books (two novels and two collections of poetry) had been banned by executive order on charges of obscenity in 1978. The petitioner, author Fakhar Zaman, then filed the Writ Petition cited above, which refuted the obscenity charges in part by arguing that what was at stake was the freedom to develop Punjabi as a literary language, to retrieve the language of Punjab, the literature of Punjabi, and the history of Punjab from an abject and subservient status. This subservient status, according to the Writ Petition, came about as the result of all histories of the region having been written first from the perspective of the former British masters, and then from the perspective of an "obscurantist" and oppressive "minority elite." The legal argument – ultimately successful – thus linked a discourse of rights with an archeological call to excavate some deeper historical and literary truth, the "spirit of Punjabiyat" to which the Punjabi language must lay claim.[1]

Zaman's Writ Petition, an extraordinary English-language document running some forty-three pages in print, exemplifies the unusual case of a language movement or language nationalism emerging from a region

---

[1] Complete text of Writ Petition and the final judgment of the Lahore High Court republished in Pakistan Academy of Letters, *Ban Lifted After 18 Years From Fakhar Zaman's 4 Books: Full Text of the Writ Petition & the Judgment of Lahore High Court* (Islamabad: Pakistan Academy of Letters, 1996).

that has long dominated political and economic power within Pakistan, Punjab. As we saw in Chapters 2 and 3, the language movements struggling against the nation, emblematized by the Urdu language, routinely place Punjab as the ethnically dominant center of their protest. Understanding the emergence of a sense of cultural subordination from within this proto-typically dominant Punjab forms the inquiry of this chapter and the following.[2]

A longer historical view on the place of culture and political legitimacy in Pakistan underscores the imbrication of this "spirit of Punjabiyat" in ongoing processes of polity formation in the country. From the days of the Pakistan Movement even prior to Partition, and explicitly so after the creation of the country in 1947, a relational cultural hierarchy symbolically linked the notion of Pakistan's legitimacy with a national cultural heritage emblematized by Urdu and its literary-cultural history.[3] That Punjabi has lacked official status, even in Punjab, provides the necessity for its revival. But the emergence of this Punjabiyat narrative suggests deeper implications for our most powerful theories charting the relationship of language to the nation and its political imagination. Although this movement bears the surface features of a classical nationalist formation – insistence upon recovering an unfairly oppressed history and literature, one unique on earth and uniquely imbued with the spirit of the local people and the local land – the structural features of this process in its elite aspects differ markedly from those we have come to understand as classical nationalisms.

The Punjabiyat movement in Pakistan has not been propelled by newly literate but disenfranchised individuals recognizing inequality or social difference as they gain education in the transition to industrial society, leading to a search to overturn an urban cultural elite in favor of a vernacular populism.[4] Given Punjab's well-noted dominance in Pakistan, it is hard to explain as an effort by political entrepreneurs seeking advantage through incorporation with, or resistance to, the "center," as is the case with classic models of language revivalism and language nationalism such as the other regional language movements in Pakistan discussed in the previous chapter.[5] Moreover, with the positions of power – social, political, economic – enjoyed by the Punjabiyat movement's actors – quite distinct from the actors of the Siraiki movement of

---

[2] Much of the material in this chapter and the chapter which follows, "The case of Punjab, part II," has appeared in modified form as Alyssa Ayres, "Language, the Nation, and Symbolic Capital: The Case of Punjab," *Journal of Asian Studies* 67, no. 3 (August 2008): 917–46.

[3] Rahman, *Language, Ideology and Power*, 262–87.

[4] Ernest Gellner, *Nations and Nationalism* (Ithaca: Cornell University Press, 1983).

[5] Laitin, *Identity in Formation*; David D. Laitin, "Language Games," *Comparative Politics* 20, no. 3 (April 1988).

southern Punjab – the explanation of symbol manipulation or theory of instrumental, even opportunistic, choice in search of electoral or other competitive gain appears an insufficient logic.[6]

As confounding, the Punjabiyat movement raises questions about the role of language, reading, and textual transmission of powerful ideas of belonging. It is hard to situate the Punjabiyat case within Benedict Anderson's sophisticated models, and seems a particularly poor fit for causal explanations involving print capitalism. It appears to be a reaction to, rather than an instance of, official nationalism, creating a confusing paradox.[7] Rather, it has been slowly growing out of the work of an urban cultural and political elite – fluent in Urdu and English as well – some of whom have maintained comfortable positions of power for some time. Yet they seek to "restore" a role for Punjabi justified entirely in terms of aesthetics, and pursued through the development of a respected Punjabi-language written public sphere. Thus the movement represents something of an inversion of the most widespread theoretical understandings of nationalism's mechanics, one well noted by Hobsbawm in his trenchant analysis of nationalism in Europe: it seems to be concerned with *creating* the key tools that theories of nationalism posit as necessary for its emergence.[8]

Given the intriguing questions this case poses about the mechanisms of nationalism, the Punjabiyat movement marks an opportunity to explore the importance of symbolic capital in driving efforts to maintain cultural forms against state efforts to forge a national identity that would supplant them.[9] Bourdieu's elaboration of the forces of symbolic domination and the working of the linguistic market – a market in which social exchange produces distinction in social value – allows us to better isolate and explain the phenomena at stake with the case of Punjab. By virtue of the dynamics of the movement's emergence from within the dominant "core" of the country, this case allows an abstraction away from the functionalist and instrumentalist explanations that have been powerfully convincing elsewhere. For we see in the case examined here precisely what Bourdieu understood as a struggle for recognition – a struggle for a particular language tradition to gain acceptance as a legitimate language – in a context entirely without the analytic interference of economic, political, or even demographic distractions.[10]

---

[6] Brass, *Language, Religion and Politics in North India*; Laitin, "Language Games."
[7] Anderson, *Imagined Communities*.
[8] Hobsbawm, *Nations and Nationalism Since 1780*, 54–63, esp. 54.
[9] Pierre Bourdieu, *Language and Symbolic Power*, trans. Gino Raymond and Matthew Adamson (Cambridge: Harvard University Press, 1991).
[10] On symbolic capital and the production of legitimate language, see especially *ibid.*, 43–65, 72–6. On Punjab's relevance for this argument, see Ayres, "Language, the Nation, and Symbolic Capital," 919, 939–42.

As a step toward such an exploration, this chapter and the following examine the dimensions of the puzzling Punjabiyat movement in Pakistan. This chapter, the first of the pair, analyzes the political literature produced by this movement and their call for historical reclamation. Chapter 5 then considers the nature of cultural products circulating in spaces of limited literacy, including work written for a less educated population, and the remarkable parallel development of new heroic archetypes in Punjabi cinema – a textual form accessible to illiterates. Taken together, we have the basis for a more expanded consideration of the implications of the "case of Punjab" for our understanding of nationalism more generally. The analysis also suggests ways the movement offers alternatives to the end-game logic that has bedeviled thinking about language and cultural nationalism in recent times.

Panjāb kā muqaddamah, "the case of Punjab"

As we saw in Chapters 2 and 3, Pakistan's difficulties forging a cohesive sense of nationality, one able to include its diverse citizenry, has been the subject of significant scholarly and journalistic work. In all of the scholarship on Pakistan's nation-region dilemmas, Punjab's dominance has been a central feature. And rightly so: Punjab is the most populous province of Pakistan, with its residents comprising 55.6 percent of the population of Pakistan according to the 1998 census.[11] With a population somewhere between seventy-seven to eighty-three million, Pakistan's Punjab would rank as the fourteenth largest country in the world – putting it ahead of Germany and Egypt – so the scale considered here resembles a major country. Punjabis dominate Pakistan's major institutions: though clear current statistics are not available, Punjabis have comprised as much as 80 percent of the Pakistani Army, and 55 percent of the federal bureaucracy, according to figures as of 1987.[12] Virtually since the country's birth, other ethnic groups in Pakistan have accused Punjab of seizing national spoils for its own benefit at the expense of others. Punjab is perceived to have "captured" Pakistan's national institutions through nepotism and other patronage networks.[13] Ideas about Punjab's dominance – it is often called a hegemon – are so

---

[11] Government of Pakistan, *Population and Housing Census of Pakistan 1998, Vols. 1–5*, 127 vols. (Islamabad: Population Census Organisation (Pakistan), 1998).

[12] Yunus Samad, "Pakistan or Punjabistan: Crisis of National Identity," in *Punjabi Identity: Continuity and Change*, ed. Singh and Talbot (Delhi: Manohar, 1996), 67.

[13] Oskar Verkaaik, "The Captive State: Corruption, Intelligence Agencies, and Ethnicity in Pakistan," in *States of Imagination*, ed. Hansen and Stepputat (Durham: Duke University Press, 2001).

commonplace that the word "Punjabistan" serves as a shorthand for the national conundrum.[14]

The "Punjabistan" idea has to do with a widespread resentment of Punjab's numerical dominance, and as importantly its prosperity and perceived greed. Pakistan's Punjab enjoys natural advantages; this land of five ("panj") rivers ("āb") is the most fertile province in a country in which some 44 percent of the population makes its living off the land.[15] But many of its man-made advantages indeed indicate preferred treatment for the province: updating Ian Talbot's earlier observations,[16] Punjab's farms have 84 percent of all the owned tractors in the entire country, as well as 94.6 percent of the tubewells, two important development indicators.[17] The literacy rate in Punjab is about the same as that of Sindh (47.4 percent and 46.7 percent, respectively), though higher than NWFP and Baluchistan (37.3 percent and 26.6 percent); Punjab's women are the most literate in the country, with 57.2 percent of the urban and 25.1 percent of the rural female populations able to read.[18] The urban female literacy rate is comparable with that of Sindh, but Punjab's rural female literacy rate is nearly twice that of Sindh and NWFP, and more than triple Balochistan's.[19] All these indicators tell us, in short, that there are more Punjabis than anyone else in Pakistan, and they are better off than everyone else, with more productive land, cleaner water, better technology, and better educated families.

The education-literacy dimension is important, not least because it is one of the core components of the two most widely cited theories about the mechanisms of nationalism, those of Benedict Anderson and Ernest Gellner.[20] Anderson's elegant theory relies upon print capitalism (in particular, newspapers and novels) as the primary vector for creating a cohesive sense of shared belonging – a shared sense of space–time – across

---

[14] Samad, "Pakistan or Punjabistan;" Ian Talbot, "From Pakistan to Punjabistan? Region, State and Nation Building," *International Journal of Punjabi Studies* 5, no. 2 (July–December 1998); Ian Talbot, "The Punjabization of Pakistan," in *Pakistan: Nationalism Without a Nation?*, ed. Jaffrelot (New Delhi, London, and New York: Manohar; Zed Books, 2002).

[15] Government of Pakistan, *Pakistan 2000 Agricultural Census* (Islamabad: Federal Bureau of Statistics, Government of Pakistan, 2000).

[16] Talbot, "The Punjabization of Pakistan," 56.

[17] Government of Pakistan, *Pakistan 2000 Agricultural Census*, Table 10.6.

[18] Amir Latif, "Alarming Situation of Education in Pakistan," *UNESCO Education for All* (2001), www.unesco.org/education/efa/know_sharing/grassroots_stories/pakistan_2.shtml.

[19] Government of Pakistan, *Population and Housing Census*; advance tabluation on sex, age group, marital status, literacy and educational attainment (figures provisional), 127 vols., vol. VI (Islamabad: Population Census Organisation, Statistics Division, 1998), iv.

[20] Anderson, *Imagined Communities*; Gellner, *Nations and Nationalism*.

large populations. Gellner's exploration of modernization and the gradual transformation of agricultural societies to industrial modes requires the expansion of bureaucracies and the "Mamlukization" of society. This functional explanation relies on a state-directed ability to institute literacy in an official language, which regional elites become aware of as a point of difference from their "own" regional language-culture complex. An obvious problem here lies in the issue of much less than universal literacy, despite Punjab's relative performance compared with other parts of Pakistan. Given that slightly more than half of Punjab is adjudged illiterate (and here we should recall that such surveys skew toward reporting higher rather than lower literacy), the situation poses clear limitations for the explanatory or catalytic value of print textual forms to engage this large population in a common sense of national belonging.[21] But in addition, what we find in Pakistan's Punjab is an extremely curious situation: formal literacy in Punjab means literacy in Urdu, for literary, official, and daily "documentary" public life in Punjab has taken place in Urdu since the British Raj. After annexing the province from the Sikhs in 1849, the British decided to substitute Urdu for Persian as the state language in the later part of the nineteenth century. This decision was, according to contemporary documentary evidence, taken despite full knowledge that many in Punjab simply did not understand the language.[22] Two historians who have worked on this period have both concluded that the decision in favor of Urdu was driven simply by the logic of standardization: the British were already educating employees in Urdu elsewhere in the Indian subcontinent, so they could be easily deployed in the newly acquired territory of Punjab if it were instituted as the language of state. That Punjabi was perceived by the colonial authorities to be nothing more than a "patois" did not help its case.[23]

The colonial policy privileging Urdu as the official language of Punjab continued with the creation of Pakistan in 1947, although a broader institutionalization of Urdu across the territories which became part of this new country – territories with longer histories of regional language use, such as Sindhi, Pashto, Bengali, Balochi, and Siraki – would require a significant capital and epistemological project on the part of the central government, as seen in the previous chapter. Historians of nationalism

[21] Satish Deshpande, "Imagined Economies," *Journal of Arts and Ideas* 25–6 (1993): 10; Hobsbawm, *Nations and Nationalism Since 1780*, 56, 62; Lisa N. Trivedi, "Visually Mapping the 'Nation,'" *Journal of Asian Studies* 62, no. 1 (February 2003): 12.
[22] Nazir Ahmad Chaudhry, *Development of Urdu as Official Language in the Punjab (1849–1974), Punjab Government Record Office Publications* (Lahore: Government of Punjab (Directorate of Archives), 1977), 169.
[23] Jalal, *Self and Sovereignty*, 102–138; Farina Mir, "The Social Space of Language" (PhD dissertation, Columbia University, 2002).

Ronald Grigor Suny and Geoff Eley have remarked on the "creative political action" necessary to forge a larger sense of collectivity from diverse populations, including the selection and adoption of national languages, and their general observation that national languages "were very far from simply choosing themselves as the natural expression of majority usage" appears most apt here.[24] Census figures illustrate that Urdu was and still is the first language of a very small percentage of the population of Pakistan overall – 3.3 percent in 1951, rising to 7.6 percent by 1981, and 7.53 percent in the 1998 census (but as high as 20 percent for urban areas). Here we must recall that the choice of Urdu as the national language for Pakistan (rather than any of the other languages which could have been selected and which had wider presences as first languages) was intimately related to a language ideology that posited Urdu as the bearer of high Muslim culture in the region – indeed, as the preferred bearer of *religious identity*, although Urdu has never been a language of religious text in the way that Arabic (for Islam) or Sanskrit (for Hinduism) could claim.[25]

But as important, Urdu is not the sole prestige language in Pakistan. As we saw in Chapter 2, in addition to the privileging of Urdu for administrative and official life, English – at varying levels of competence – has been regarded since at least the late nineteenth century as a necessary tool for elite economic and social advancement. The confluence of two prestige languages with official patronage has created an unusual situation for Punjabi, rendering it peripheral to the longer history of an Urdu-language official sphere and the unceasing dominance of the English language at the upper levels of bureaucratic life. Thus Punjabi is truly doubly marginal, *despite being the first language of the majority of the country's population*. Given this prestige hierarchy, it is indeed surprising that the Punjabi language not only perdures in Pakistan but has sustained an effort to forge authorized space for it.

Examined in terms of direct economic or social benefit, the Punjabiyat movement does not easily fit into any of our theoretical categories of explanation. From an instrumentalist perspective, the movement does not make any sense, as noted sociolinguist Tariq Rahman observed in frustration.[26] As we shall see particularly with respect to the literary

---

[24] Geoff Eley and Ronald Grigor Suny, eds., *Becoming National* (Oxford: Oxford University Press, 1996), 7.
[25] The linguistic anthropology concept of language ideology was introduced earlier in Chapter 1. For an excellent and accessible introduction, see Woolard, "Introduction: Language Ideology as a Field of Inquiry." For the seminal essay on this concept, see Silverstein, "Language Structure and Linguistic Ideology." For the impact of language ideology on the identification (indeed, creation) of languages, see Gal and Irvine, "Boundaries of Languages."
[26] Rahman, *Language and Politics in Pakistan*, 191, 208–9.

elite, this movement is not about seeking power: the movement's key protagonists are all successful public intellectuals based in Lahore, whose advocacy for the language *followed* their success in electoral or bureaucratic politics, or in the private sector. It does not appear to be about financial gain, given the limited arena of Punjabi publishing. Although Punjabiyat activists have been called anti-national,[27] the Punjabiyat movement itself does not claim a separatist agenda, and it has not been linked in any way with the Khalistan movement of the 1980s in India. (Indeed, the association of Punjabi regionalism with "anti-nationalism" as a category of thought likely has more to do with the historical legacy of the Unionist Party, which, as noted in Chapter 1, sought to preserve a unified Punjab in opposition to the Muslim League's call for partition and the creation of Muslim Pakistan.)[28] The Punjabiyat activists instead want Punjabi to claim its rightful inheritance as one of the great world languages. Its rhetoric is entirely framed in terms of affect, and the urgency of recovering a "lost" identity. Indeed, as sociolinguist Sabiha Mansoor noted, "A growing number of Punjabis ... feel that in Pakistan no regional language has suffered at the hands of the vested interests as Punjabi has ... creating a cultural alienation of the worst kind."[29] That Punjab, widely perceived as the most "vested" of Pakistan's "vested interests" should nurture a growing ethnic nationalism eager to rehabilitate itself from a perceived cultural alienation perpetrated by some *other* vested interests suggests the need for more inquiry into the reasons for the emergence of this "case of Punjab."

Cultural revival

During the two decades after independence, a small group of Lahore's Punjabi-language enthusiasts maintained a literary group devoted to Punjabi, although the gatherings did not gather steam nor attain greater public attention, likely due to government restrictions on such organizations.[30] The sense of urgency that marks the movement today appears to have come to the fore during the latter half of the 1980s which,

---

[27] Punjabi proponents Fakhar Zaman, Aitzaz Ahsan, and Mohammad Hanif Ramey have all spent time in jail; Najm Hosein Syed was removed from his position as head of the Punjabi department at Punjab University during the Zia regime, under the same accusation. See also Tariq Rahman, "The Punjabi Movement in Pakistan," *International Journal of the Sociology of Language* 122 (1996).

[28] On the Unionists, see especially Talbot, *Khizr Tiwana*.

[29] Sabiha Mansoor, *Punjabi, Urdu, English in Pakistan: a Sociolinguistic Study* (Lahore: Vanguard, 1993), 17.

[30] Rahman, "The Punjabi Movement in Pakistan;" Christopher Shackle, "Punjabi in Lahore," *Modern Asian Studies* 4, no. 3 (July 1970).

as detailed in Chapter 2, was a period immediately following a decade of important geopolitical changes within and outside Pakistan.

In this context of the past three decades, Punjabi writers developed and nourished their project of literary-historical reclamation. As is typical in cases of cultural revival worldwide, the Punjabiyat project's roots can be traced to lone intellectuals – cultural entrepreneurs – working in the 1960s.[31] Among them, Najm Hosain Syed (1936–) was central. He began actively creating new literary works in Punjabi – criticism, poetry, and plays – in the late 1960s, with several of his key texts emerging in the next decades. Syed was a core participant in the Majlis Shah Hussain, a literary association celebrating Sufi poet Shah Hussain (1539–99 CE) through literary readings and an annual festival, the *cirāghān dā melā*.[32] Syed's writings clearly inaugurated the discourse of recovery which marks all the Punjabiyat efforts. His narrative forms drew from old Punjabi poetry and folktales, using them as alternative historical sources, and insisted upon a representation of Punjab *as heroic*. Importantly, Syed established his notion of Punjabi heroism in opposition to what he viewed as the received wisdom of Punjab as a land and a people of submission – a view that stands in sharp contrast to the English-language typology of Punjabis as a "martial race" and indeed a region from which the British colonial authority recruited heavily for its British Indian Army. This belief that Punjab has been characterized as submissive and stripped of its historical valor redounds throughout the Punjabiyat texts, as I will elaborate upon later.

In the earliest of the Punjabiyat texts aiming to recover a lost past, Najm Hosein Syed made use of essays and plays to articulate his historical revisionism. For example, in essays written in Punjabi and English,[33] Syed wrote of the *vār*, a Punjabi epic-martial verse form,[34] composed by Qādiryār, a nineteenth-century poet (*c*.1800–50) whose verses recovered the story of the pre-Islamic hero Puran of Sialkot (*c*.100–200 CE).[35]

---

[31] Ronald Grigor Suny and Michael D. Kennedy, eds., *Intellectuals and the Articulation of the Nation* (Ann Arbor: University of Michigan Press, 1999).

[32] Shackle, "Punjabi in Lahore."

[33] Najm Hosain Syed, *Sidhāṉ*, 2nd edn (Lahore: Majlis Shah Hussein, 1973 [1968]), 77–121.

[34] Malik defines the vār as "an epic poem or the narrative ballad of resistance." See "Note on the Var," Fateh Mohammad Malik, *Punjabi Identity* (Lahore: Sang-e-Meel, 1989).

[35] See also "Puran of Sialkot" in Najm Hosain Syed, *Recurrent Patterns in Punjabi Poetry* (Lahore: Majis Shah Hussein, 1968), 73–112. For the Punjabi text, see Qadir Yar, *Puran Bhagat/Qādir Yār*, trans. Taufiq Rafat (Lahore: Vanguard Books, 1983). Tahir suggests that the story of Puran Bhagat draws upon the Greek legend of Hippolytus via its invocation of an incestuous stepmother; see *ibid.*, 26–9. Also see Athar Tahir, "A Coat of Many Colors: The Problematics of Qadiryar," ed. Singh and Thandi (New Delhi: Oxford University Press, 1999).

Syed then composed his own *vār*, *Takht-e-Lāhor* ("Throne of Lahore," 1972), which used Shah Hussain's poetry as historical source material for a drama based on the character Dulla Bhatti.[36] Dulla Bhatti, leader of a revolt against Mughal emporer Akbar, was hanged in 1599. In the annals of received history, he was a criminal, but in the verses of his contemporary Shah Hussain, Dulla Bhatti was a resistant hero of the land: his dying words as recorded by Shah Hussain were "No honorable son of Punjab will ever sell the soil of Punjab."[37] Syed published a series of poetry collections in the 1970s, as well as another drama exemplifying this new Punjabi heroism in 1983. Syed's *Ik Rāt Rāvī Dī* featured Rai Ahmed Khan Kharal (1803–57 CE), a participant in the 1857 revolt against the British, as a hero for Punjabis to call their own. As with *Takht-e-Lāhor*, *Ik Rāt Rāvī Dī* drew upon alternative historical sources, in this case folk songs of the Ravi riverbank area – Kharal's birthplace – to fashion a hero where the British state had seen a criminal.[38] By employing these indigenous forms, with sons of the soil reinterpreted heroically via the textual source of Punjabi poetry rather than the annals of the Mughal victors, Syed presented a new kind of Punjabi person – strong, valiant, unfazed by confronting authority. Most importantly, this new Punjabi person could lay claim to his own language as the form most appropriate for cultural expression.

During the early to mid-1970s, under the country's first democratically elected government, headed by Zulfiqar Ali Bhutto (1972–7), a sense of intellectual openness coincided with the search for national redefinition in the aftermath of the 1971 truncation. During this short half-decade, a greater emphasis on the legitimacy of local ethnic identities – in no small part attributable to Bhutto's own recognition of Sindh's unique cultural heritage, one underemphasized on the national stage – resulted in the state creation of institutions like Lok Virsa (1974), and regional literary boards such as the Pakistan Panjabi Adabi Board. Writers like Fakhar Zaman, Munnoo Bhai, and Shafqat Tanveer Mirza began to establish themselves in Punjabi. Mohammad Hanif Ramey, whose work will be engaged below, served as chief minister of the Punjab during the Bhutto years. Yet following General Zia ul-Haq's military coup in 1977, opportunities to openly write about a "Punjabi identity" (or any

---

[36] Najm Hosain Syed, *Takht-e-Lāhor: Dulla dī Vār* (Lahore: Majlis Shah Hussein, 1972). On poetry as an alternative historical source, see "Introduction: A Palette of Histories," in Velcheru Narayana Rao, David Shulman, and Sanjay Subrahmanyam, *Textures of Time* (New Delhi: Permanent Black, 2001), 1–23.
[37] See Mohammad Hanif Ramey, *Panjāb kā muqaddamah* [The Case of Punjab] (Lahore: Jang Publishers, 1985), 111–30.
[38] Najm Hosain Syed, *Ik Rāt Rāvī Dī* (Lahore: Rut Lekha, 2000 [1983]).

other) were curtailed, particularly during the first half of his decade of dictatorship. Poet/fiction-writer Fakhar Zaman saw his works banned. (Despite this, they still received attention and circulation: his translator, Khalid Hasan, noted that books like *Bandīwān* still circulated because the Pakistani government was not a very efficient censor.)[39]

By the mid 1980s this ethnoliterary project took on a more openly declared agenda through treatises that expanded upon the themes of the literary forms. Mohammad Hanif Ramey returned from self-imposed exile and penned *Panjāb kā muqaddamah* ("The Case of Punjab"), published in 1985.[40] Manifesto-length responses from other regions followed within two years.[41] 1985 also witnessed Fateh Muhammad Malik's *Punjabi Identity*.[42] In 1986 the World Punjabi Congress, spearheaded by Fakhar Zaman, convened its first World Congress.[43] 1988 brought *Panjābī zabān nahīn maregī* ("The Punjabi Language Will Not Die"); 1989 *Panjāb kā maslah: 'depoliticization' aur awāmī tahrīk kā na calnā* ("The Problem of Punjab: Depoliticization and the Non-movement of the People's Movement"); 1992, *Āo, panjābī ko qatl karen!* ("Come, Let's Kill Punjabi!"), and Shafqat Tanveer Mirza's *Resistance Themes in Punjabi Literature*.[44]

Though this literature has not been examined in any detail in the academic analyses of center–province relations in Pakistan, it is a rich source – in some cases, explicitly describing the relationship between the Punjabi people and their language in filial terms; in other cases, making use of powerful, violent allegory to convey such affect; and most of all, establishing a set of iconic figures to embody a new notion of Punjab and the Punjabi language as strong and resistant. These texts offer important examples of the way Punjabi language, history, ethnicity, and thereby concepts of the Pakistani nation are undergoing revision.

---

[39] Telephone interview with Khalid Hasan, March 19, 2003.
[40] Ramey, *Panjāb kā Muqaddamah*.
[41] Syed Masood Zahidi, *Pākistān kā muqaddamah* (Lahore: Classic, 1988); Shakil Ahmed Zia, *Sindh kā muqaddamah: Hanif Ramey ke muqaddamah-e-Panjāb par ahl-e-Sindh kā jawāb-e da`va* (Karachi: Shabil Publications Limited, 1987).
[42] Malik, *Punjabi Identity*.
[43] The World Punjabi Congress inaugurated its global activities with the 1986 conference, another in 1989, and gatherings throughout the 1990s. By the late 1990s the frequency of these increased to annually. They now meet several times a year in different locations all over the world (Toronto, London, Lahore, Amritsar, etc.).
[44] Farrukh Suhail Goindi, *Panjāb kā maslah: depoliticization aur awāmī tahrīk kā na chalnā* (Lahore: Jamhuri Publications, 1988); Saeed Ahmad Farani, *Panjābī Zabān Nahīn Maregī; Panjābī kā muqaddamah Panjāb men* [The Punjabi Language Will Never Die: The Case of Punjabi in Punjab] (Jhelum: Punjabi Esperanto Academy, 1988). Kahut, *Āo, Panjābī ko Qatl Karen*; Shafqat Tanveer Mirza, *Resistance Themes in Punjabi Literature* (Lahore: Sang-e-Meel, 1992).

The hegemon's lost self

The most surprising aspect of the Punjabiyat literature is the extent to which the Punjabi language is characterized as "lost," lost through the oppression of Urdu. This stance turns upside-down the idea of "Punjabistan" as an oppressor, presenting instead a Punjab in need of self-reclamation. In this view, the Punjab of Punjabiyat is itself a kindred spirit to the other ethnic victims of the state, making common cause with Bengal and Bengali in particular. One dimension of the relationship between Punjab and Urdu-Punjabi languages lies in the fact that the Punjabi language has had a more limited role in print life, particularly in its Arabic script form.[45] The Punjabiyat literature points to these separate spheres of language life in Punjab as evidence of an internal loss of self. At the same time, however, these writers frequently address the paradox of a lost self alongside the dominant idea of Punjabistan, acknowledging the acquiescence of many Punjabis themselves in the oppression of other language-ethnic groups in Pakistan through a sort of false consciousness:[46]

[1]... Punjabis ... became a participant in profiteering and opportunism, swinging their axe on their own two feet ... For the sake of murderous Urdu, first they slit the throat of our Punjab and murdered hundreds of thousands of Punjabis. Then, for this man-eating language, [they] wanted to make the Bengalis slaves. They tried to rob them of their freedom. And having become the spokesmen of the other brothers, they spilled the blood of Bengalis ... And not just Bengalis, but for this murderous language they also fired bullets upon Sindhis, the next-door neighbors for thousands of years.[47]

[2] Having given up their identity, and through Punjab built a tradition of living as a Pakistani, in this way, they became intellectually developed but their emotional development remained halfway, and they became the prey of several such dreams, on account of which not just they but Pakistan as well was harmed ... Punjab's new generations are not proud of Punjabi, but are excluded from it; in a bid to walk like a swan, the crow forgot its own gait.[48]

[3] I was one in a midst of those people who became aliens right in their own homeland. This sounds strange – but this is the real truth and reality.[49]

---

[45] This hierarchization resembles the high (*krama*) and low (*ngoko*) Javanese social roles in Indonesia, speaking high or low. See James T. Siegel, *Solo in the New Order* (Princeton: Princeton University Press, 1986).

[46] See the theory of the "intimate enemy," a psychology of the post-colony where those who collaborated with the colonizers confront a "loss of self." Ashis Nandy, *The Intimate Enemy: Loss and Recovery of Self under Colonialism* (Delhi: Oxford India, 1983).

[47] This passage is from the introduction to Farani, *Panjābī Zabān Nahīn̲ Maregī*, 7.

[48] Ramey, *Panjāb kā Muqaddamah*, 76, 97.

[49] My reading is from the Urdu translation of *Bewatna*: Fakhar Zaman, *Bewatan (Urdu translation)*, trans. Sitar Tahir (Lahore: Classic, 1988). For the Punjabi original, see

[4] I am also a migrant. I am from Faisalabad. My home is a true United Nations: the cook is Bengali. The servant is Sri Lankan. The driver is a Pathan and the gardener is a Sindhi. My children speak Urdu, not Punjabi. When I started to put a tape of Punjabi songs on in the car, my four-year-old son said "Please turn it off." I asked "Why?" He said "Only dogs speak this language." ... We don't live in Pakistan, our place is air-conditioned. Air-conditioned cars and videos. We have a satellite antenna; we have lost our link and connection with our own country.[50]

These four passages, all taken from texts that appeared in the mid 1980s to early 1990s, are linked by the notion that a process of identification with the nation – Pakistan and its national language – brought disaster upon themselves as well as the nation. Speaking Urdu rather than Punjabi is something alien [3], or a forgotten inner essence [2]. The novel which contains passage three, Fakhar Zaman's *Bewatna* ("Stateless" or "The Alien") narrates the tale a lost self, a lost Punjab. Zaman's powerful allegory encapsulates the crux of the problem: Punjabis have become aliens on their own soil. The violent and deep-seated resentment expressed in passages [1] and [2], with characterizations of Urdu as "murderous" and "man-eating," point to a disaffection within Punjab itself that the "Punjabistan" model of Pakistan does not adequately express. For how does an ethnic group said to be politically and culturally dominant in a polity suffer from a "lost" self?

The late Mohammad Hanif Ramey's *Panjāb kā Muqaddmah* ("The Case of Punjab") gives extended attention to the problems of a dual-consciousness and loss of self, arguing that this loss forms Pakistan's core problem. His treatise, a 159-page manifesto as well as a revisionist history of Pakistan, attributes the breakup of Pakistan in 1971 to Punjabis' false identification with the idea of Pakistan instead of Punjab. In the chapter *"wan yūniṭ aur mashriqī pākistān"* ("One Unit and East Pakistan"), he lays the blame for the secession of East Pakistan squarely on the shoulders of Punjab – as do most Bangladeshi accounts of that history – but for an entirely different set of reasons:

[5] If the people of Punjab had demonstrated such love for the Punjabi language, to which it was entitled by status of being our mother tongue, then the situation would not have deteriorated, it would have become apparent to all that Urdu, if it wasn't the language of the Baluch, nor of the Pathans, nor of the Sindhis, wasn't the Punjabis' either. And if the peoples of the four provinces would have kept their respective mother tongues, then they would have been ready to accept Urdu as their national language, so then it may have been

---

Fakhar Zaman, *Bewatna (Punjabi; original)* (Lahore: People's Publications, 1987 [1984]). A very poor English translation is available; see Fakhar Zaman, *The Alien (English translation of Bewatna)*, trans. Asif Javeed Mir (Lahore: Panda Books, 1995).
[50] Kahut, *Āo, Panjābī ko Qatl Karen*, 253.

possible for the Bengalis also to accept Urdu as their national language while also having their own mother tongue. I blame myself above all, and then all the Punjabis, for having betrayed our mother tongue Punjabi. We not only erected the language problem in Pakistan, but also caused terrible damage to Urdu ... The truth is that, after having been the object of imperialism at an international level, and having felt political oppression and social exploitation at a national level, the one thing that broke Pakistan into two pieces was language.[51]

What we can glean from the passages selected above is the sense in which this "lost self" interpretation depends on the perception of Punjab as having sacrificed itself – its tongue, its way of being – in service to the unmet promise of Pakistan. This notion of sacrifice is compounded by ethnolinguistic assertion from other regions (including the distinct Siraiki-speaking areas of southern Punjab, discussed in Chapter 3), resulting in the existence of primary-level regional language education in every province but Punjab.[52] Instead of conceptualizing the strong presence of Urdu in Punjab as advantageous in an "Urdu-speaking" nation-state, these writers instead locate their national, provincial, and personal struggles in the psychological discourse of language loss as a loss of self.

New voice through new literature

Fakhar Zaman makes use of the trope of honor to paint a disturbing allegorical portrait of a country quite literally violating its own mother, and cynically authorizing this rape in the name of the army and Islamic authority. Zaman's *Bewatna* – a Punjabi-language novel in the high modernist style of Kafka – reads as a straightforward allegory in which the protagonist, the alien in his own homeland, chronicles the brutish state of the world around him and refuses to accept the justifications authorities make for their deeds. This novel, comprised of twenty-nine chapters that hang together like short scenes in a film, takes as its central character a bastard boy born in a prison of a mother rendered mute. The value of this Punjabi-language political fiction lies in its characterizations: the alien and the mute mother as a Punjabi bereft of his "mother tongue."

The suffering mother figure recurs throughout the novel. In a horrifically violent subplot, another mother suffers the wrath of her violent military son – an army general – aided by a corrupt religious judge:

Sometimes he slapped his mother, other times he pulled her hair. One time he kicked his mother so hard with the toe of his heavy boots that it was as if she broke in half ... Then one night all hell broke loose ... the general-son entered

---

[51] Ramey, *Panjāb kā Muqaddamah*, 93–4.
[52] The exception in sparsely populated Balochistan dispensed with its short-lived "Mother Tongue" education programs as of 2000.

his mother's room in the middle of the night, totally drunk. He told her she had better stop all her crying or else ... The general hit her over and over; she was covered in blood. When she didn't quiet down, he then ... his mother's eyes turned to stone. Her body was completely lifeless. The general stomped the floor hard with his jackboot and said "Now will you beat your chest? Now your honor has been soiled, you hunchback." For one second life returned to the mother. She laughed like a lunatic, and said, "Sons are born to be victorious over their mothers! Congratulations, you man in uniform!"

Without explicit details, Zaman signals through the silence of ellipses that the general, in his rage, did the unmentionable: he raped his mother. He "soils her honor" to silence her both through violence and the attendant shame of this act. But the allegory does not end here. Zaman's general seeks absolution in the name of Islamic authority:

The news that the general-son had defiled his hunchback mother while drunk spread through the city. The man in uniform wasn't bothered in the least by his actions, but he found it necessary to search for the legitimacy of his actions. That night he went to the house of a friend who was the most esteemed *qazi* (religious judge) in the city. The general related the whole incident. The *qazi* assured him that he would help. The next day a *fatwa* was issued!:

Whenever fits of insanity descend upon a mother, whenever she wails, pounds her chest, or cries aloud, at that time the uniformed general can kick her with his heavy boots until she's covered in blood ... this is exactly in keeping with the Doctrine of Necessity,[53] according to its constitution, and is permissible in the eyes of the law.

Thus the city faced the incident.[54]

We see here a disturbing, provocative metaphor in which a powerful agent of the state is so depraved as to rape his own mother, and the *qazi* has no qualms authorizing the obviously immoral act, one illegal by any measure of Islamic jurisprudence. The overt message here is that the military and the Islamists, two of Pakistan's powerful institutions, have colluded to despoil that which has given them life, the Punjabi language – and lost all moral bearings in the process.

Building particularly on the notions described above of the "lost self," the question of honor and valor come into play. Punjabiyat literature

---

[53] Zaman clearly refers here to a provision that developed in Pakistani legal reasoning to permit the suspension of constitutional authority, the "Law of Civil Necessity" (justifying the first civilian coup of Ghulam Muhammad in 1952) and later the "Doctrine of Necessity" (justifying Zia's military coup in 1977). See Paula R. Newberg, *Judging the State: Courts and Constitutional Politics in Pakistan* (Cambridge: Cambridge University Press, 1995), 35–68; also McGrath, *The Destruction of Pakistan's Democracy*, 210–11, 285n84–5.

[54] English text translated from the Urdu with reference to the Punjabi original. See Zaman, *Bewatan (Urdu translation)*, 43–7; and Zaman, *Bewatna (Punjabi; original)*, 47–51. Less felicitous English translation available; see Zaman, *The Alien (English translation of Bewatna)*, 33–7.

82   Speaking Like a State

asserts that the project of recovering Punjabi language for the psychological well-being of the Punjabi people must go hand-in-hand with a recovery of Punjab's history. I will say much more about the question of historiography in Chapters 6 and 7, looking particularly at state education policy that explicitly undertook to write a history of the nation-state without reference to the deep regional pasts of the provinces. Yet here I want to look in particular at depictions of heroism embodied in these texts and films. One strand of this thinking focuses on the literary merits of Punjabi writers, primarily the devotional poetry of Sufis and the romance tales – the famed *Hīr-Rānjha, Sāhibān -Mirza, Sohnī-Mahiwāl*, and *Sassī-Punnūn* in particular.[55] Another strand places greater emphasis on re-narrating the history of Punjab out of some received notion of martial weakness and into some notion of valor and strength.

With respect to rehabilitating the great works of Punjabi literature and energizing these works into popular consciousness, the *Hīr-Rānjhā* romance of Waris Shah (c.1722–98 CE) and the mystical poetry of Bulleh Shah (c.1670–1758 CE) are important points of reference, cited routinely.[56] Farani contrasts the "reign" of Urdu literature in Punjabi schools with the injustice that excludes Punjabi literature – Waris Shah, Bulleh Shah, Shah Hussain, and Baba Fareed.[57] Kohut named the press which published his *Come, Let's Kill Punjabi* "Waris Shah Publications." Shah Hussain's grave continues to be the setting for the annual *cirāghān dā melā* in Lahore. Zaman, in his *Bandīwān*, develops this line of thinking into an extraordinary argument about language and literature, depicted as the bondage and oppression of subjectivity. His Punjabi revolutionary protagonist resists the anti-Punjabi bureaucratic state by suffering terrible tortures, sustained by a faith in Punjabi language.

Bandīwān is a political manifesto in the form of a novel, and resembles nothing so much as Kafka's *Trial*, a novel it repeatedly invokes not only stylistically but by name as well.[58] It opens with the central character,

[55] Sikh literature, for the most part, does not find a place in this canon-in-formation. However, in 2000 an Arabic-script transliteration of the writings of Guru Nanak (the founder of the Sikh religion) was produced in Lahore. The volume is enormous, some thousand pages, and nearly three times the cost of an average book in Pakistan.
[56] According to Farina Mir, *Hīr Rānjha*, a Punjabi-language romance dating from at least the sixteenth century was widely hailed as a seminal text for Punjabis during the colonial period. See Mir, "The Social Space of Language," 1–2; also Mirza, *Resistance Themes in Punjabi Literature*, 210.
[57] Farani, *Panjābī Zabān Nahīn Maregī*, 27. Note that Baba Fareed is claimed both by Punjabi enthusiasts as well as Siraiki ethnonationalists.
[58] *The Trial*'s protagonist is known only as "Herr K." In one early scene in *Bandīwān*, Z imagines writing "Kafka's Joseph K should be asked" in one of the forms he is filling out. Zaman, *The Alien (English translation of Bewatna)*, 31; Fakhar Zaman, *Bandīwān (Punjabi original)*, 2nd edn (Lahore: Nigarshaat, 1987), 49; Fakhar Zaman, *Qaidī (Urdu translation of Bandīwān)*, trans. Shaista Habib (Lahore: Classic, 1989), 39.

"Z," in solitary confinement, awaiting trial and punishment under the accusation of conspiracy to commit murder. Z claims he has committed no crime, only that he has written in "the people's language," having rejected the national "double standard," and with his writing seeks to battle the "inverted subjectivity" which is the great enemy of Pakistan. In the novel's climactic fourteenth chapter, we find Z placed on a rack, enduring repeated floggings. After each lash, Z expounds upon his philosophy of Punjabi language and its centrality to restoring proper psychic health to political life in Pakistan. There are twenty such lashes, and Z's proclamations are so extensive that when the late Khalid Hasan translated this novel from Punjabi into English he deliberately eliminated much of the political rhetoric, in order to make the novel a lighter read.[59] The Pakistani bureaucracy comes under scathing criticism for arbitrary and unjust exercise of power. As in *Bewatna*, Zaman again castigates Islamic authority for its hypocrisy, citing homosexual pedophilic rape to undermine a *maulvi*'s legitimacy to deliver moral verdicts.[60] But it is surely Z's long speeches about Punjabi, while undergoing lash after lash of a leather whip, which form the novel's centerpiece. Each lash unleashes progressively more impassioned speeches about language and Pakistani nationalism:

The fourteenth lash: "The unfortunate part of this double standard is that creative writing in the local languages – Pashto, Balochi, Sindhi, and Punjabi – are deliberately reviled. In fact, the thoughts of these writers are deemed anti-national and they are banned..."

The fifteenth lash: "Scorning today's Sindhi poet is like belittling yesterday's Shah Abdul Latif Bhitai... These very writers are the basis of national existence. Killing them amounts to weakening the federal system... This 'inverted subjectivity' is the great enemy of this county."

The sixteenth lash: "... Unfortunately, for several generations the history of Punjabi was written according to the whims of the white rulers, and Punjabis were called obedient and 'devoted servants...' The current batch of Punjabi poets, writers, and intellectuals have completely re-analyzed Punjabi character and its history ... they have shown it the poetry of opposition, against oppression and domination."[61]

---

[59] Interview with Khalid Hasan, March 19, 2003.

[60] The *maulvi* who blesses the whip prior to "Z"'s flogging is "that same *maulvi* who was caught in his chamber with a boy." Zaman, *Bandīwān (Punjabi original)*, 135; Zaman, *Qaidī (Urdu translation of Bandīwān)*, 110. Hasan translates this slightly differently; see Fakhar Zaman, *The Prisoner (English translation of Bandiwan)*, trans. Khalid Hasan (New Delhi, Bombay, Calcutta, and Madras: Allied Publishers Private Limited, 1984), 90. A chapter of *Bewatan* similarly unmasks the depravity of a *maulvi* with not only a young boy, but a goat and a chicken as well. See Zaman, *Bewatan (Urdu translation)*, 39–42.

[61] Zaman, *Qaidī (Urdu translation of Bandīwān)*, 118–19. Zaman, *Bandīwān (Punjabi original)*, 147–9. Note the similarity with Zaman's Writ Petition, cited at the beginning of this chapter.

84   Speaking Like a State

By the end of the novel, the character "Z" has been sentenced to death, convicted of trumped-up charges designed to rid society of his revolutionary interpretations of what and who comprises Pakistan, i.e., Punjabi and other regional languages – and the novel closes with him in a cell on death row. This novel remains banned in Pakistan.[62]

Old stories, new heroes

Zaman uses a fictional protagonist who can suffer terrible tortures with his faith in Punjabi in order to demonstrate valor. Other writers mine Punjabi history in order to propagate new ideas about Punjabi "character." Literary critic Shafqat Tanveer Mirza authored a book on "Resistance Themes" found in romance literature, oral tales, and poetry to similarly assert some kind of strength and valor in the essence of Punjab.[63] As mentioned earlier, Najm Hosain Syed wrote two Punjabi plays featuring historical Punjabi figures as protagonists, and presenting their lives as ones of resistance rather than criminality. Man of letters Safdar Mir, for many years a columnist featured in the English-language paper *Dawn*, wrote a play, *Nīlī Dā Aswar*, featuring Sialkot's pre-Islamic hero Raja Rasalu (*c*.100–200 CE).[64] Mohammad Hanif Ramey argued the case for Punjabi valor as well, though in a departure from Zaman, Farani, and Mirza he separated his vision of Punjab's history valor from the *qisse* romance literature.

Ramey devoted two chapters of his manifesto to refuting the stereotype of Punjabi subordination and subservience. In one chapter, "*tārikh kā tashaddud*" ("The Terror of History") he chronicles the millenia of invasions Punjab has suffered, and asserts that over time Punjabis – though a valiant people – learned to adapt to the constant invasions. Having suffered invasions from the Aryans to Alexander the Great up through the British, Punjabis became psychologically downtrodden.[65] Ramey also claims, in a departure from Zaman, that the stories of Punjabi valor have been lost due to the colonial policies of the British. Not only did the British establish Urdu as the language of state in Punjab, but they also instituted a system of landlordism (presumably by building the canals which irrigated the lands more widely and resulted in an early green revolution).[66] When the Punjab, in Ramey's historical narrative,

---

[62] According to Pakistan Academy of Letters, *Ban Lifted After 18 Years*.
[63] Mirza, *Resistance Themes in Punjabi Literature*.
[64] "Safdar Mir Passes Away," *Dawn*, August 10, 1998.
[65] Ramey, *Panjāb kā Muqaddamah*, 39–50.
[66] For the history of the creation of the "canal colonies" under the British – and resulting changes to Punjab's political economy and society through land grants to certain

transformed into a landlord-administered agricultural instead of a pastoral economy, and as the cultivators maintained more sedentary, less nomadic lifestyles, the stories of battle gave way to romance tales.[67] Thus not only did the British steal the land of Punjab from the Punjabi people, and sideline the Punjabi language through state language policy favoring Urdu, but also caused Punjabis to be excluded from their own sense of historic bravery. Shafqat Mirza echoes the interpretation, stating that Punjabi Muslims were "cut asunder from their rich political past" by losing their language.[68]

To arm Punjabis once again with the fearlessness to recover themselves, Mirza assembles 228 pages of tales of bravery. Ramey decides to focus more narrowly, and retells the stories of five valorous Punjabi youth. Ramey's "*pānc jawān mard panjābī*" ("Five Valiant Punjabi Youth") thus excavates five men from the margins of Punjabi consciousness and proclaims their centrality. He recounts short tales of the battle-demonstrated bravery of Raja Poras (*c.*326 BCE) who fought, and lost to, Alexander the Great but met his gaze not with shame but with pride; Dulla Bhatti (ordered executed by Mughal emperor Akbar); Rai Ahmad K͟hān Kharal (who led the rebellion against the British in Punjab in 1857); and the twentieth-century rebels against the British, Nizam Lohar (*c.*1900) and Bhagat Singh (1907–31). In each of these stories the important point is not the fact of victory, for they all lost their battles, but the bravado with which they demonstrated their Punjabi valiance. They are to be reinstated as models for Punjab, as Punjabis who fought with their heads held high, and as narratives to be told to Punjabis for their self-recovery. The tales of Raja Poras, Dulla Bhatti, Rai Ahmed K͟hān Kharal, and Puran of Sialkot/Raja Rasalu appear to be particularly salient throughout these works; this is not just one man's uncorroborated ravings about Punjab's heroic past. A "Dullah Bhatti" institute has even been set up to advocate the Punjabi cause.[69] An important point is that these resistant heroes, elaborated in these texts precisely so that contemporary Punjabis can take pride and inspiration, have been drawn from all periods of Punjab's history. The idea of claiming "Punjabiyat" does not limit itself to a post-Islamic world, something rather unexpected in light of official state narratives. In fact, this is precisely where the Punjabiyat debate cross-cuts that of the nation-state: where the state locates heroism in the great men of the Pakistan movement, the coming of Islam

---

castes – Imran Ali's book is unsurpassed. See Imran Ali, *The Punjab under Imperialism, 1885–1947* (Princeton: Princeton University Press, 1988).
[67] Ramey, *Panjāb kā Muqaddamah*, 39–50.
[68] Mirza, *Resistance Themes in Punjabi Literature*, 42–3.
[69] Mansoor, *Punjabi, Urdu, English in Pakistan: a Sociolinguistic Study*, 17.

to the subcontinent, and the Muslim rulers of pre-Partition India – all chronicled in an overtly supra-regional Urdu or English textual corpus – the Punjabiyat hero reclamation project explicitly seeks to re-narrate heroes marginal to national memory by drawing from folk songs and poetic forms.

While these efforts have been advanced through an unexpected quarter, the Lahore-based group of successful, highly educated elite, a parallel phenomenon has been taking place in the arenas of very low literacy. The existence of a "counterpublic" in the Punjabi language within Punjab offers additional evidence for a convergence of sentiment between the elite and the popular. Chapter 5 thus examines the intriguing phenomenon of Punjabi-language popular culture, and connects the theoretical implications of the work of the literary elite analyzed here with the implications of the popular allegiances as well.

5 The case of Punjab, part II: popular culture

> "So, this Punjabi is whose language?"
> "It's the hicks' language."
> "Who are these hicks?"
> "The people who live in villages."
> "What percentage are they?"
> "They're about seventy-five percent."
>
> "Skit Number 5," *The Punjabi Language Will Never Die*

The Punjabiyat movement has arisen due to the work of cultural entrepreneurs focused on crafting "high" literature in their language to give it a voice in culturally prestigious arenas, an important aspect of the argument that the language deserves its rightful place on the world stage (not to mention the national stage). At the same time, an intriguing development has been unfolding in the segments of Punjabi-speaking Pakistan that illustrates perduring attachment to the language even in the face of a national hierachization that places it at subordinate levels. The brief skit which begins this chapter encapsulates the symbolic economy: the questioner runs through a whole cast of Pakistani ethnic ideal-types, first asking a Sindhi what language he likes to speak ("Sindhi"), then a Pashtun and a Baloch (who answer "Pashto" and "Balochi"). But when the questioner poses the same question to a Punjabi, the latter answers "Urdu." When the questioner presses the Punjabi ethnic type further on the matter of the Punjabi language – who speaks it, and where – he receives answers designed to highlight the peculiar relationship between Punjabi, Urdu, and the Punjab.[1] The region with the great preponderance of the population (rural Punjab's 75 percent quoted above) suffers from the most extensive sense of language loss, with respondents unable to offer up an ethnically-marked language of their own, and worse still, bearing the markings of outcast status.

In this polemic, *Panjābī Zabān Nahīn Maregī* ("The Punjabi Language Will Never Die"), Saeed Ahmad Farani provides an inside view into

---

[1] Farani, *Panjābī Zabān Nahīn Maregī*, 25–6.

the quotidian life of a non-elite Punjabi speaker, one unable to socially negotiate the bilingual terrain successfully navigated by Urdu-literate Punjabi speakers. Indeed, the author's declared biography suggests his intention to explore low-status social life in Punjab: his biographical notes list occupations such as: "laborer, *caprāsī* [gopher], typist, phone operator, fruit seller, accountant, newspaper reporter, officer-manager (Habib Bank)."[2] One skit focuses on the humiliation a low-level Punjabi-speaking functionary faces from the scorn of an Urdu-speaking officer in what appears to be a government office. The Punjabi-speaker, when called, answers using words common to Urdu and Punjabi alike, but with syntax typically considered coarse or impolite in Urdu.[3] While the rustic answer – "Main jī" instead of "Hān jī," or better, "Jīhān" – hardly stands as an egregious impropriety, the worker's boss shames him for his lack of grace.

Farani's narratives illustrate how Punjabi-speakers fare poorly in status consciousness, a finding that coincides with the surveys carried out by sociolinguist Sabiha Mansoor as well. Her survey asked various groups of students (Punjabis in both Urdu- and English-medium schools) to rate their "native language groups" on aspects such as "social grace," "modern," and "cultured" – and contrary to her guiding hypothesis, found that the Punjabi students consistently rated themselves lower in these aspects than they rated their Urdu-speaking peers.[4]

This sense of dual-consciousness is portrayed here as a burden, one weighing particularly on the backs of Punjabis whose linguistic and cultural limitations in Urdu apparently mark them as inferiors, and who are simultaneously denied knowledge of literatures in their own language. Through this narrative, the idea of "Punjabistan" evaporates and we see instead the mask of the Pakistani nation-state as an ethnic oppressor. This view would come as quite a surprise to many Pakistanis outside Punjab, who would find it difficult to view Punjabis as having experienced oppression. And despite the fact that within the gross ethnic grouping of "Punjabi," which encompasses thinner slices of difference – the Siraiki of southern Punjab, of course, or even highly localized speech forms like "Jhangi" – the markings of Punjabi serve to stigmatize the speaker outside the elite strata despite the aggregate ethnic, numeric, and political dominance of this province.

---

[2] Back cover of *ibid*. Also see Mirza, *Resistance Themes in Punjabi Literature*, 228.
[3] See "Mukālma Nambar 5," Farani, *Panjābī Zabān Nahīn Maregī*, 32.
[4] Mansoor, *Punjabi, Urdu, English in Pakistan*, 46–57.

On the outside: language defines deprivation

Whereas the Punjabiyat literary efforts focus on prestige hierarchies and reclaiming what they believe to be their language's due, one strand of the pro-Punjabi argument perceives the language as a cause of socio-economic disadvantage. Again, this perception is hard to understand if viewed through the lens of a Pashto-speaker in Peshawar, for in terms of agrarian development and every other social indicator, Punjab is far more prosperous than any other province of Pakistan. But in the "lost" self understanding, Punjabis face hardship purely by virtue of the language they were born to speak first. In recent years, statistics on unemployed Punjabi-language youth seems to have become an important feature in public addresses made by writer Fakhar Zaman. His more recent addresses advocate the use of Punjabi language for official debates in the Punjab Assembly, and adopting Punjabi as the medium of education at primary levels. This idea of Punjabi economic desperation is possible not by juxtaposing Punjabi wealth with Balochi deprivation, but instead through comparison with the English- and Urdu-speaking elite. The interpretive sleight-of-hand can be seen in political cartoons from Farani's *Panjābī Zabān Nahīn̲ Maregī* ("The Punjabi Language Will Never Die") (see Figures 2, 3, 4, and 5).

Figure 2 Cartoon: throne of education.

Figure 3 Cartoon: "This is the journey to reach the economic goal in the Islamic Republic of Pakistan?" (One furlong for the English speaker, one mile for the Urdu speaker, but three miles for the Punjabi speaker.)

Figure 4 Cartoon: Punjabi? Urdu, English inside?

In Figure 2, we see the English-educated Western-suit wearing elite closest to the throne of education. Close behind we see a man wearing a "Jinnah cap," a sherwani, and shalwar. This is the stereotypical image of an Urdu-speaking elite, and the "national dress" proffered by textbooks.

Figure 5 Cartoon: "Untitled."

Behind him and farther back we see a rural villager, the Punjabi-speaker, in lungi, kurta, and pagri. The cartoon obviously comments on the villager's uphill struggle, beginning with a significant disadvantage, to reach the seat of power: education. Figure 3 depicts a similar scenario, though in the form of a race to reach the "economic destination." Figure 4 shows the Punjabi language embodied as a Punjabi villager, one shivering without cover in a cold desert night while Urdu and English (indicated not only by the caption but by the Jinnah cap and the necktie on the camel) lie protected in a tent. Finally – and grotesquely – the extraordinary image of Figure 5, perhaps fortunately captioned "Untitled," depicts the Urdu- and English-speakers drinking milk directly from a cow's udder while hapless regional ethnic types stand watching, unable to wrest a drop for themselves.[5]

The sentiments expressed in these political cartoons invert the standard understanding of Punjab as a "Punjabistan" in a self-portrayal as a victimized subaltern, one singled out for oppression. Reading these political cartoons against social statistics and human development indicators which clearly establish Punjab as the most privileged provides

---

[5] All cartoons reproduced with permission of the author, Saeed Ahmad Farani. Author Farani drew each of the bystanders in Figure 5 to represent the four major language-based ethnicities of Pakistan – Punjabi, Sindhi, Pashtun, and Baluchi.

insight into the degree to which ideas about prosperity are linked to those of prestige, and are as much imagined as real.

It is worth noting that in a country with low literacy rates overall, the Punjabi language has a print life only at the lowest levels and in arenas marginal to formal education and "official" life. Indeed, the number of quality books published in Punjabi is miniscule, although due to the Punjabiyat efforts the numbers are slowly increasing. As well, a daily Punjabi newspaper, *Khabrān*, was launched by the Khabrain Group in 2004. The paper's circulation has been increasing, likely accounting for the 67 percent increase in Punjabi-language newspaper circulation enumerated by the Audit Bureau of Circulations in 2004, growing by 62 percent over the previous year in 2005, and by another 53 percent over the year before in 2006. Even with the circulation boosts of these past years, however, Punjabi-language newspaper circulations measure a mere fraction of Urdu and of English-language circulations: in 2005, just 0.45 percent of Urdu dailies' circulation, and 3.3 percent of English. These climbed slightly to 0.68 percent of Urdu and 4.8 percent of English circulations in 2006. While the trendline is increasing, the figures show the marginality of the language in the printed world.[6]

In the world of "chapbooks," or small stapled books, the best available survey – albeit more than a decade old – shows that approximately 39 percent of such printed artifacts are written in Punjabi, compared with 36 percent in Pashto and 23 percent in Urdu. Their content ranges from poetry (religious and secular) to romance stories, film songs, magical spells, humor, and the lives of religious figures.[7] Again, the prevalence of written Punjabi circulating primarily within this quasi-literate sphere serves to illustrate the doubly marginal dimension of Punjabi in Pakistan. What the Punjabiyat proponents advocate is a qualitative change in Punjabi's relationship to official state institutions, for a simple quantitative change would not achieve the goal of gaining respect, recognition, and the symbolic capital the Punjabiyat proponents see as its due. As Farani offers as a summary in one of his morality plays, "In the schools of Punjab, Miyan Mohammad Bakhsh, Baba Bulheh Shah,

---

[6] Federal statistics group Punjabi and Siraiki as one for the sake of circulations, although the national census enumerated Siraki as a language only in 1981. The boost between 2004, when *Khabrān* began publication, and the year before was very significant: from a circulation of 10,000 to some 17,000-plus. Government of Pakistan, *Average Circulation of Newspapers and Periodicals by Language/Type, 1996–2006* (Federal Bureau of Statistics, 2007); available from www.statpak.gov.pk/depts/fbs/statistics/social_statistics/periodicals_by_language.pdf.

[7] William L. Hanaway and Mumtaz Nasir, "Chapbook Publishing in Pakistan," in *Studies in Pakistani Popular Culture*, ed. Hanaway and Heston (Lahore: Lok Virsa and Sang-e-Meel, 1996), 364–6.

Waris Shah, Baba Fareed, and Shah Hussain aren't allowed admission. And Ghalib, Mir Dard, Mir Taqi Mir, Dagh, and Jigar all reign. Isn't this a shame?"[8]

In the aural realm of the textual spectrum a phenomenally successful development of the Punjabi language has been underway. Let us recall that even with the most literate population in Pakistan, Punjab's literacy rate hovers only slightly under half the population. The "masses" appear to have declared their allegiance to a contemporary heroic character that, though he does not explicitly reference historical figures, could have been drawn from any of the heroes featured in the Punjabiyat literature. This hero, "Maulā Jaṭ," has transformed Pakistani popular cinema.

The rise of the popular violent Punjabi hero

During the 1980s, and no less importantly for our purposes, Punjabi cinema rose to a position of market dominance, primarily through a new hero, the iconic revenge-seeking peasant-warrior, "Maulā Jaṭ," played by Sultan Rahi (1938–96) (see Figures 6 and 7). By the mid 1990s he so overdetermined the aesthetic, linguistic, and narrative content of Punjabi cinema as to embody the genre. His first major success hit the theatres in Punjab with a bang in 1979: *Maulā Jaṭ*, a rough-and-tumble extravaganza of violence, catapulted him to the very top of Pakistani cinema. The film's unequalled success – spawning numerous sequels and knock-offs – resulted in Punjabi cinema eclipsing Urdu as the most prolific and highest grossing in Pakistan. Sultan Rahi's importance earned him an entry in *Encyclopedia Britannica*, where he is defined as the one who "established Punjabi as the major language of Pakistani cinema."[9] This was an unusual turning point, for the Pakistani film industry had long indulged the genteel poetic Urdu aesthetic, epitomized by actors like Nadeem: handsome, well-spoken, educated, often dressed in Western suits, and clean-shaven. Rahi's *Maulā Jaṭ* character could not have been more different: rough, dressed in the lungi-kurta of a Punjabi peasant, a skilled horse rider as well as master of the *gaṇḍāsā* (the long-handled axe pictured below, typically used to cut sugarcane),

---

[8] Farani, *Panjābī Zabān Nahīn̲ Maregī*, 27. All the figures denied admission to schools in Punjab are well-known Punjabi writers of the past two centuries. Those who "reign" in Punjab's schools are important Urdu literary figures, most of whom made their homes in what is today's north India.

[9] The *Maula Jaṭ* and *Maula Jaṭ* in London film posters reproduced here are from a private collection, and appear here with the permission of owner Omar Khan. On Rahi, see "Rahi, Sultan" Encyclopædia Britannica from Encyclopædia Britannica Online. Via www.britannica.com/EBchecked/topic/489642/Sultan-Rahi.

Figure 6 Film poster for *Maulā Jaṭ*.

possessing an enormous and obviously hypermasculine moustache, and given to demonstrations of brute physical strength. Sultan Rahi quickly came to symbolize a new privileging of Punjab and Punjabi in the non-official, low-prestige arenas of Pakistani public life. The Zia ul-Haq military regime tried to ban the film, yet somehow the film's producer managed to get a two-year "stay order" against its prohibition. It went on to a record run, marking a visual as well as literal vernacularization of the cinema.[10]

But this demotic shift did not take place to universal acclaim; the criticism of a prominent Pakistani social and literary critic clearly partisan to the highbrow Urdu aesthetic, Gilani Kamran, summarized the genre's problems. He castigated the Punjabi film industry for "defin[ing] the Punjabi culture as something primitive, noisy, vociferous, and highly pugnacious … The choice of the language is still another major defect of these films: it is crude, vulgar, morally degrading and without any

[10] See "*Maula Jaṭ* – The Director's Cut" from *The Hot Spot Online*. (The Hot Spot website is the most comprehensive source of film reviews, billboard images, and trivia relating to Pakistani cinema. This company has acquired VCD distribution rights to *Maula Jaṭ* and many other films, which are now available for purchase. See www.thehotspotonline.com/moviespot/bolly/reviews/m/Maulajat.htm.)

Figure 7 Film poster for *Maulā Jaṭ in London*.

decorum."[11] While Kamran may not be alone in his sentiments, the question arises as to whether some different aesthetic is at work here, one more 'true' to Punjab than he cares to admit – precisely because of the widespread prevalence of the features Kamran describes as crude and vulgar. In his own words, "Even in Punjabi novels and short stories the same defects may be traced without any exception."

Against Kamran, those who loved the *Maulā Jaṭ* genre found the "choice of language" the very source of cheer, especially an aspect of the performance that drew upon a type of Punjabi-language verbal

---

[11] See "An Interesting Punjabi Novel" in Gilani Kamran, *Pakistan: A Cultural Metaphor* (Lahore: Ravian English Masters Association and Nadeem Book House, 1993), 247. Gilani Kamran is a well known Pakistani critic.

duel called *barrak*. According to Pakistani film director and historian Mushtaq Gazdar, barrak instantiated a Punjabi bellicosity:

> The verbal brawl called barrak, in Punjabi slang, is the hallmark of the movie. It can be taken as comic or serious, real or grotesque, depending on the nature of the audience. But such scenes stir audiences immensely. Barrak is a high-pitched, full-throated, threatening yell, a sort of warming up, a prelude to a brawl ... [it is] a part of Punjabi life and culture. It is a bold challenge to the opponent.[12]

Not only does the *Maulā Jaṭ* character engage in this particularly Punjabi behavior, but every aspect of his character showcases a strong, brave, Punjabi masculinity. He fights his enemies in hand-to-hand combat, using a traditional agricultural implement (the *gaṇḍāsā*, notably pictured in both film posters above). He combats evil, personified by a fictionalized version of a real Punjabi village don, Nuri Nath. He rescues a Punjabi girl about to be raped, when other "sons of Punjab" refuse out of fear. He displays physical strength, pulling a heavily loaded oxcart out of a bog, so all can see that he is *stronger* than an ox.

The Jat films are especially interesting because they eclipsed Urdu as the primary language of Pakistani cinema, and also because Punjab rather than Pakistan seems to structure the landscape. Characters refer to Punjab, not Pakistan, being very big, or that "all of Punjab" will come to a festival – the horizons of experience are focused exclusively on Punjab. The central hero invokes, by name alone, pre-Islamic caste identities native to Punjab, primarily Jats and Gujjars. In contemporary Pakistan, these groups are called *birādarī* networks; they are traditional agricultural castes, which exist both in Pakistan as well as today's Indian Punjab. Thus ethnic as well as linguistic horizons valorize Punjab, not Pakistan, and pay little heed to the necessity of defining Pakistan in national terms, terms which have come to ignore the non-Islamic dimensions of social life.

Maulā Jaṭ and the many spin-offs (*Maulā Jaṭ in London*, *Maulā Jaṭ te Nūri Nath*, *Jaṭṭī dā Vīr*, *Jaṭ Gujjar*, *Jaṭ Gujjar te Nath*, *Makhā Jaṭ*, *Bālī Jaṭṭī*, *Ik Dhī Panjāb Dī*, *Desān dā Rājā*, *Wehshī Jaṭ*, and *Wehshī Gujjar* – to name just a few) represent a major rethinking of the language of cinema in Pakistan and the representation of heroism – a preoccupation of the literary efforts as well. Just as Ramey, Mirza, and Syed sought to reclaim strong Punjabi heroes for the current generation, Maulā Jaṭ became the cinematic embodiment of Punjabi strength mediated by the pugnacious pleasures of the Punjabi language. Maulā Jaṭ is noble, honorable,

---

[12] Mushtaq Gazdar, *Pakistan Cinema 1947–1997* (Karachi: Oxford University Press, 1997), 134.

protective of women's chastity, and above all is victorious in battle. If the proponents of Punjabiyat worried about reclaiming a Punjabi *imaginaire* in which Punjab would no longer be viewed as submissive, Punjabi cinema fulfilled this wish from the 1980s forward. From 1979 until his death in 1996, Sultan Rahi's Punjabi hero dominated Pakistani cinema and destroyed in a bloody frenzy anyone who crossed his path. These films are gore-laden, with legs and arms flying off after a *gaṇḍāsā* chop; the visual representations of Rahi in every billboard and advertisement (the most famous two reproduced above) depict him either covered with blood himself or holding a *gaṇḍāsā* dripping with blood. Punjab indeed found itself a hero who could not be called submissive.

Through this visual narrative reassessment of heroic representation, particularly appropriate for the large illiterate population, we can see the outlines of a society demanding to see itself represented in a different way from what the national aesthetic demanded. The new hero cared little for Urdu and reveled in the Punjabi vernacular imagination, and that too of the most aggressive sort. Maulā Jat was literally a man of the village, battling rural problems of landlordism and domination by brute force. This changing face of the Pakistani film hero was not a single occurrence; rather, with every Jat-type filmic success Sultan Rahi further confirmed the desires of his fans.[13] Following Rahi's shocking murder in 1996 – he was killed by highway bandits while he stopped to fix his car – the Punjabi film industry hit a slump, but has again revived, particularly buoyed by the successes of a younger star, Shaan, who has taken on the roles Rahi used to play. Shaan's roles like *Makhā Jat* and a remake of *Wehshī Jat* have again brought Punjabi film box office success. For an industry nearly fatally done in by Rahi's death, coupled with the increasing availability of better-quality films on video from Bombay and Hollywood, the popularity of this resurrected Jat genre signals a meaningful attachment to the sort of hero it portrays.

The Jat characters clearly depended on an overtly (indeed excessively) masculine notion of heroism. Of the films in the genre, only a few focused on female protagonists, typically a heroine willing to carry out violence just like a man. (Film posters of *Bālī Jattī* and *Jattī dā Vīr*, for example, depict Rubenesque women brandishing guns, in bloodstained clothes). In part we can attribute this to the social restrictions that inhibit women from attending films in cinema halls in Pakistan – this is a male domain, without any doubt, and producers/directors play

---

[13] The Jat films did little business outside Punjab and upper Sindh (where many Punjabi – indeed Siraiki – speakers live). It was a regional phenomenon, but because this is the most populous region, the box office proceeds were dramatic.

to their audience. But we can take the analysis a step further by recognizing the degree to which this trope of masculine heroism works in the service of establishing a public sphere for a mode of being – speaking Punjabi – that fares poorly in public prestige hierarchies dominated by the Urdu-speaking genteel.

In the broader region of South Asia, the analogy between language and motherhood is not uncommon. We saw that the literary Punjabiyat writings analogize the relationship between ethnic essence and language as one between children and a mother, creating a filial bond between Punjabis and their language, a bond necessary to defend. The metaphor bears remarkable resemblance to the idea of the life-giving Tamilttay, the female goddess of Tamil language described in Sumathi Ramaswamy's *Passions of the Tongue*. This history of "language devotion" describes conceptions of language as deity, a mother, and an eroticized lover – in all cases, ideologized as some kind of powerful female presence.[14] In perhaps the most noted political speech on the subject, Gandhi used the simile in an address to a Hindi organization, even extending the trope to liken the mother tongue to the purity of "mother's milk."[15] While the Punjabiyat understanding of self and language does not fashion the language into a physically representable presence like Tamilttay (and given the Islamic context, such a personification would be extremely unlikely), the linkage of person to the "mother tongue" receives elaboration, in analogies such as Farani's "The child which … drinks milk from her breasts … the language which it hears is that very language called the mother tongue,"[16] and Ramey's "For the Punjabi people, in place of the mother there was Punjab, and for the father, Pakistan."[17] The necessity of "protecting" the language-mother thus falls neatly into pre-existing notions of feminine virtue, chastity, and honor, all perennially in danger of violation, and therefore in need of chivalrous protection. Where the literary Punjabiyat writing sought to recover the heroism of Punjab's past, the cinema does this visually and aurally, standing in for and reclaiming a mode of being that valorizes the agrarian rustic life, and the

---

[14] See Sumathi Ramaswamy, *Passions of the Tongue* (Berkeley: University of California Press, 1997).
[15] See M. K. Gandhi, *Our Language Problem [Collected Writings, 1918–1948]*, ed. Hingorani, Pocket Gandhi Series, No.13 (Bombay: Bharatiya Vidya Bhavan, 1965), 12–13.
[16] Farani, *Panjābī Zabān Nahīn Maregī*, 45. Here the usage of "mother tongue" is so explicitly linked to an actual mother that it is worth recalling Joshua Fishman's study, which found only twenty languages in the world for which this filial metaphor existed. Joshua A. Fishman, *In Praise of the Beloved Language* (Berlin and New York: Mouton de Gruyter, 1997), 34.
[17] Ramey, *Panjāb kā Muqaddamah*, 76.

honorable protection of women's virtue. In this economy of belief, the virile Jat characters do double work: simultaneously asserting an ethnic strength to triumph over the adversity of a prestige deficit, alongside the ever-present need for "rescuing" and "protecting" feminine honor – the undercurrent parallel of protecting one's cultural-linguistic self.

This brief foray into cinematic representations of heroism brings us back full circle to the puzzle of Punjabiyat in Pakistan. The emergence of Maulā Jaṭ as a hero and the Punjabi film aesthetic's eclipse of Urdu offer a proxy point of comparison to the literature being produced by the elite actors of the Punjabiyat movement. Yet despite their social disconnect, and while occupying other ends of the literacy spectrum, both forms of Punjabi text from the 1980s forward mirror the incomplete quality of attachment to the national authorized culture. Indeed, the intriguing convergence of Punjabi heroic representation in popular cinema – entertainment for (male) illiterates – and the heroic and historical reclamation project articulated by the intellectuals of the Punjabiyat movement suggest very interesting implications for Pakistan's national project as well as our understanding of language and nationalism, and the functions thereof.

Theoretical lessons from the case of Punjab

Nearly sixty years have passed since Pakistan's creation, six decades that have witnessed challenges to the official national vision from virtually all corners – East Bengal, Balochistan, Sindh, and NWFP's recurrent Pashtun nationalism. Each of these challenges have fit the region versus center model, and in each one, the center has been ethnically labeled as Punjabi. Now we find the "Case of Punjab," as it were, which bears the markers of a classic nationalist movement: an elite undertaking "reconstruction of the historical consciousness of the nation and ... achievements of its language, art, and literature," to quote an apt formulation.[18] But its surface appearance belies a different underlying structure. Indeed, this elite is not one that we would expect to find engaging in such a process of cultural revival, for the idea that Punjab and Punjabis have a politically, culturally, and economically dominant existence in Pakistan has become a virtual truism. It is as if the protagonists are in opposition to themselves, adopting the stance of a minority or regional elite against some majority or center oppressor. In fact, one of the more self-conscious arguments of the Punjabiyat literature is precisely this, that they must battle "inverted subjectivity" or the "loss of self." The

---

[18] Brass, *Language, Religion and Politics in North India*, 29.

long-assumed "center" of political power finds the national legitimate language *insufficient*, illustrating the limits of symbolic domination, even over decades, and even on the consciousness of those exercising dominance within the nation-state itself. In this way, the case of Punjab offers the unusual situation of a living counterfactual: without clear instrumental motivations, or other functionalist explanations that rely on the usage of language politics to achieve other kinds of power, it becomes easier to perceive that the Punjabiyat ethno-reclamation project is a movement to elevate a Punjabi linguistic and literary sphere from a position of marginality in the national aesthetic order – again, a strategy entirely focused on increasing symbolic capital as *an end in itself.*

But this perception leads to a number of related questions about the ideological effects that structure nation-forms and spaces of national subjectivity; it also suggests that attention must be paid on the margins to perduring historical memory beyond the nation-state; and finally, it suggests the need for more inquiry into the relationship of text to ideas of national belonging, particularly in spaces of less than universal literacy.

As we saw above in the previous chapters, Pakistan's early leaders chose to pursue a national language project that relied upon a language ideology that portrayed Urdu as the appropriate language of South Asian Islam. Other language traditions in Pakistan, despite being those of Muslim populations in Bengal, Sindh, NWFP, and Baluchistan, were subordinated, and in the cases of Bengali and Punjabi, perceived as having non-Islamic linkages (Hinduism, Sikhism) that made it difficult for them to achieve recognition as equal cultural participants in the nation. This underscores the force of language ideologies in making language policy choices in a modern polity, and how those choices impact ideas about cultural spaces and their relative value. Perhaps as important, this relational language hierarchy has been reproduced in the economic sphere, where against all social statistics to the contrary, Punjabiyat proponents conceptualize themselves as victims, oppressed, lost, and deprived. These ideas about Punjabi as being an inferior language to Urdu have led to a movement that seeks specifically to refute these same contentions through forging new literature that draw upon the contributions of Islamic Sufi thinkers. This move works to undo the boundaries between "high" Urdu culture and "low" Punjabi by highlighting the philosophical contributions of the latter, and the effort has performative analogues, such as the annual celebration at Shah Hussain's tomb, which invokes the Punjabi past while simultaneously flagging Punjabi's role in furthering Islamic traditions as the language of creative Sufi thought. This focus on elevating Punjabi language and cultural traditions, typical of all classic nationalist efforts, within a *purely symbolic economy* (rather than as a proxy for the pursuit of other forms of power) goes against the grain of functionalist explanations. Functionalist/instrumentalist views on language politics treat these efforts as levers for broader political mobilizations that have other goals at their endpoints: political dominance, bureaucratic hegemony, political-economic success. Yet as we saw in Chapter 4, the structural relationship of Punjab to Pakistan's other regional ethnicities has been and remains one of overt dominance. For this reason, the case of Punjab offers compelling real-world data that underscores the importance of symbolic capital as a motivating force in contexts where this force simply cannot be dismissed as epiphenomenal.

The second intriguing lesson from the case of Punjab relates to perduring historical memory and the unsatisfying primordial versus constructivist dichotomy for explaining cultural formations. Punjab's much longer (nearly seventy years longer) experience with Urdu as an official language would perhaps have pointed to a more extensive displacement – or even atrophy – of Punjabi, particularly given the language ideological hierarchy that has relegated Punjabi to the low end of this prestige scale. That Punjabi has not experienced a more extensive erosion suggests some limits on a wholly constructivist position, for if that were the case, the national language/national culture project in Pakistan should have been a far easier task with far greater impact. But again, even during colonial rule, the historical record shows that Punjabi never "disappeared" without state patronage; it simply moved to, and was maintained in, spheres beyond those constrained by state practices.[19] One does not need to posit a sort of romantic primordialism or Herderian rapture over the autarkic existence of national cultures in order to make sense of this, but we certainly need to recognize that the production and reproduction of a particular cultural space, via oral poetic forms, historical tales that "pass down" exemplary heroes, and texts (written or oral) invested with spiritual authority, illustrate the conceptual importance of symbolic value of a language-culture complex, particularly when placed in a relational hierarchical matrix that assesses that value negatively in relation to others.[20]

The close, indeed legitimizing, relationship of history to the modern nation-state requires that the national past tell a story that results in the creation of the national present.[21] Gramsci noted the central role

---

[19] Mir, "The Social Space of Language."
[20] For elaboration on these theoretical problems in the context of premodern India, see Pollock, *Language of the Gods*, 550–60.
[21] Duara, *Rescuing History from the Nation*; Ronald Grigor Suny, "History," in *Encyclopedia of Nationalism*, ed. Motyl (San Diego: Academic Press, 2001).

played by literature in crafting history that naturalized the nation and offered cultural unity; language and literature serve states by legitimating a national culture which, in turn, suggests the inevitability – indeed, the wholly inescapable – outcome of the nation's present form.[22] But this teleological lens, with its narrow field of vision, always excludes other kinds of stories, especially if those other stories exist in a linguistic medium without state patronage. Thus the historiographical effort of the Punjabiyat movement to "reclaim" important figures from a Punjabi-language regional past has led to a new canon of heroes: Raja Poras, Dulla Bhatti, Rai Ahmed K͟han Kharal, Puran of Sialkot, and his half-brother Raja Rasalu, to name a few. These resistant fighters, featured precisely to "rescue" Punjab from a self-perception of submissive victim, have been drawn from all periods of Punjab's history and from other kinds of literatures not present in official life. As Sheldon Pollock notes, "Linguistic particularity and aesthetic difference, to say nothing of the actual stories about particular spaces and their reproduction across these spaces, produce powerful ideational effects, and have done so for a long time."[23] Powerful ideas, when denied formal recognition, grow all the more conspicuous by their absence. Notably, this movement's idea of claiming "Punjabiyat" does not limit itself to a post-Islamic world, something rather unexpected in light of official Pakistani state narratives. In fact, this is precisely where the Punjabiyat debate cross-cuts that of the nation-state: where the state locates heroism in the great men of the Pakistan movement, the coming of Islam to the subcontinent, and the Muslim rulers of pre-Partition India – all chronicled in an overtly supra-regional Urdu or English textual corpus – the Punjabiyat hero reclamation project explicitly seeks to reincorporate heroes marginal to national memory by drawing from folk songs and poetic forms, forms that can perdure through oral transmission even if excluded from formal historiography. The growth of this movement illustrates how processes of national legitimation through literary-historical exclusions that clearly sideline the contributions of constituent peoples creates the perceived need to carve space for their inclusion.

This leads us to the insight that the case of Punjab has to offer regarding nationalism and communication. The recent history and growth of the Punjabiyat movement in Pakistan is occurring in a space in which print textual forms simply cannot support theories of nationalism's mechanics which posit causality between the expansion of printed

---

[22] Gramsci, *Selections from Cultural Writings*, 256–7.
[23] Sheldon Pollock, "Introduction: From Literary History to Literary Cultures in History," in *Literary Cultures in History*, ed. Pollock (Berkeley: University of California Press, 2003), 27.

texts and the rise of nationalist consciousness, such as in Anderson's print capitalism theory. Given the social statistics obtaining in Punjab – let us recall here that the province has a 47 percent literacy rate, and slightly less than half the population are employed in agriculture – it is very difficult to see how Gellner's industrialization thesis can explain the situation, either. To further complicate matters, a very limited print life for Punjabi has meant that much of what the Punjabiyat movement focuses on is the creation of a high culture and literary sphere to enhance its symbolic capital. While the case of Punjab cannot resolve these matters decisively, it does point to the need for further investigation into the processes through which a social-cognitive understanding of cultural belonging takes place in places that do not fit the theoretical models. The communicative work of textual forms that do not require literacy, specifically, festivals and other large gatherings in which performed text features prominently – such as the *cirāghān dā melā* celebrating Shah Hussain, or the rambunctious Punjabi cinema – would appear to be fully capable of reproducing a notion of cultural specificity or belonging as something marked, different, from the official national culture offered by the state. In other words, that Maulā Jaṭ and the high-culture literature produced by the Punjabiyat litterateurs appear to invoke similar tropes of resistant heroism with a strong Punjabi specificity does not appear to be a coincidence.

Finally, the case of Punjab offers a lesson that may point to a future of regional coexistence rather than the replication of end-game exclusion that has been the source of so much bloodshed. The Punjabiyat movement does not argue for a separate state to cohere with its culturally-distinct sense of self – particularly since it already commands the dominant province of Pakistan – but it wants to supplement its already-existing political and economic dominance within the country by achieving national recognition for Punjab's language, culture, and regional history. In this sense, the effort wants to amend the nation-form to achieve greater pluralism rather than replace it with some other narrow vision. As we saw with Fakhar Zaman's Writ Petition earlier, the nationalist effort of the Punjabiyat movement seeks "rediscovery of the rational basis of the national identity ... to be a Punjabi is to be as much a Pakistani as Punjab is an integral part of Pakistan." Because this movement demands a widening of the cultural basis for Pakistan's political legitimacy – not a replacement of one with another, but a reframing of that basis as something inherently plural to begin with – this effort has the potential to reduce the internal ethnic competition that has plagued the country since inception. Moreover, because the movement disrupts the national ideology that fuses Pakistan's Islamic heritage with the traditions of Urdu, it also permits a reclamation of cultures and traditions that the province shares with Indian Punjab without impugning Punjab's Islamic legitimacy. On a small scale, the ability to recognize a shared past with India has already led to an increase in cultural exchanges and people-to-people links between Indian and Pakistani Punjab that would have been unimaginable a decade ago.[24] In a region where ideologies of nationalism have led to violent conflict in the past six decades, any mechanism that undoes such exclusionary logic offers a real glimmer, however small, of hope.

[24] Alyssa Ayres, "Two Punjabs: A Cultural Path to Peace in South Asia?" *World Policy Journal* 22, no. 4 (Winter 2005–6).

6 History and local absence

> What is our past, and what is our relationship to it? Are we the logical result of the past's historical flow?
>
> Dr. Jamil Jalibi, *Pākistānī Kalcar* (1964)

Seventeen years after Pakistan's birth, and some twenty-four years after the Lahore Resolution demanded Pakistan as the necessary political expression of the Indian Muslim nation, esteemed scholar of Urdu literary history Dr. Jamil Jalibi penned *Pākistānī Kalcar* in an effort to reason through the problematic of what precisely comprised the national culture of Pakistan. Jalibi's inquiry took as axiomatic the idea that a nation-state must necessarily have a culture which is national in order to evidence its status as a nation:

This question by itself is troubling, because without a national culture, we have no right to be called a nation, nor can we demonstrate the creative power in our individual and collective lives.[1]

The peculiarity of Jalibi's statement illustrates a contradiction, one central to our concerns here: Pakistan was created, even naturalized, as the expression of a nation, but that very nation self-consciously lacked a "national" culture well after its founding. As with debates concerning the national language, the idea of a national culture held the status of a problem despite its prominence as a rationale for the creation of the new state – a sort of causality conundrum. The solution to this problem would be to craft a national past for dissemination to citizens of this new country, a past which would assert the authenticity of Pakistan as an organic entity with long claims to existence, yet somehow in a long phase of dormancy – what Ronald Grigor Suny refers to as the "Sleeping Beauty" theory of the nation – before its emergence into the world of nation-states in 1947.[2]

---

[1] Jamil Jalibi, *Pākistānī Kalcar: Qaumī Kalcar Kī Tashkīl Kā Maslah* (Karachi: Mushtaq Book Depot, 1964), 70. See also Jamil Jalibi, *Pakistan: The Identity of Culture*, trans. Hadi Husain (Karachi: Royal Book Company, 1984), 46.

[2] Ronald Grigor Suny, *The Revenge of the Past* (Stanford: Stanford University Press, 1993).

This chapter examines historiography in Pakistan as a way to make sense of the growth of new histories re-situating Pakistan and its past with reference to specific regions, histories which explicitly argue for the primacy of territory and locality. These concerns are not merely academic. In 2006, Pakistan's Ministry of Education issued new curriculum guidelines directing the various state-level curriculum boards to re-introduce material on minorities, Hinduism, and pre-Islamic civilization – after years of public debate about the ideological quality of national history proffered by the state. Historiographic debates thus have immediate and urgent relevance to the country's internal politics. To contextualize these debates about the politics of history, I look first at the ways this nation-state was first imagined prior to its existence, and then trace the state policy planning process that crafted a history disconnected from the territory of the new country. This chapter thus uses state documentation to examine the steps that resulted in the regional movements for cultural recognition, and which have led to new historiographic efforts asserting new versions of Pakistani history, told through the regions.

Imagining Pakistani antiquity

Much of the narrative groundwork for this national past had already been lain by the various proponents of the Pakistan Movement, for in the two decades leading up to Partition a number of Muslim nationalists had authored treatises drawing direct linkages from the Arab invasion of Sindh in 712 CE to the establishment of Muslim rule in the north of India, through to the contemporary political environment. In those narratives, Muslims – either as invaders or as converts – were defined as an always-already separate entity, by birth as well as belief, and therefore deserved a county to be administered by themselves.[3] The most exaggerated of such claims to national antiquity was proffered by the man who coined the name Pakistan, Choudhary Rahmat Ali, in his 1935 book-length pamphlet, *Pakistan: The Fatherland of the Pak Nation*. Though his pamphleteering was at the time dismissed – by Jinnah himself – as the "ravings" of a student, his assertions are in many ways now standard fare in Pakistan. His actual texts, however, are rarely consulted today, and he remains little more than a footnote.

---

[3] That this same narrative was propagated as well by Hindu nationalists – as evidence for the necessity of asserting a Hindu polity – should not be overlooked. See Vinayak Damodar Savarkar, *Hindutva: Who is a Hindu?*, 4th edn (Poona: S.P. Gokhale, 1949).

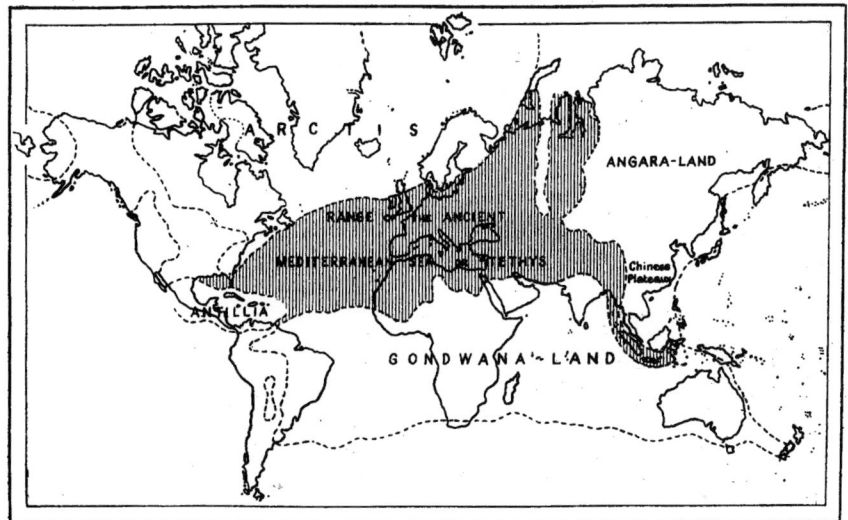

Figure 8 Rahmat Ali's Pakistan in geological times.

Pakistan: The Fatherland of the Pak Nation (1935) depicted the "Pak Nation" in its changing shape over millennia, beginning chronologically with "Pakistan in geological times" (see Figure 8).[4]

It is unclear whether Rahmat Ali intended the reader to identify proto-Pakistan in the ancient Mediterranean of mythic Tethys, or somehow across Gondwana Land, shown above in its Jurassic-era state following the breakup of Pangea. Regardless of the map's denotative intentions, it served to locate a twentieth-century nationalist idea in a physical history that would seem, by its very anachronism, to assert a primordial existence.[5] Rahmat Ali then brought time forward from this geological era to the "dawn of history" (see Figure 9), which in its representation of territory suggests the early eighth-century incorporation of land into the Umayyad caliphate. The labeling of this moment as the "dawn" of history manages – for starters – to displace the Indus Valley and Gandharan periods in an astonishing reconfiguration of

[4] See Choudhary Rahmat Ali, *Pakistan: The Fatherland of the Pak Nation*, 3rd edn (Cambridge: Pakistan National Liberation Movement, 1946 [1935]). Also reprinted in K. K. Aziz, ed., *Complete Works of Rahmat Ali*, vol. 1 (Islamabad: National Commission on Historical and Cultural Research, 1978).
[5] Map scanned from "Pakistan in Geological Times," Rahmat Ali, *Pakistan: The Fatherland of the Pak Nation*, 30.

Figure 9 Rahmat Ali's Pakistan at the dawn of history.

history's emergence on the subcontinent. He moved then to claim as "Pakistan" various territorial progressions as follows (Figures 9 to 23).

One can readily identify the work of reification here; the visual representation of Pakistan's great past – even if concocted by the author – gave a legible, visible form, even boundaries, to an abstract idea,[6] and neatly effaces the centuries of varied political history into a progression of Pakistan from the dawn of time to his contemporary present. In the face of such an ancient "nation," the Two Nations Theory gained strength, and in fact the boundaries of Pakistan delineated at Partition hew fairly closely to Rahmat Ali's final map, the "Pak Millat 1942."

Yet we cannot get around the salient problem of contemporary Pakistan: these claims to national unanimity – of language, of people, of history – came to be contested in Pakistan's independent

[6] Maps 9–23 from Rahmat Ali, *Pakistan*, 172, 179, 181, 183, 185, 187, 189, 193, 196, 198, 200, 201, 226, 247, 272.

Figure 10 Rahmat Ali's eighth century AD.

existence. The precise elements invariably centered on questions of language and history as evidencing ethnic incommensurability with the national forms on offer. As we saw in Chapters 2 and 3, virtually from its founding the regions contested the cultural/linguistic idea of Pakistan presented by the state. Chapters 4 and 5 then showed, in an example of further modular spread, how the very people identified by the "regions" as the captors of the nation-state have begun to assert a local imaginary: Punjabiyat proponents present a past in need of recovery by the archaeological assistance of the Punjabi language and literature. We can get better purchase on these phenomena by taking another tack, that of the relationship between territory and the past. The earth – territory – becomes an important dimension of the contested past in Pakistan.

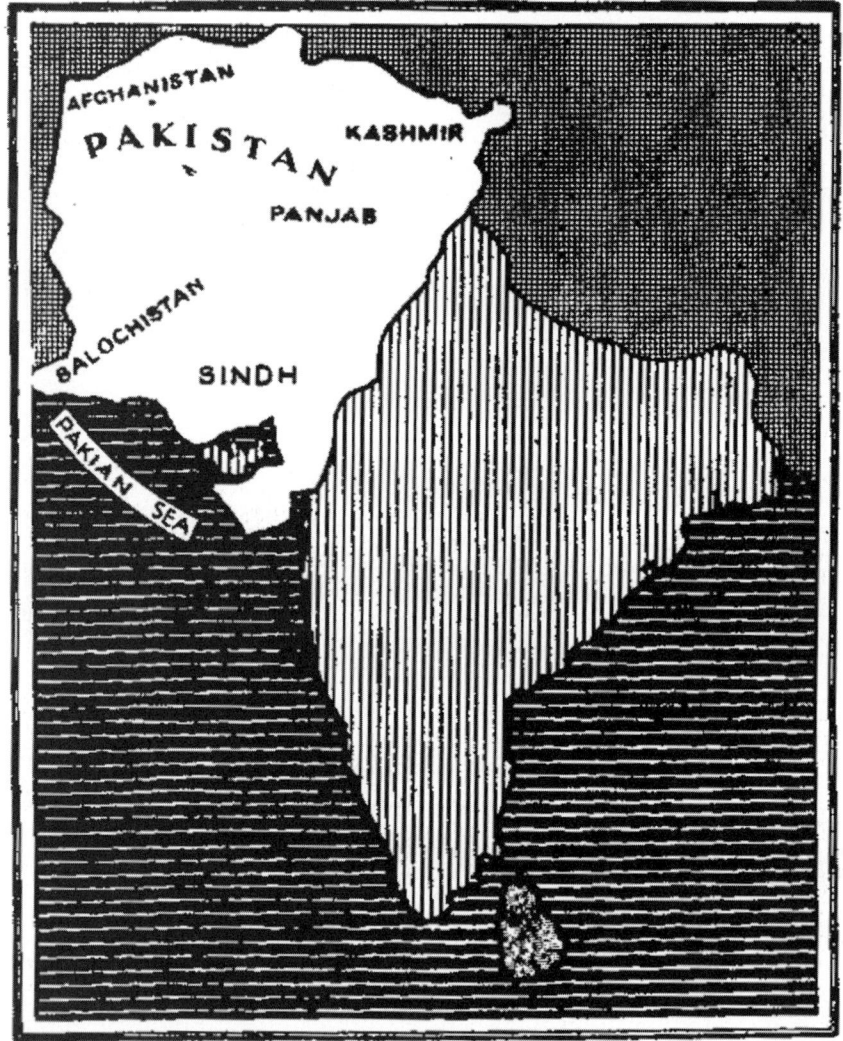

Figure 11 Rahmat Ali's eleventh century AD.

The national past

Pakistan's experience is by no means unusual in its insistence on a national past authorized from the vantage point of its later political creation. The history of the nation-state as a form is a history of unitary narratives employed as "proof" of primeval – national – existence.

History and local absence 111

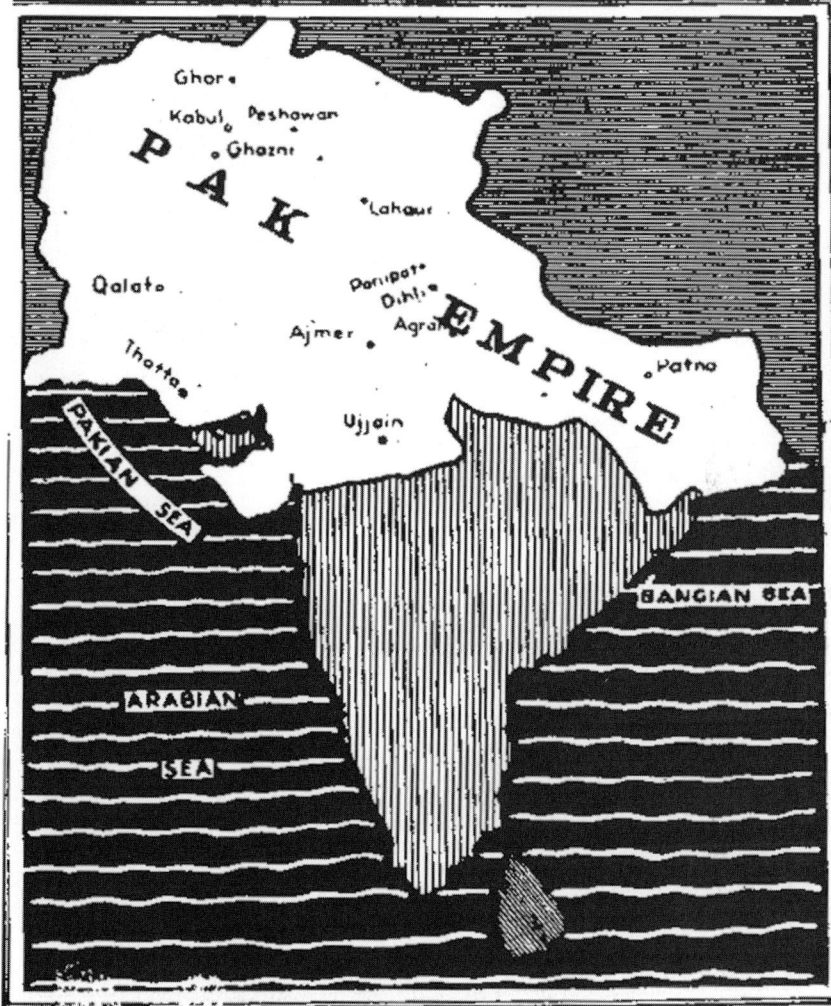

Figure 12 Rahmat Ali's Pakistan in the thirteenth century AD.

In Gramsci's formulation, "History was political propaganda, it aimed to create national unity – that is, the nation – from the outside and against tradition, by basing itself on literature. It was a *wish*, not a must based on already existing conditions."[7] From the very beginnings of

---

[7] See especially 256–7 of "People, Nation and Culture," Chapter 6 of Gramsci, *Selections from Cultural Writings*, 196–286. For excellent discussions on the question of history as

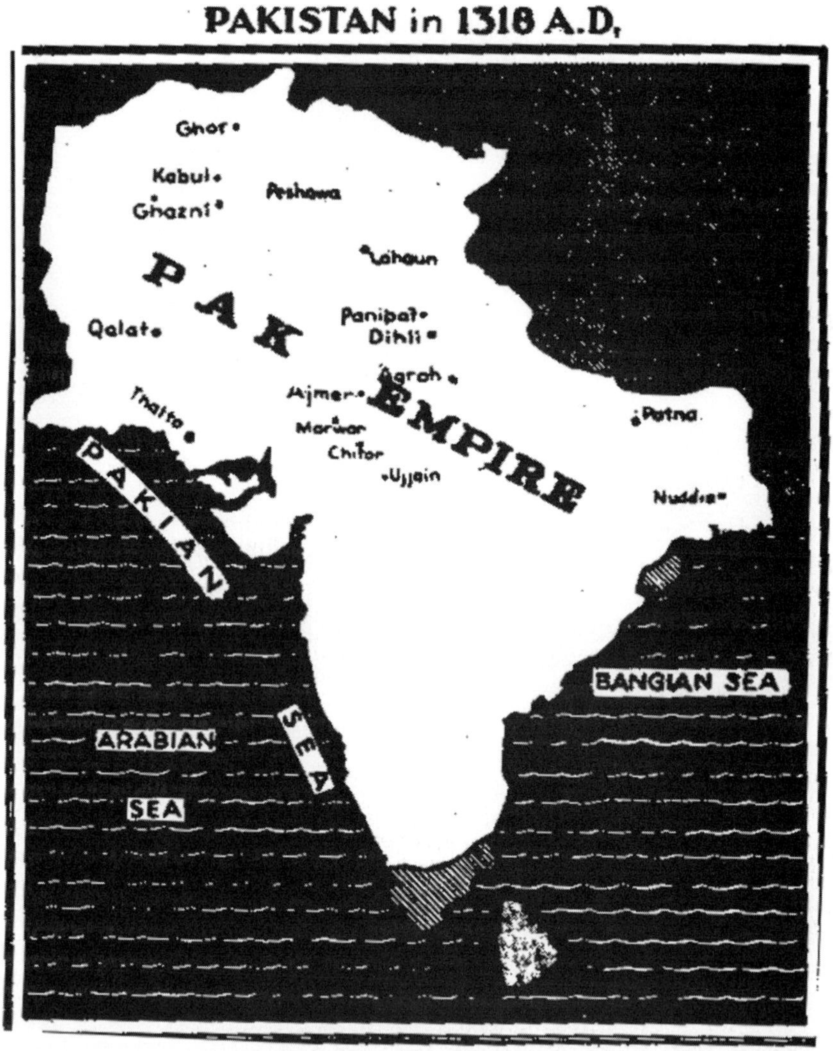

112 Speaking Like a State

PAKISTAN in 1318 A.D.

Figure 13 Rahmat Ali's Pakistan in AD 1318.

the Pakistan Movement in pre-Partition India, the history of Islam in the Indian subcontinent provided historical fodder for an ideology

wish with respect to India, see Sudipta Kaviraj, "The Imaginary Institution of India," in *Subaltern Studies VII*, ed. Chatterjee and Pandey (Delhi: Oxford University Press, 1992), 23. See also chapters 4 and 5, "The Nation and Its Pasts" and "Histories and Nations" in Chatterjee, *The Nation and its Fragments*, 76–115. For a discussion of the imbrication of history, nation, and nationalism more generally, see Suny, "History."

History and local absence 113

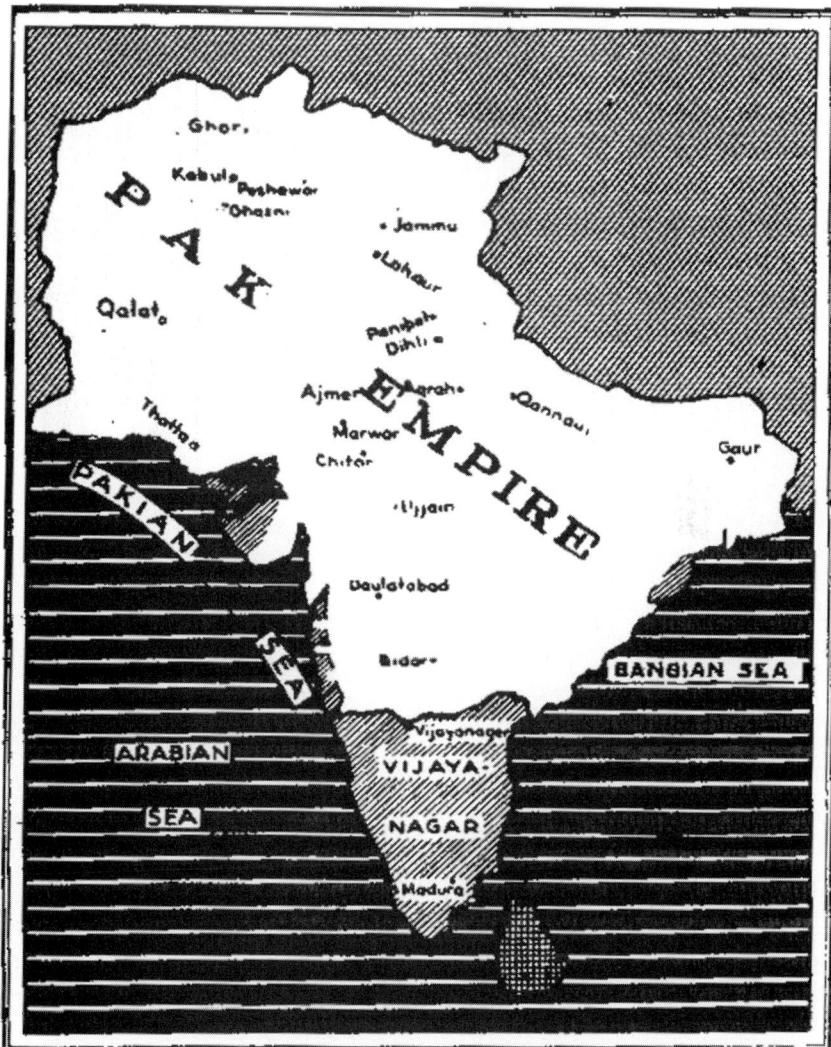

Figure 14 Rahmat Ali's Pakistan in AD 1398.

of a unified nation claiming to be distinct (culturally, racially, *nationally*) from the Hindu majority.[8] What marks this nationalism as a

---

[8] The origins of what is termed "Muslim separatism" in north India are not agreed upon, and are beyond the scope of this research. See Robinson, *Separatism among*

114 Speaking Like a State

PAKISTAN in 1525 A.D.

Figure 15 Rahmat Ali's Pakistan in AD 1525.

more unusual case in the twentieth-century history of nationalism and state-formation lies in the question of territory and its disjunctures. Pakistan must surely feature among the world's most obvious cases

Indian Muslims. Amrit Rai blames the language issue on Muslims in his *A House Divided*.

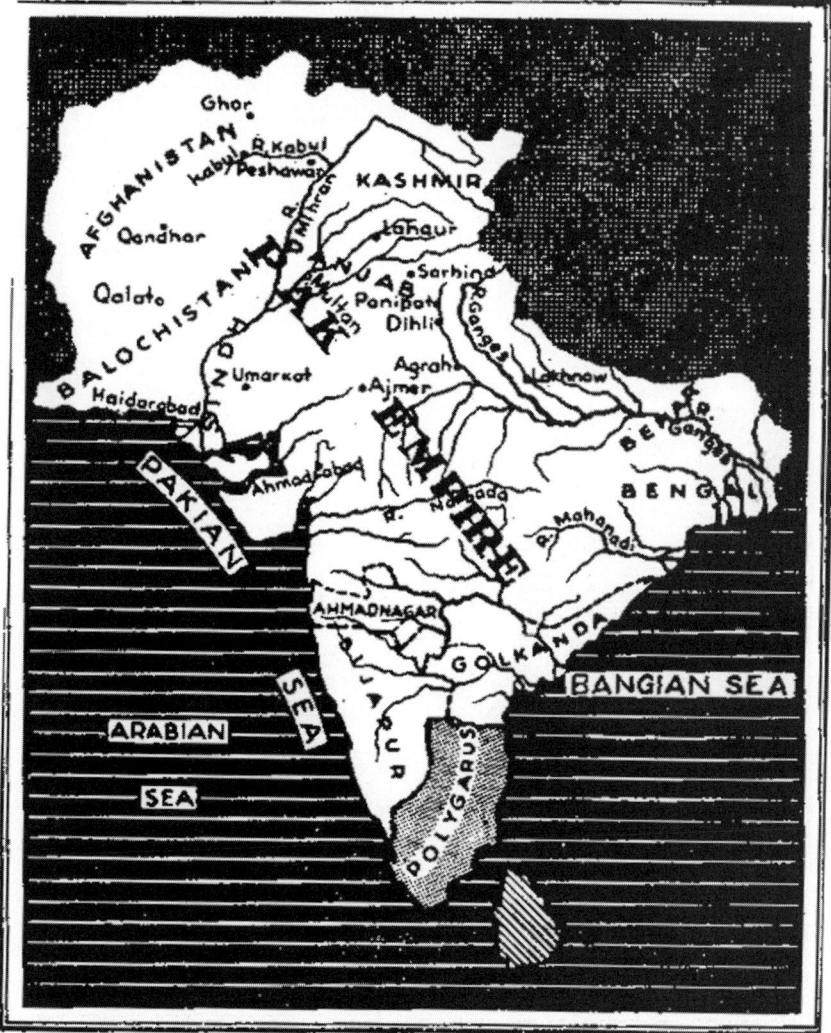

Figure 16 Rahmat Ali's Pakistan in AD 1605.

of constructed primordialisms, which gives us all the more reason to examine processes of revisionism that take the task of constructing primordialisms to a second-order level.[9]

[9] See Suny, "Constructing Primordialisms."

116   Speaking Like a State

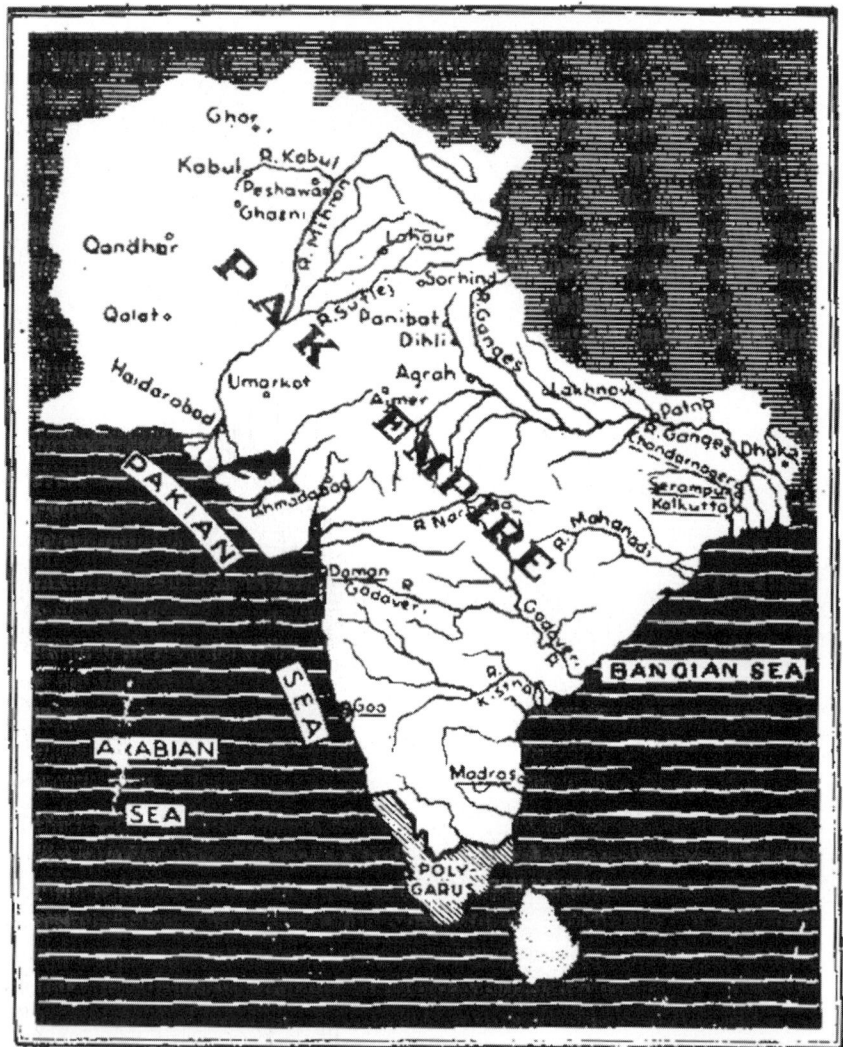

Figure 17 Rahmat Ali's Pakistan in AD 1700.

Creating the national past

Muslims lived in all parts of British India, and prior to Partition comprised approximately 20 percent of the empire's total population. They were not, however, distributed equally throughout the territory: more

History and local absence 117

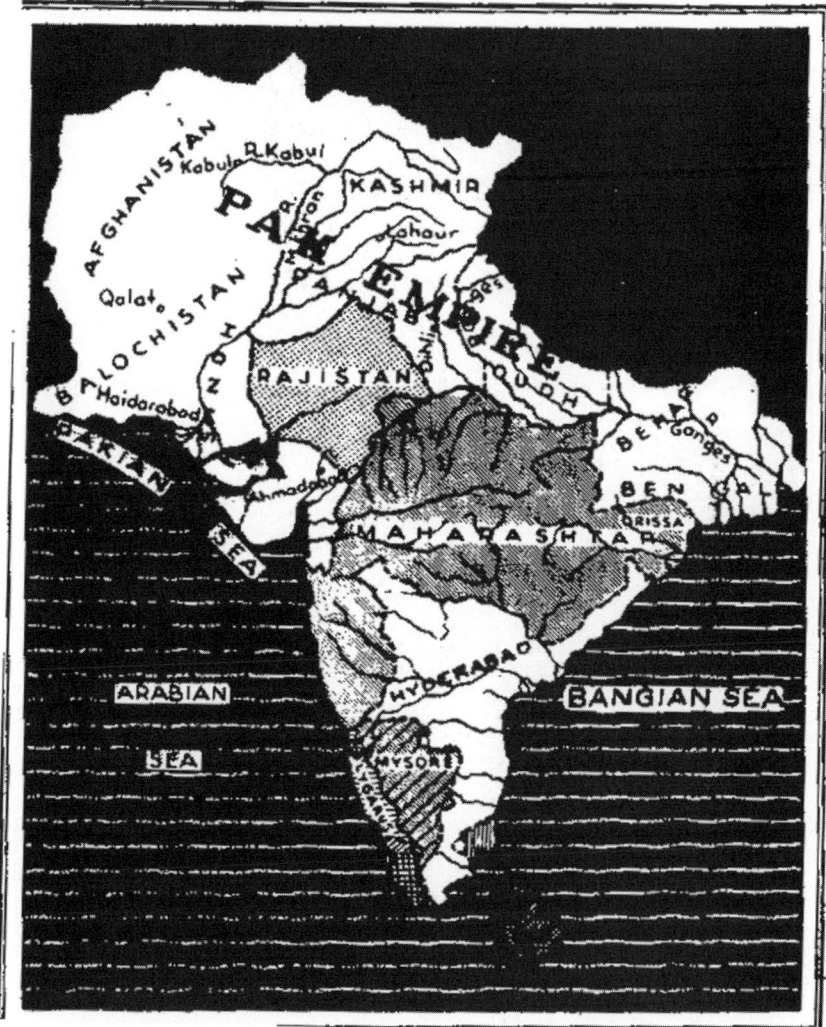

Figure 18 Rahmat Ali's Pakistan in AD 1751.

Muslims resided in the north, and in greater concentrations in cities as well as in the northwest territories and East Bengal. In the northwest territories (Sindh, Balochistan, the Northwest Frontier Province) and in East Bengal, Muslims were the majority of the population. As a Muslim freedom movement demanding political sovereignty began to

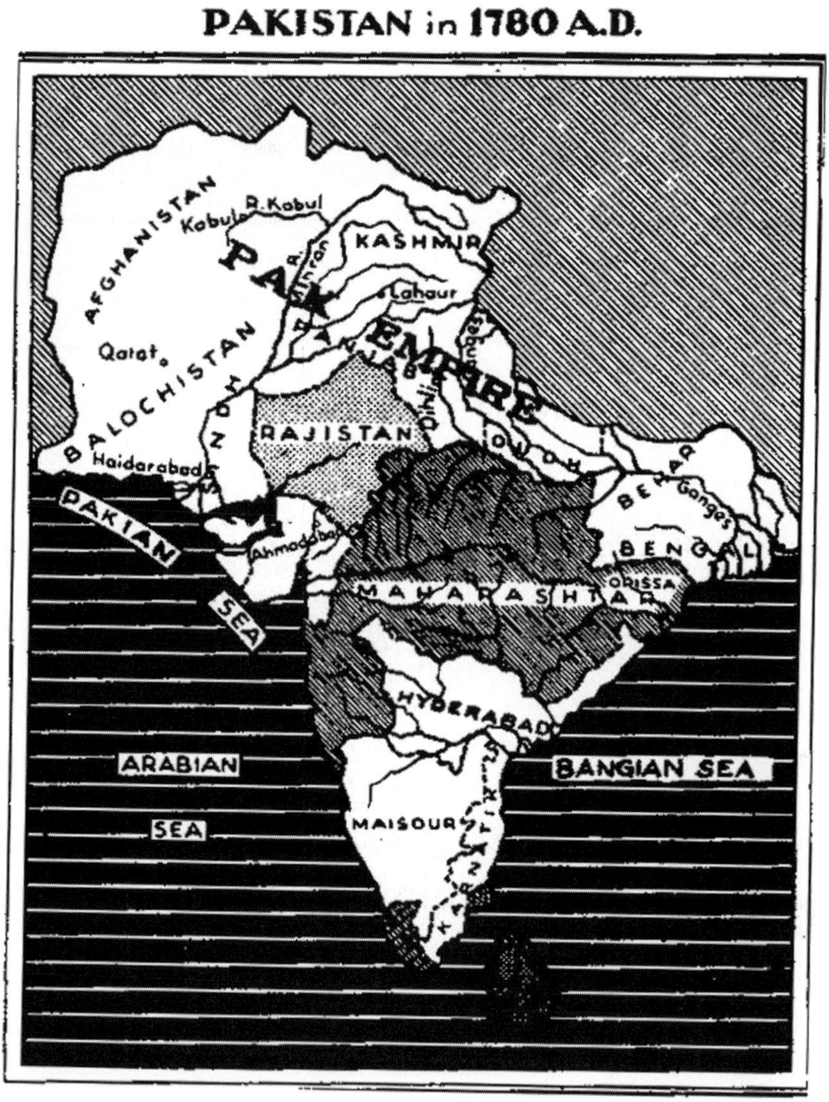

118   Speaking Like a State

PAKISTAN in 1780 A.D.

Figure 19 Rahmat Ali's Pakistan in AD 1780.

take shape, ideas about the possible territory for such a political space began to emerge, taking the Muslim-majority areas of the northwest as the claimed territorial homeland.

It was on this basis that the first maps for a then-imaginary Pakistan, though looking largely like today's country, began to circulate – in

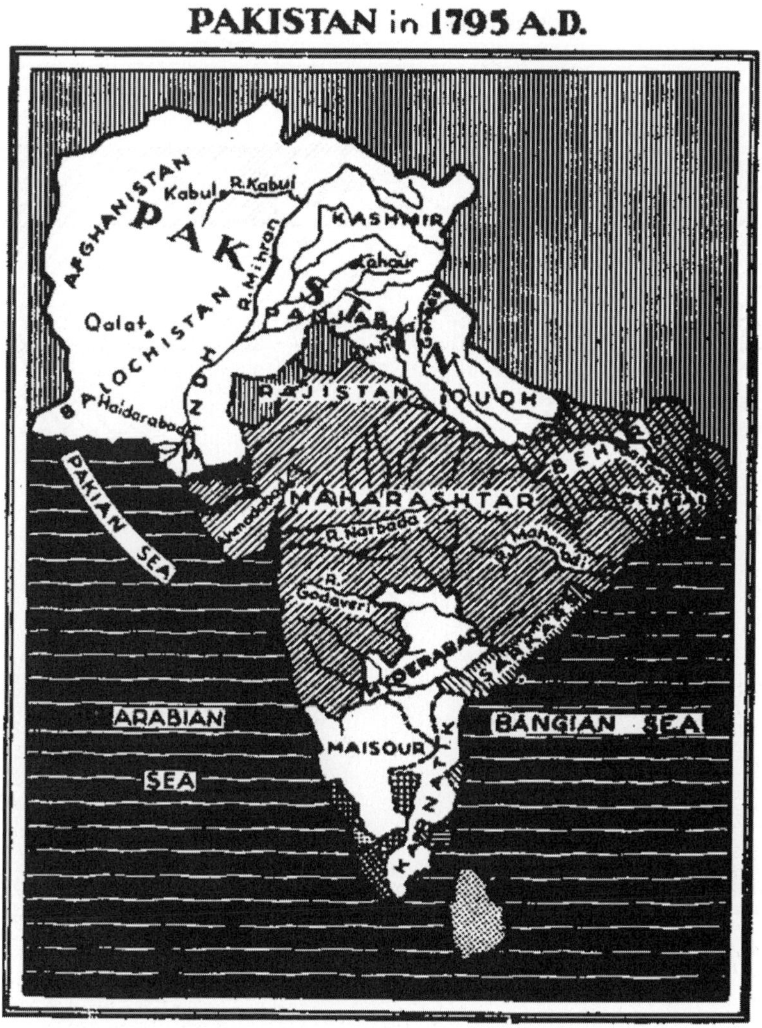

PAKISTAN in 1795 A.D.

Figure 20 Rahmat Ali's Pakistan in AD 1795.

Rahmat Ali's pamphlets above, as the letterhead for the like-minded Majlis-e-Kabir Pakistan (a Lahore-based fringe group, which penned endless letters to major figures of the Indian National Congress and the Muslim League advocating the Pakistan cause),[10] and as the possible

---

[10] For reproductions of the 1939 entreaties to Jinnah, Gandhi, and Nehru from the Majlis-e-Kabir, see Sarfaraz Hussain Mirza, *Tasawwar-e-Pākistān se Qarārdād-e-Pākistān*

Figure 21 Rahmat Ali's Pakistan in AD 1933.

territory for Muslim sovereignty in the pre-Partition, ultimately unsuccessful "Cultural Zones Scheme." The physical maps envisioned a state of Muslim sovereignty, following more or less the ultimate territorial shape that would become West Pakistan in 1947. Accompanying narratives of this Islamic primordial nation, however, did not place particular emphasis on that same territory.

All of this has been covered in much greater detail in a number of thorough histories of the period, particularly with respect to the

Tak [From Imagining Pakistan to the Pakistan Resolution] (Lahore: Pakistan Study Center, Punjab University, 1983), 278–303.

History and local absence 121

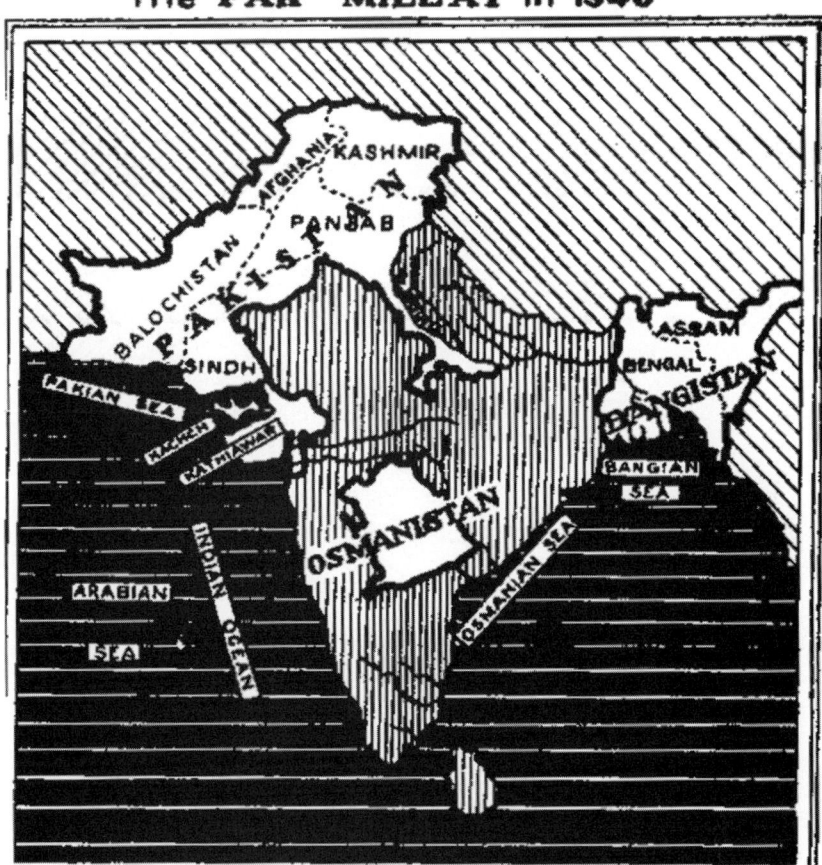

Figure 22 Rahmat Ali's Pak Millat in 1940.

emergence of a philosophy of Muslim nationalism.[11] My purpose in briefly referencing the Pakistan Movement lies in locating the roots of what would become official state ideology, state educational policy, state history, and state language policy in Pakistan. The elaboration of this state policy, now explicitly referred to as "Pakistan ideology," pays little attention to the regions comprising the territory of the current country,

[11] See Jalal, *Self and Sovereignty*; Jalal, *Sole Spokesman*; Sayeed, *Pakistan: The Formative Phase*. Bimal Prasad, *The Foundations of Muslim Nationalism* (New Delhi: Rajendra Prasad Academy and Manohar, 1999); Bimal Prasad, *A Nation Within a Nation* (New Delhi: Rajendra Prasad Academy and Manohar, 2000), esp Chs. V–VI.

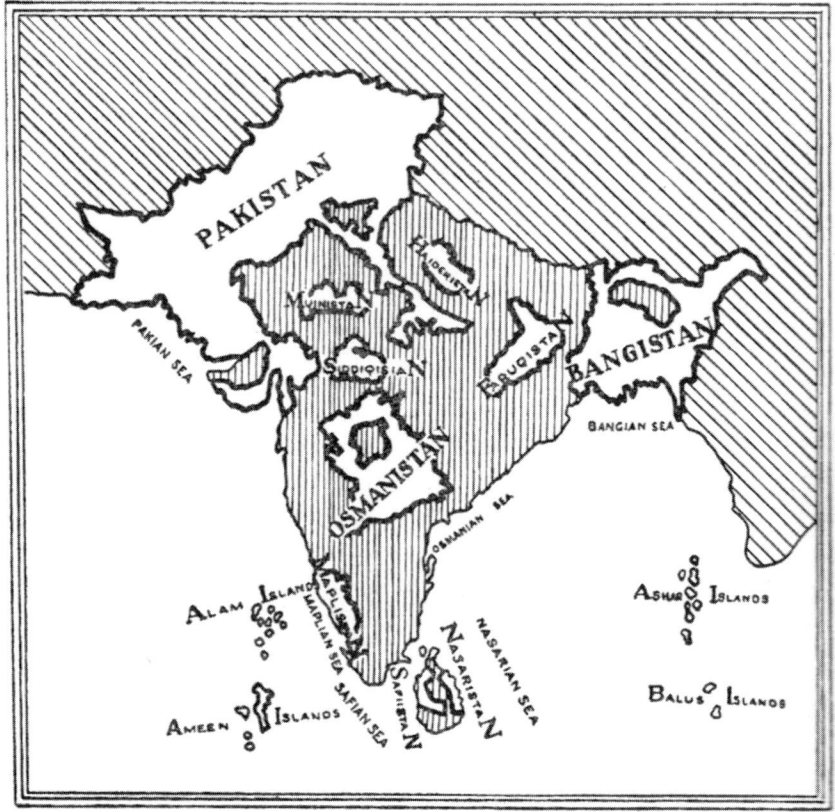

Figure 23 Rahmat Ali's Pak Millat in 1942.

instead investing its all in chronicling the development of Muslim rule in north India, the Urdu language, and the high-water marks of Indo-Muslim artistic traditions. This would produce a national past thoroughly disconnected from the territories that it actually came to occupy; not only that, but this new past derived the greater part of its historical narrative from achievements in lands of today's India, producing a confusing national epistemology. If Muslims of the Indian subcontinent existed as a separate people, the very separateness of which provided the rationale for a nationalist movement seeking autonomy from India, the invented past pointed instead to the cultural history rooted in that very India from which the new Pakistan had effectively seceded! By proffering a past located outside the geographical boundaries of the new Pakistan, the territory contained within was in important ways deprived of a notion of cultural heritage, of a past, connected with its own soil. The emergence of revisionist histories reinserting regional pasts illustrates a response to the phenomenon of a national history that saw no reason to include them at the outset. Before examining the revisions, however, we should understand exactly what ideological conditions produced them.

The history of Pakistani history

Pakistani national history is an explicitly state-directed, top-down project, institutionalized and disseminated through the education system and the government-controlled electronic media following specific curriculum requirements set by the Ministry of Education. The ministry's Curriculum Wing has its roots in the very first national conference on education held in 1947. Point 19 of Fazlur Rahman's inaugural address to the 1947 Pakistan Educational Conference called for the establishment of a national curriculum bureau to get away from the practice of "entrusting their preparation to commercial firms." The Curriculum Wing has authority over content through the 1976 "Federal Supervision of Curricula, Text-books and Maintenance of Standards of Education Act."[12] Its recommendations, uniform throughout the country, must be followed by the provincial-level textbook boards charged with writing and printing books.[13] Concerns about curriculum content have in recent years gathered attention, ultimately leading to the 2006 revision of the "Pakistan studies" content and the launch of a reform agenda, not yet complete. Pakistan's Sustainable Development Policy Institute (SDPI) published perhaps the most comprehensive assessment of the curriculum and its problems, with a 2002 report that amply details the biases and historical limitations which have influenced young minds for

---

[12] Complete text of act reprinted in Ministry of Education (Bureau of Educational Planning and Management) Government of Pakistan, *Major Trends in Education: Report Presented at the 36th Session of the International Conference on Education, IBE/UNESCO Geneva, September* 1977 (Islamabad: Printing Corporation of Pakistan Press, 1977), 27–8.

[13] See Jacob Bregman and Nadeem Mohammad, "Primary and Secondary Education – Structural Issues," in *Education and the State: Fifty Years of Pakistan*, ed. Pervez Hoodbhoy (Karachi: Oxford University Press, 1998), 77; Pervez Hoodbhoy, "Preface: Out of Pakistan's Education Morass: Possible? How?," in *Education and the State*, 11; Nayyar and Salim, *The Subtle Subversion*, 5. On the Curriculum Wing, see Pakistan Educational Conference, *Proceedings of The Pakistan Educational Conference, Held at Karachi, From 27th November to 1st December 1947*, reprint edn (Islamabad: Government of Pakistan, Ministry of the Interior (Education Division), 1983 [1947]), 12.

decades.[14] Their survey of all texts (in English and Urdu) for grades one through ten covering the subjects Urdu, Pakistan studies, social studies, and Islamiyat propelled them to one inescapable conclusion: "for over two decades the curricula and the officially mandated textbooks in these subjects have contained material that is directly contrary to the goals and values of a progressive, moderate, and democratic Pakistan ... A large part of the history of this region is also simply omitted, making it difficult to properly interpret events, and narrowing the perspective that should be open to students."[15]

The SDPI report translates the concerns of academic historians and education specialists into a framework for revision. Its findings drew upon the work of historians K. K. Aziz, Pervez Hoodbhoy, Ayesha Jalal, Abdul Hameed Nayyar, and Tariq Rahman, all of whom have carried out serious critique of the problem of national history and education policy in Pakistan.[16] In *The Murder of History in Pakistan,* Aziz covers in compelling detail a survey of some sixty-six textbooks (social studies, Pakistan studies, and history), finding appalling errors in virtually all. Aziz pursues his task by identifying individual errors of fact that lead to errors of interpretation, rather than examining intellectual assumptions that permit such factual errors to make contextual sense. He looks in particular at the claims made by textbooks regarding Pakistani culture and the Urdu language. Aziz found that "wild and impossible claims" were made on behalf of Urdu; among them, that "Urdu was the spoken language of the entire South Asia" and "the spoken language of the common people of the subcontinent." In "The Road to Ruin," Aziz examines the problem of Pakistan's territorial past disconnected from its present, through lessons which attribute the creation of Pakistan solely to Aligarh and the United Provinces. Moreover, "Most of the textbooks ... persist in preaching that the United Provinces [in today's India] was the home of Pakistani culture ... but nobody explains what it is, beyond the Urdu language."[17]

Hoodbhoy and Nayyar see a different sort of pattern at work destroying truthful representations of Pakistan's past. In their view, official history of Pakistan experienced an epistemological rupture with General Zia ul-Haq's 1979 National Education Policy, one which formally mandated courses in "Islamiyat," "Pakistan studies" (Mutala-e-Pakistan),

[14] See Nayyar and Salim, *The Subtle Subversion,* iii.
[15] *Ibid.,* i.
[16] See Aziz, *Murder of History*; Pervez Amirali Hoodbhoy and Abdul Hameed Nayyar, "Rewriting the History of Pakistan," in *Islam, Politics and the State,* ed. Mohammad Asghar Khan (London: Zed Books, 1985); Jalal, "Conjuring Pakistan"; Rahman, *Language, Ideology and Power,* 488–528.
[17] Aziz, *Murder of History,* 171, 198, 200.

and introduced a number of administrative changes that dramatically affected the relationship between state education and religion. For example, *madrasa* degrees were formally recognized as the equivalent of a BA degree; Urdu-literacy programs held at local mosques with *mullah*s as instructors were instituted; Arabic became a compulsory subject in schools; Pakistan Television launched Quranic literacy lessons; and "Pakistan studies" was created as a mandatory subject for students in all schools.[18] It was this education policy which, in their narrative, brought the idiom "ideology of Pakistan" into schools as an explicit focus.[19] They trace this notion to increased involvement of the Jamā`at-e-Islāmī in lobbying for an increased presence of Islamic teachings in public education and, ultimately, a theocratic state. They argue that the "ideology of Pakistan" was a phrase drawn from the 1951/1969 manifesto of the Jamā`at; through the creeping influence of such Islamists that Pakistani history underwent revision such that Partition would come to be the endpoint of a "historic inevitability with the first Muslim invasion of the subcontinent."[20]

Ayesha Jalal's essay, "Conjuring Pakistan: History as Official Imagining," takes a metahistorical perspective on the competing claims to national origin and its historical moment of inception according to official historiography. She found, for example, that "officially approved textbooks display an exasperating degree of confusion as to when and where to begin cataloging Pakistani history." Some writers locate Pakistan's origins in Arabia (through the intellectual inheritance of Islam), yet others begin the national narrative with Mohammad bin Qasim's arrival in Sindh; still others, such as K. Ali, choose to include the pre-Islamic past while projecting the existence of an "Indo-Pakistan" backwards through time when discussing events in 2000 BCE.[21] Here, Jalal identifies the core conundrum of the national history project in Pakistan. It is also the most salient dimension of historical revisionism over the course of the last fifty years.

Yet examining the range of textbooks and education policy documents, particularly in comparison with the more recent regional revisions arguing against them, suggests a slightly different understanding of the representations of national origin. The relationship of the present territory to its past likely has deeper roots than is generally understood,

---

[18] The Jamā`at-e-Islami's Institute of Policy Studies issued an evaluation in 1981 of the 1979 education policy, finding that it was *insufficiently* implemented particularly with respect to mandated prayer in schools, study of Islam, and Urdu as the medium of study. See Hafeez-ur Rahman Siddiqi and Ahmed Anas, *Tālimī Pālisī, 1979: Do Sālah Amaldarāmad, Jaiza aur Tajāvīz* (Islamabad: Institute of Policy Studies, 1981), 41.
[19] Hoodbhoy and Nayyar, "Rewriting History," 166–7.
[20] *Ibid.*, 167, 176.
[21] Jalal, "Conjuring Pakistan," 77–9.

and relates to the received form of historical representation of "Indian history" dominant since 1770.

Periodizing the subcontinent: Hindu/Muslim/British

History textbooks from Pakistan that were written in the 1960s, and which in some schemas include descriptions of the pre-Islamic subcontinent, follow an intellectual organization that has a specific lineage. Two sets of history textbooks from the mid 1960s, in Urdu and English, illustrate the form nicely: K. Ali's English-language volumes, *A New History of Indo-Pakistan*, *A New History of Indo-Pakistan Since 1526*, and *A History of Muslim Rule in Indo-Pakistan*; and Sahibzada Abdur Rasool's three volumes, *Tārīkh-e-Pāk-o-Hind: Hissa Awwal ta 1707* ("History of Pak-Hind, Part One to 1707"), *Tārīkh-e-Pāk-o-Hind: Hissa Duwam 1707 ta 'Ahd-e-Hāzrah* ("History of Pak-Hind, Part Two: 1707 to the Present Era") and *Pāk-o-Hind kī Islāmī Tārīkh* ("The Islamic History of Pak-Hind").[22]

Both versions broadly mirror each other in form as well as content. In the one volume of each which includes the "ancient history" of the subcontinent, the most striking aspect is the analytical framework of presentation, which differs significantly from the presentation of post-Islamic history to the subcontinent. The "ancient history" segments offer thumbnail sketches of Hindu law, concept of caste, art, literature, Buddhism, and brief descriptions of the Sanskrit epics *Mahabharata* and *Ramayana*. This material appears as a backgrounder, the "what was" in advance of the real history, which begins either with reference to Muhammad bin Qasim landing in Sindh, or with Mahmud of Ghazni and then moves forward in a juggernaut of rulers and their battles for power. The *Mahabharata* and *Ramayana*, for example, are presented as literary works one should know about, and brief summaries (notably, the presentation of the Pandava and Kaurava families of the *Mahabharata*) follow – but there is no claim that these epics comprise part of a cultural continuum, nor that they might be of interest to any later Muslim ruler. The effect is a very dramatic partitioning of time and "cultural era" in the subcontinent into the ancient Hindu age, then the Muslim age, then the British age, a sense of periodization that more recent historiographic

---

[22] K. Ali, *A New History of Indo-Pakistan*, 2nd edn (Dacca: Ali Publications, 1968); K. Ali, *A New History of Indo-Pakistan: Since 1526*, 3rd edn (Lahore: Aziz Publishers, 1977); K. Ali, *A Study of Muslim Rule in Indo-Pakistan*, 3rd edn (Dacca: The Famous Publishers, 1963); Abdur Rasool, *Pāk-o-Hind Kī Islāmī Tārīkh* (Lahore: M.R. Brothers, 1964); Abdur Rasool, *Tārīkh-e-Pāk-o-Hind, Hissa Awwal: ta 1707* (Lahore: M.R. Brothers, 1965); Abdur Rasool, *Tārīkh-e-Pāk-o-Hind, Hissa Duwam: 1707 ta 'Ahd-e-Hazrah* (Lahore: M.R. Brothers, 1966).

work has come to question.²³ That these broad periods overlap amongst each other is a missing piece of information; that this schema would be untenable for a history told from the perspective of the Tamil-speaking south or even the Punjab goes without mention; and that composite cultural forms were forged in the subcontinent which cannot be understood without reference to Hindu and Muslim traditions does not arise.²⁴

In fact, this abrupt sense of periodization mirrors that employed by James Mill's 1817 publication, *History of British India*.²⁵ In Mill's schema, Indian history could be cleanly partitioned into three phases – the Hindu, the Mohammadan, and the British – and in his account, this periodization appears to have cleanly demarcated moments with little overlap in each; for each phase, the appropriate historiographical sources could be found in Sanskrit, Persian, and then English sources. In the ten-volume reprint of Mill, for example, the first third of British Indian history covers the Hindus and the Mohammadans largely in terms of brief descriptions of Hindu culture, laws, religion, the arts, and literature, and then the rise and fall of Muslim kings. The formal parallels with the schema of history presented in Pakistani textbooks in the first two decades are dramatic.

Working still backwards, Mill's sense of periodization appears to borrow heavily from Alexander Dow's English translation of Mohammad Qasim Farishta's history of the subcontinent, which would have been one of the best-known histories of India at the time in English.²⁶ As Romila Thapar notes, Dow's translation of Farishta was widely read as

---

²³ See Partha Chatterjee, "The Social Sciences in India," in *The Cambridge History of Science*, ed. Porter and Ross (Cambridge: Cambridge University Press, 2003), 492. See also Sumit Sarkar, "The Limits of Nationalism," *Seminar*, no. 522 (February 2003). A recent effort to write history without the tripartite-era scheme is David Ludden, *India and South Asia: A Short History* (Oxford: Oneworld Publications, 2002).

²⁴ Muzaffar Alam describes cultural borrowing between Muslims and Hindus throughout the premodern era, including translations of Hindu texts into Persian for circulation throughout the Persianate world; this history of cosmopolitan borrowing has, on both sides, been conveniently ignored in favor of more communitarian rememberings. See Alam, *The Languages of Political Islam in India*.

²⁵ See James Mill, *History of British India*, ed. H.H. Wilson, (Wilson reissue with continuation from 1805ff.) 10 vols. (London: James Madden, 1858 [1817]), vol. 2, 177. As Romila Thapar points out, the British historical schema such as Mill's appears to have been extremely influential in affecting the formal qualities of Indian (and obviously Pakistani) representations of its own past. See Romila Thapar, *Somanatha: The Many Voices of an Indian History* (New Delhi: Penguin / Viking, 2004), 169–201.

²⁶ See Alexander Dow, *The History of Hindostan; Second Revised, Corrected and Enlarged Edition with a Prefix on Ancient India based on Sanskrit Writings; Translated from Persian*, reprint edn, 3 vols. (New Delhi: Today and Tomorrow's Printers & Publishers, 1973 [1770]). I consulted the Urdu translation of Farishta, Mohammad Qasim Farishta, *Tārīkh-e-Farishta*, trans. Abdul Hai Khwaja, Urdu edn, 2 vols. (Lahore and Karachi: Shaikh Ghulam Ali and Sons, 1962 [c.1607]).

the history of India; British historians like Mill and Gibbon accepted Persian chronicles as "historically accurate" due to their familiarity of form and narrative.[27] Farishta's organization of time and period contains a prefatory pre-history of the Hindu age prior to moving into the beginnings of the chronicles of kingship and power with Muslim rulers. (Farishta, however, presents the *Mahabharata* with a note that Abu-ul Faiz 'Faizi' translated the epic into Persian, a bit of information that does not make its way into post-1947 Pakistani accounts.)[28] Broadly, there appears to be an inherited notion of cleanly separated periods, with the serious history of power beginning with the coming of Islam to the subcontinent, and anything prior to that is relegated to the domains of aesthetics: literature, religion, and the arts. This forms the template for the way history appears in Pakistan when the "ancient era" is included. The "ancient era" does not make its way into every textbook, however, and we see its elimination from textbooks by the 1970s. The process of eliminating the ancient past was that of a distinctly national agenda, and it is here we must now return to the education bureaucracy for a more careful examination of the process of writing history through the nation.

National history as ideology

Who caused "the murder of history in Pakistan?" Virtually all observers attribute the Zia regime with the inauguration of an epistemic shift in national consciousness in Pakistan, through extensive efforts to Islamicize the state. Yet an examination of documents from the Pakistani education policy bureaucracy from 1947 to the present suggests that General Zia ul-Haq's 1979 National Education Policy was not a moment of dramatic rupture, but instead the fruition of a particular vision of the nation quite apparent from the very start. If Zia's policies brought Islam front and center, this was not such a remarkable break from the foundational desires of policymakers prior to Zia's regime – at least not according to policy planning documents of 1947, 1952, 1960, and 1972.

Pre-1979 education policy planning documents reveal an extensive concern with ideology and nation-construction virtually since inception. While it is true that the terminology "ideology of Pakistan" did not appear in history books and texts as relentlessly as it would after 1979, a concerted focus on the study of Pakistan comprised a central preoccupation of all curricula and education plans since the country's birth.

---

[27] Thapar, *Somanatha*, 170.
[28] See Farishta, *Tārīkh-e-Farishta*, 83.

Moreover, the documents show that it was the democratically elected government of Zulfiqar Ali Bhutto, not the Zia regime, which effectively instituted the Islamiyat and Pakistan studies programs.

The proceedings of the first Pakistan Educational Conference, held in December 1947, show that the new state's education planners felt it urgent to forge a truly *national* culture, something they clearly felt could not exist within the terms of regional ethnicities:

> We have been far too prone in the past to think in terms of Bengalis, Punjabis, Sindhis and Pathans and it is to be deeply regretted that our education has failed to extirpate this narrow and pernicious outlook of provincial exclusiveness which, should it persist, will spell disaster for our new-born State. There cannot be a greater source of pride and a better object of undivided loyalty than the citizenship of Pakistan, no matter what political, religious or provincial label one may possess.[29]

It was this conference at which the national language policy decision, and the decision to impart education on the basis of "Islamic ideology" were put into formal language, and religious education was deemed mandatory for Muslim students. Though only brief statements, they became the cornerstones on which later education policy documents referred; by 1952, the Six-Year National Plan for Education Development in Pakistan had drawn up budget planning figures relying on the 1947 proceedings for guidance in content.

The Six-Year National Plan released in 1952 called for the "adoption of Islamic ideology as a basis of the educational system ... a thorough research in Islam's contribution to the various aspects of life and its bearing on modern problems in the fields of economics, social and political relations," and to develop materials for this adoption, proposed establishing a Central Institute of Islamic Research.[30] The Six-Year plan further advises:

> As has been claimed, Pakistan stands for an Islamic way of life ... Civilization today is passing through a crisis. There is not only physical insecurity but, what is worse, moral and spiritual anarchy ... To the challenge of this moral crisis of civilization, Pakistan's response is firm and unequivocal. Its education is to be inspired by Islamic values, for these values constitute a valid and coherent philosophy pervading all aspects of life ... It will suffice to mention here that the Central and Provincial Governments as well as the Universities are engaged

---

[29] Inaugural address by Fazlur Rahman, then-Minister for Interior, Information and Broadcasting and Education, Government of Pakistan. See Pakistan Educational Conference, *Proceedings of the Pakistan Educational Conference*, 8.

[30] Education Division Government of Pakistan, *Six-Year National Plan of Educational Development for Pakistan*, 2 vols. (Karachi: Government of Pakistan Press, 1952), Part I, p 111.

in recasting the existing syllabi and curricula and it is to be hoped that, with a similar revision of the teacher's training courses which is in progress, the educational system will correspond more or less closely to the ideological *rationale* of Pakistan. [emphasis in original][31]

This proposal suggests the seeds of what becomes the emphasis on Islamic history that by necessity begins with Muhammad bin Qasim's arrival in Sindh in 712 CE, and thereafter devotes its intellectual attentions to territory in India.

By 1960, two key objectives of the *Report of the Commission on National Education* was for education to "play a fundamental part in the preservation of the ideals which led to the creation of Pakistan and strengthen[ed] the concept of it as a unified nation ... we must strive to create a sense of unity and of nationhood among the people of Pakistan."[32] The planning report makes quite obvious the strong links identified by the planning bureaucracy between national cohesion and the state's ability to disseminate a vision of that cohesion in order to effect it. The commission recommended the formation of a National Book Trust to encourage publications and the development of a "national" literature; this Trust would work with the Writers' Guild, "already formed," to produce more books.[33]

Bhutto, remembered as a great populist, instituted a number of policy changes that accelerated the narrow definition of Islam in Pakistan's education policies. Bhutto came to power in the wake of a national truncation, with East Bengal having formed independent Bangladesh after the genocidal 1971 war. The loss of East Bengal illustrated the inadequacy of the Two Nations Theory as Pakistan's national glue; more pronounced statements of Islamic piety emerged from the Bhutto regime in efforts to legitimize the basis of the truncated nation. It was Bhutto in 1974, for example, who acceded to Islamist demands for legislation to legally render followers of Ghulam Ahmed (known as 'Qadianis,' or 'Ahmedis') non-Muslims, punishable with death for offenses of blasphemy if, for example, caught with a Quran.

[31] *Ibid.*, Part I, 4–6.
[32] Ministry of Education Government of Pakistan, *Report of the Commission on National Education, January-August 1959* (Karachi: Government of Pakistan Press, 1960), 10–11.
[33] On the matter of the creation of "national literature," that presupposes the existence of both a nation as well as its literary expression, see Pollock, "Literary Cultures in History." Citation from Government of Pakistan, *Report of the Commission on National Education, January-August 1959*, 220. This Writers' Guild was in fact the state-instituted replacement for what had been the Progressive Writers' Association. Information about the formation of the Writers' Guild was provided by Fateh Mohammad Malik, Chairman of the National Language Authority, in an interview on October 15, 2002. The Ayub regime dissolved the Progressive Writers' Association in Pakistan in 1954, said by some due to American pressure to contain communist influence. See Sibte Hasan, *The Battle of Ideas in Pakistan*, 218.

Bhutto's Education Policy (1972–80) was most noted for nationalizing the private schools, a policy to offer "free and universal" access to education, a move intended to offer greater equality in educational opportunity, and establishing Urdu as the national language with constitutional status. What is not widely acknowledged is that this education policy created the state-approved curriculum for religious studies in schools, thus instituting the curricular concept of Islamiyat (something articulated in previous policy plans yet not developed): "The study of Islamiyat will be compulsory for Muslim students up to Class X. Steps will be taken to ensure that the curricula and textbooks ... do not contain anything repugnant to, or inconsistent with, the cultural and ethical values of Islam."[34] The Islamiyat curriculum was apparently finalized in 1973–4, and available for use thereafter.[35] This same education policy called for the innovative use of electronic media as non-formal extensions of the education system:

> a massive distribution of radio and television sets will be undertaken ... separate radio and television channels will be established for broadcasting educational programmes to schools and adult literacy centres. On these channels, substantial time will be allocated to the recitation and translation of the Holy Quran so as to saturate the air with the message of God and further forge the bond of national cohesion among the Muslims in different parts of the country.[36]

That the electronic media were conceptualized not as an opportunity to educate Pakistani citizens about the cultural diversity and historical heritage of the country – in the wake of having lost half of itself – appears dramatic against the choice of programming interests. (Regional transmission stations for television and radio would allocate a few hours per week for regional language programming, but these programs were not broadcast nationally and were of limited duration.) More interestingly, the phrase "ideology of Pakistan" appears on the very first page of the New Education Policy 1972–80, as the first objective of the state's education policy: "Ensuring the preservation, promotion and practice of the basic ideology of Pakistan and making it a code of individual and national life."[37] This is the first occurrence of the phrase in curriculum planning documents, clearly identifying as a Bhutto-era shift what is generally attributed to Zia. Two years later, in the Curriculum Wing's

---

[34] Ministry of Education Government of Pakistan, *The Education Policy, 1972–1980* (Islamabad: Government of Pakistan, 1972), 37.

[35] See note (b), Ministry of Education (Curriculum Wing) Government of Pakistan, *Development of Education in Pakistan, 1973/75* (Islamabad: Government of Pakistan, Ministry of Education (Curriculum Wing), Examination Reforms and Research Sector, 1975), 49.

[36] Government of Pakistan, *The Education Policy, 1972–1980*, 29.

[37] *Ibid.*, 1.

report, a new subhead for "Ideological Studies" emerges as the curricula framework for studying national history:

Ideological studies

On several occasions, the Government of Pakistan has rightly emphasised the need for including a compulsory paper on "Islam and Pakistan" in the educational curricula right upto the degree stage for the purpose of ideological orientation of the youth ... We have proposed that 30 per cent of the reading material to be provided for the study of Urdu and English must consist of themes on (i) Pakistan Government as reflected through the speeches of Quaid-e-Azam and other stalwarts of the movement, (ii) Islam as the ideological base of Pakistan, and (iii) the lessons of Muslim History, it being understood that the material on these themes will be an advancement over what may have been taught ... Moreover, all books should have an introductory note on the Muslim contribution to the branch of knowledge with which the book deals in order to inculcate pride in our cultural heritage. This imperceptible way of ideological orientation, is belived [sic], will be much more effective than the direct method.[38]

This policy anticipates the Zia's regime's "Pakistan studies" innovation in full: it clearly delineates national history as the culmination of some Islamic telos, against which anything not fully compatible with that narrative could be discarded. Against the backdrop of these developments in curriculum policy planning, General Zia's education policy would mark a change in degree but not in kind.

In addition to instituting mandatory charity contributions (*zakat*, or Islamic tithing, one of the five pillars of the faith), creating Islamic shariat courts, and implementing the Hudood Ordinances as part of a broad series of steps to make the Pakistani state practice a stricter form of Islam, General Zia's plans for educating his citizens revolved around ways to purify their religious practice. Finding that the effort to spread Urdu – endowed as the sole bearer of Islam in Pakistan rather than any of the regional languages – more thoroughly throughout the country as a bona fide national language had not been achieved, he created the Muqtadira Qaumi Zaban, or National Language Authority. The 1979 National Education Policy, devised after a large conference in 1978, contained nine top-level "aims," four of which emphasized Islam's role in literally producing the people:

a) To foster in the hearts and minds of the people of Pakistan in general and the students in particular a deep and abiding loyalty to Islam and Pakistan and a living consciousness of their spiritual ideological identity thereby

---

[38] Government of Pakistan, *Development of Education in Pakistan, 1973/75*, 61.

strengthening unity of the outlook of the people of Pakistan on the basis of justice and fairplay.

b) To create awareness in every student that he, as member of the Pakistani nation is also a part of the universal Muslim Ummah and that it is expected of him to make a contribution towards the welfare of fellow Muslims inhabiting the globe on the one hand and to help spread the message of Islam throughout the world on the other.

c) To produce citizens who are fully conversant with the Pakistan Movement, its ideological foundations, history and culture so that they feel proud of their heritage and display firm faith in the future of the country as an Islamic State.

d) To develop and inculcate in accordance with the Quran and Sunnah, the character, conduct and motivation expected of a true Muslim.[39]

The new dispensation requirements created "Pakistan studies" as a separate subject area for the required courseload, which already included "Islamiyat," for students of all ages.[40] This new subject thus built on a set of ideas already contained in earlier policy plans, ideas about the necessity for this new nation to know a particular representation of its history (that which had led to its creation) and therefore appreciate the struggles that had led to its independence.

Thus we can better understand how more recent presentations of national history have evolved. The ideological requirements resulted in a revised presentation of Pakistan's past that begins explicitly with "Ideology of Pakistan." To make national history correspond to the "Ideology of Pakistan," now extremely narrowly defined, the previous separate subjects of history and geography were eliminated, with only some of their curriculum covered in the new subject of "Pakistan studies." As Ahmed Salim put it in the SDPI report, "Muslim heroes and discussions of the superiority of Islamic principles replaced the subjects of history and geography. All history that concerned Pre-Islamic events of the territory, which is now Pakistan, such as Mohen Jo Daro and Texila [*sic*], the old Hindu and Buddhist empires, etc, was eliminated from textbooks."[41]

A quick glance, for example, at the *A-One Textbook of Pakistan Studies*, in its second edition in 1991, provides a clear picture of the problem of history under erasure. This is a text approved for "Pakistan studies" for BA, BSc, BCom, BE, MBBS, and CCS degree students, so it is intended to comprise part of the education of some of the country's best educated.

---

[39] Ministry of Education Government of Pakistan, *Development of Education in Pakistan (1978–80); Country Report for the 38th Session of International Conference on Education, Geneva, 10–19 November 1981* (Islamabad: Government of Pakistan, Ministry of Education, 1981), 13–14.

[40] *Ibid.*, 23–8; for primary classes, see 23; for middle classes see 24; for secondary school requirements, see 24A–28.

[41] Ahmed Salim, "Historical Falsehoods and Inaccuracies," in *The Subtle Subversion*, 69.

The national past is broached as follows: "The nation along with its ideology was already there for centuries but the country came into existence afterwards. Hence Pakistan's geography is a result of its ideology."[42] This statement then flows immediately into an explanation of the Two Nations Theory, which requires a telescoping backward to a focus on the "Evolution of Partition Idea" and an outline format summary of various phases under the British, leading up to Partition. Immediately after this material, all presented in Chapter 1, we come to "the Arab conquest of Sind, by Muhammad bin Qasim in 711" [sic] which "gave the Muslims a foothold on the subcontinent."[43] There is a mention of "Pre-Islamic Civilization," for three and a half pages, and it covers Soan culture, the Indus Valley, Aryan civilization, Gandharan Culture, Buddhism, and Ashoka, before coming to the Arab conquest of Sindh.[44]

For our concerns, the most important dimension of forging the national past through the lens of the "Ideology of Pakistan" is that the history of Pakistan's regions must be ignored, altered, or refuted when they contradict the national logic. If Jamil Jalibi was able to muse in 1964 about whether Pakistan was the "natural result of the past's historical flow," after reworking the national past, the state-produced representation of that historical flow was cast such that the only obvious outcome could be an Islamic Pakistan. This reworking required emphasizing an amorphous history of Islam in the Pak-Hind subcontinent, where the glory of the Delhi Sultanate receives heavy attention, the Mughals are a prominent focus, but Ranjeet Singh, the Sikh ruler of Punjab, is an embarrassment and must be cast as an oppressor. Projecting national heroes through the "Ideology of Pakistan" magic lantern requires the inclusion of Islamic reformists like Shaikh Ahmed Sirhindi, Shah Walliullah, Sir Syed, and the Ali brothers of Khilafat fame – but Raja Poras and Raja Rasalu of Punjab's earlier history are either mentioned in passing or not at all. Unable to avoid mention of the many Sufis whose devotional poetry forms the various canons of regional language literatures, and whose graves, or *dargah*s, are sites of pilgrimage for millions of Pakistanis whose religious practices remain "heterodox," they receive mention in a laundry list of some four pages. Hopelessly repetitive chapters present the development of the Two Nations Theory over and over again; the Pakistan Movement as told here is a chronicle of actions by the Muslim League, the results of the Cabinet Mission Plan, Congress' treachery in withdrawing its support for the proposal, and

---

[42] Mirza Muhammad Yousaf, *A-One Textbook of Pakistan Studies* (Lahore: A-One Publisher, 1991), 2.
[43] *Ibid.*, 17.
[44] *Ibid.*, 35–7.

Partition. Thus, in a brief exposition on "The Role of the Muslims of NWFP, Baluchistan, Sind, Punjab" one learns that:

> It can be said that all the Muslims all over the sub-continent took an active part in the struggle for Pakistan, an independent homeland for the Muslims of the subcontinent.
>
> But on the close study and scrutiny of the struggle, it is an affirmed observation that the Muslims of those regions in which they had been living as minorities, were more active as compared to their fellow breathren in the Muslims-majority provinces ... It is a universally acclaimed fact that the Muslims of the subcontinent who were in minorities in the regions, waged a persistent struggle for the Pakistan.[45]

The requirements of the national past eliminated deep knowledge of pre-Islamic civilizations in the territory comprising contemporary Pakistan, but as importantly, the legitimate political debates *among Muslims* of the Indian subcontinent in the run-up to Partition were similarly erased. It is a truism among observers of Pakistani national history that figures such as Maulana Azad, an opponent of Partition, a friend to Gandhi and a towering figure in the Indian National Congress, cannot find a home in representations of Muslim history from the Pakistani perspective. What is more troubling is that the very heroes of so many of Pakistan's territorial pasts cannot be recognized either.

Two examples illustrate this problem: the politics of Partition amongst the Muslims of NWFP and Punjab. The national past cannot contain the unruly history of NWFP: a province which only in the last month before Partition voted in favor of accession to Pakistan, and in which half the eligible voters did not participate.[46] One of the most important figures of twentieth-century Pukhtun politics, Khan Abdul Ghaffar Khan, is eliminated from the subject matter of Pakistan studies precisely because explaining that his party favored an independent Pukhtunistan rather than subordination to Pakistan or India suggests that Muslims of the Indian subcontinent were not fully in agreement about the formation of Pakistan. So Pakistani national history must ignore his party, the Khudai Khidmatgars, and instead explain that the Pathans "are devout muslims ... noted for religious inclinations and are universally acclaimed the freedom-loving people besides being noble and upright ... they were treacherously made to fall prey to the supremacy of the sikhs and the Hindus."[47] Accusing Ghaffar Khan, popularly known as the "Frontier Gandhi" of being duped by non-Muslims dismisses the sophisticated

---

[45] *Ibid.*, 153–4.
[46] See especially 243–4 of Chapter 9, "The Triumph of the Muslim League, 1947" in Rittenberg, *Ethnicity, Nationalism, and the Pakhtuns*, 217–48.
[47] Yousaf, *A-One Textbook of Pakistan Studies*, 158.

political debate about primacy of ethnicity, territory, and sovereignty that he represented. In perhaps the most egregious example of erasure, a new official history of the NWFP's contribution to the Pakistan Movement, part of the "Golden Jubilee" fiftieth anniversary celebration of the Lahore Resolution, does not even feature this man in the extensive *tazkirah* (book of brief biographies) of important Pukhtun figures which comprises two-thirds of the volume.[48] Perhaps as revealing is the fact that even according to the most extensive bibliographic database available, of the four biographies published on Khan Abdul Ghaffar Khan in the past two decades, three were from India.[49]

Like NWFP, Punjab faces the same dilemma: how can the national past be reconciled with a regional political history that includes the Unionist Party and public support coming very late for the Muslim League's demand for Partition? The Muslim League's efforts to gain power in Punjab – the territory which it *had already claimed* as the substantial part of the imagined Pakistan – pitted it against a strong multireligious Unionist Party which did not favor Partition. As historian Ian Talbot puts it, "Such opponents as the Unionist Party Prime Minister Khizr Hayat Tiwana were denounced as 'infidels' and 'traitors' to Islam."[50] Again, legitimate and extremely serious political differences about the dispensation for the region cannot figure in the national version of Pakistani history, and are instead portrayed as follows: "Sir Khizar Hayat Tiwana, who in collusion with the congress and the British, managed to cripple the activities of the All-India Muslim League. They invented all kinds of measure and contrivances to foil the muslims [sic] aspirations and their desires for a separate homeland."[51]

Thus with the focus solely on a very restricted interpretation of the "Islamic" dimensions of the nation, combined with the intellectual inheritance of British tripartite-era schemas of subcontinental history deriving from British versions of the subcontinent's past, the idea of

---

[48] See Muhammad Shafi`a Sabir, *Tahrīk-e-Pākistān Men Subah-e-Sarhad kā Hissah* [NWFP's Part in the Pakistan Movement] (Peshawar: University Book Depot, 1990). Despite its omissions, this is an important book for its calls to recognize some 185 notable Pukhtuns, including ten women, and their contributions to the creation of Pakistan.

[49] Of these four commemorative volumes, three are Indian. See Midrarullah Midrar Naqshbandi, *Khān Abdul Ghaffār Khān: siyāsat aur `aqā`id* (Mardan: Idarah-yi Isha`at Midrarul`ulum,, 1995); Nehru Memorial Museum and Library, "Khan Abdul Ghaffar Khan : a Centennial Tribute" (New Delhi, 1995); Girdhari Lal Puri, *Khan Abdul Ghaffar Khan, a True Servant of Humanity* (New Delhi: Congress Centenary (1985) Celebration Committee, AICC(I), 1985); N. Radhakrishnan, *Khan Abdul Ghaffar Khan: the Apostle of Nonviolence* (New Delhi: Gandhi Smriti and Darshan Samiti, 1998).

[50] See Talbot, *Pakistan: A Modern History*, 12.

[51] Yousaf, *A-One Textbook of Pakistan Studies*, 170.

a "Punjabi" history or a "Sindhi" history or their contributions to the nation were deemed literally too provincial to merit mention. In this sense, we can see that intellectual Jamil Jalibi's earlier plea for the creation of a national culture was partially successful:

> Now, we should recognize the fact that prior to 1947, Pakistan was not a nation – we must make it one. Before 1947 Pakistan was not a country – we must make it one. It is this that is our most important and fundamental problem. In this light, the question of "what is Pakistani culture?" is meaningless. Our only problem is this: that on a national level no Pakistani nation exists; we must elevate it above the level of local nationalism and make a nation.[52]

Yet in so doing, the state program for making Pakistan a nation with a coherent national culture managed to denude itself of the level of the local. It did not, however, manage to wholly erase local nationalisms and local attachments. In fact, it is in response to this homogenizing tendency – inherent in the nation-form itself – that we now come to the emergence of new regionally-focused historical revisions.

---

[52] Jalibi, *Pākistānī Kalcar*, 71. See also Jalibi, *Pakistan: The Identity of Culture*, 46.

7 Bringing back the local past

> If we have created Pakistan – a land which has deep roots in history – there must be the history of the land and of the people who have lived and laboured here.
>
> Dr. Ahmed Hasan Dani, "Discovery of Pakistan" (1996)
>
> Our earth, we are told, was not our own until people from distant lands came and conquered it (and us), for us. Our ancient heroes cannot be our heroes because they preceded our own conversion to our faith.
>
> Aitzaz Ahsan, *The Indus Saga and the Making of Pakistan* [1996]

Beginning in the mid-1980s but coming into a sort of efflorescence by the 1990s, a series of serious books offering new, regional perspectives on Pakistan's past began to appear. Some of these works reclaim wholesale the pre-Islamic history of the region,[1] some take a *longue durée* approach to their regional-ethnic history – thus necessitating the inclusion of religions, beliefs, and poetry excised from official state narratives – while still others re-examine the Pakistan Movement from the perspectives of Punjab, Sindh, or NWFP. A brief listing of the works considered here illustrates this emerging climate of historical revisionism:

> Ahsan, *The Indus Saga and the Making of Pakistan* (1996).
> Amjad, *Tārikh-e-Pākistān: Qadīm Daur* ("History of Pakistan: The Ancient Era," 1989).
> Awan, *Tahrīk-e-āzādī men Panjāb kā Kirdār* ("Punjab's Role in the Freedom Movement," 1993).
> Chauhdry, *Tahrīk-e-Pākistān Men Panjāb kā Kirdār* ("Punjab's Role in the Pakistan Movement," 1996).
> Leghari, *Jidd-o-Jahd-e-āzādī men Sindh kā Kirdār* ("Sindh's Role in the Independence Struggle," 1992; this book does not contain pre-British history).

---

[1] Aitzaz Ahsan, *The Indus Saga and the Making of Pakistan*, 3rd edn (Lahore: Nehr Ghar Publications, 2001 [1996]), is best known. See also Professor Dani's review, "The Discovery of Pakistan" in *Dawn Magazine*, September 6, 1966, the source for the epigraph above.

Leghari, *Tahrīk-e-āzādī men Sindh kā Kirdār, 2 Vols.* ("Sindh's Role in the Freedom Movement," 1992; this book contains additional historical material on Sindh).

Malik, F. *Punjabi Identity* (1989).

Malik, *Tārikh-e-Panjāb: Qadīm Daur ta Jang-e-āzādī 1857* ("History of Punjab: The Ancient Era to the War of Independence, 1857," 1990).

Nanak, *Kalām-e-Nānak* ("The Writings of Nanak," 2001 [d.1539]).

Qureshi, *Tārikh-e-Makhzan-e-Panjāb* ("History of the Treasures of Punjab," 1996 [1828]).

Manzoor, *The Pakistan Problem: Historical Backwardness of Punjab and Consolidation of Pakistan* (1993).

Ramey, *Panjāb kā Muqaddamah* (1985).

Sabir, *Tārikh-e-Subah-e-Sarhad* ("History of NWFP," 1986; contains "ancient times").

Sabir, *Tahrīk-e-Pākistān Men Subah-e-Sarhad kā Hissa* ("NWFP's Part in the Pakistan Movement," 1990).

Zulfaqar, *Jidd-o-Jahd-e-āzādī men Panjāb kā Kirdār* ("Punjab's Role in the Independence Struggle," 1996).

Each of these works writes against the dominant state-instantiated "Ideology of Pakistan" narrative to offer new (or old, in some cases) perspectives on the national past, and as such are nothing short of radical. This chapter examines in greater detail the historiographic dimensions of these new texts, all chosen because they exemplify the phenomenon of reinserting the regional past.[2] Works considered here are only those which have appeared in Urdu and English; the discussion might be even more expansive should scholars map similar terrain in Sindhi, Punjabi, Pashto, or Balochi.

Cultural continua: the regional imperative

The question of why such a phenomenon of regional reassertion should have emerged when it did demands attention. Clearly, the death of

---

[2] There are, of course, a number of additional texts that I have encountered concerned with further detailing local aspects of Pakistan's history which have not featured in public memory; for example, a history of Sialkot's role in the Pakistan Movement, and a history of Sindh and the Red Shirts, but due to limitations of time they will not be considered here. See Abu Salman Shahjahanpuri, *Khutūt, tahrīk-e Reshmī Rumāl aur Sindh: tārikh-e āzādī-e vatan kī ek azimushan tahrīk* (Lahore: Fiction House, 1997); Khvajah Muhammad. Tufail, *Tahrīk-e Pākistān men Siyalkot kā kirdār* (Siyalkot: Idarah-yi Matbu'at-i Tahrik-i Pakistan, 1987).

General Zia, in a still-unexplained plane crash, along with then-US Ambassador Arnold Raphel in 1988, and the subsequent decade of democratic rule removed some of the severe restrictions on cultural expression so characteristic of the Zia era. Only one of the texts examined here, for example, was published during the Zia years (1977–88), Mohammad Hanif Ramey's *Panjāb kā muqaddamah*, and that too after he had already spent time in self-imposed exile abroad. All the rest of the "new histories" appeared following Zia's death. Yet while the abrupt end of his regime can explain a more permissive atmosphere, it cannot explain why a significant number of Pakistanis sought to reinscribe the history of their regions upon the national past around that time. Perhaps the emergence of these revisionist histories represents a delayed effect from a conference on Pakistan's history that took place in 1972, and at which a regional critique to the dominant strand of national history was first articulated. According to Professor Fateh Mohammad Malik, it was this conference, held at Quaid-i-Azam University, at which scholars like Dr. Kaniz Fatima Yusuf criticized the historiography of the Pakistan Movement as being "dominated by Urdu-wallahs" such as Professor I. H. Qureshi.[3] Professor Malik believes the phenomenon of new histories such as "Sindh's Role in the Pakistan Movement" and "The Freedom Struggle and Punjab's Role" dates to this conference. That virtually all such revisionist historiographies appeared much following the Bhutto as well as the Zia years suggests that the combination of a long incubation period plus an overt repression of "separatist" writings during the latter's rule inhibited the appearance of such work.

Of the texts listed above, several are animated by a project of reclaiming the long history of civilization in the lands that comprise contemporary Pakistan. While this may sound Westphalian rather than radical (a subject to which we will return later), in fact it requires a complete jettisoning of the received "Ideology of Pakistan." Instead of envisioning, as did Choudhary Rahmat Ali, an always-already Pakistan projected backwards, one extant in "Geological Times," the revisionist histories interested in making the past more inclusive are fully prepared to discuss the region's changes over time. Yahya Amjad's *Tārikh-e-Pākistān*, for example, presents a natural-history approach to the land and its past, explaining the emergence of prehistoric animals like mammoths (*"mamath hāthī"*) and trilobites (*"kīrā"*), to the evolution of human life, the emergence of tribes, the Indus Valley, the Rig Veda, the Buddhist and Jain religions – all fully under the umbrella of Pakistani history.[4]

---

[3] Interview with Dr. Fateh Mohammad Malik, October 15, 2002.
[4] See Yahya Amjad, *Tārikh-e-Pākistān: Qadīm Daur* (Lahore: Sang-e-Meel Publications, 1989).

The presentation differs considerably from earlier histories such as those by K. Ali, where the ancient Hindu past was sort of prefixed to the emergence of real history; in this case, we have 626 pages covering nothing but the pre-Islamic history of the region.

Two works in particular have received extensive media coverage such that we could call them historical "interventions" in the public sphere of debate: Muhammad Hanif Ramey's *Panjāb kā Muqaddamah* and Aitzaz Ahsan's *The Indus Saga and the Making of Pakistan*.[5] Two other books, though less prominent, similarly re-establish Punjab as within a long historical continuum; they are *Tārikh-e-Panjāb: Qadīm Daur* and *The Pakistan Problem*.[6] Ramey's book, analyzed in Chapter 4, was written and published in Urdu by the press of the largest newspaper group in Pakistan, distributed widely, and spurred at least two book-length responses (*Sindh kā Muqaddamah* and *Pākistān kā Muqaddamah*).[7] Similarly, *The Indus Saga* by Aitzaz Ahsan has undergone at least eight reprintings (hardcover and paperback combined), a translation into Urdu (as *Sindh Sāgar*) and has been the object of much debate in Pakistan's public sphere.

What both Ramey and Ahsan share, and what is present as well in the Malik and Manzoor works, is a deep sense of a cultural heritage as something special, to be cherished, and having been forged over many millennia through the unusual nature of Punjab's geography. The revisionist pasts envisioned by these works clearly reject a politics of secessionism – but just as clearly, articulate a demand for Pakistan's national past to include that of the territory which it occupies. As a result, Punjab's territory features prominently as a key defining feature of the pasts they proffer. Ramey, for example, takes a genealogical view of Punjab's special geography, connecting himself corporeally with the soil:

> I have always felt a strong sense of deep resemblance between my existence and Punjab's existence. Just as the blood of my body flows from the hairs on my head down to the toenails of my feet, and finally reaches my heart through the veins and arteries, in the same way all the water of the five rivers of Punjab and their tributaries gather in the Panjnad [territory where the five rivers meet].[8]

Ramey goes on further to explain that just as Punjab has five rivers, his mother has five sons – in keeping with the gendered allegory of Punjab as a mother. This sense of physical connection to the soil is what drives his

---

[5] Ramey, *Panjāb kā Muqaddamah*, and Ahsan, *Indus Saga*.
[6] See Akram Ali Malik, *Tārikh-e-Panjāb* (Lahore: Salman Matbu'at, 1990); Manzoor Ahmed Manzoor, *The Pakistan Problem: Historical Backwardness of Punjab and Consolidation of Pakistan* (Lahore: The Frontier Post Publications, 1993).
[7] For the responses, see Zahidi, *Pākistān kā muqaddamah*; Zia, *Sindh kā muqaddamah*.
[8] Ramey, *Panjāb kā Muqaddamah*, 13.

search for a history of the land and the people of Punjab; with the focus literally on the physical territory, he claims for the long continuum of Punjabi history everything from the Indus Valley forward. In Ramey's vision of Punjab's past, even the Hindu god Shiva can be claimed:

> The picture of an ox is drawn over and over again on the Harappan seals. The ox is always associated only with Shiva. This is a sort of proof of his "Punjabiness" because for centuries the association of the ox with the people of Punjab has continually been made.[9]

This extraordinary statement, mocked mercilessly by Shakil Ahmed Zia in a book-length response,[10] thoroughly undermines the national past and sets new parameters for a regional history of Punjab, one which eclectically incorporates all religions, to create a long civilizational chain of Punjabi being.[11] To claim Shiva as Punjabi is to unravel the Ideology of Pakistan, in which the Hindu enemy is capable only of trickery and deception and surely a separate and unrelated species possessing only a vague pre-history of a past; Ramey instead claims a deity of that enemy for the history of the most populous province of Pakistan. As important, by refusing to condemn the Hindu past as outside the pale of faith, Ramey admits an intellectual genealogy that acknowledges itself as composite and therefore not pure.

Similarly, Aitzaz Ahsan weaves a deeply detailed history around an entirely new historio-geographical concept: that of the "Indus" region and the "Indus" person. By this he intends the entire region of today's Pakistan, along what he called the Gurdaspur-Kathiawad Salient, a line demarcating the Indus cultural area from the Indian. In Ahsan's telling, the Indus region, *unlike the nation-state of Pakistan*, has always been a "nation" and has always had a history distinct from both India as well as from Arabia. His macro-project is to assert another kind of primordial nation to which Pakistanis, or Indus peoples, can lay claim without having to juggle the epistemological confusion of a national Islamic history contemptuous of the local histories of the present territorial state.[12] For Ahsan, again as with Ramey, the civilizational continuum can incorporate diversity of religions, diversity of cultures and practices, all under an ethnic umbrella of the Indus.[13]

---

[9] *Ibid.*, 41. Harrapa is indeed within the boundaries of today's Punjab, though Mohenjodaro is in upper Sindh.

[10] See Zia, *Sindh kā muqaddamah*, 11.

[11] E. Valentine Daniel distinguishes "history" from "heritage": "The one is sharply defined and clearly instatiated, even if only in the imagination; the other is a vague, though rich, potentiality." E. Valentine Daniel, *Charred Lullabies: Chapters in an Anthropography of Violence* (Princeton: Princeton University Press, 1996), 27.

[12] Ahsan, *Indus Saga*, Preface (unnumbered).

[13] See Dani, "The Discovery of Pakistan," review of Aitzaz Ahsan – *The Indus Saga and the Making of Pakistan*, *Dawn Magazine*, September 6, 1996. Professor Dani's work on

Also of note is that Malik's *"Qadīm Daur"* takes a long civilizational approach to retelling Punjab's history, as does Manzoor in *The Pakistan Problem*. In one section of *The Pakistan Problem*, Manzoor goes against the grain of positing a Pakistani-nation-in-situ in Islamic South Asia, and instead asserts that 95 percent of Punjabis must be the descendents of Indus civilization and Aryan invasions, leaving only 5 percent "pure" Muslim descendents from Arab or Mongol invasions, a matter of genealogy not often presented in such a straightforward manner in Pakistan. He calls for recognition of this past as the key to the future, thus providing the rationale for his inclusion of history as far back as the Indus Valley.[14]

Aside from the inclusion of pre-Islamic history, another dimension worth commenting upon is the inclusion of more than a brief derisive reference to the Sikh period in Punjab's history. In yet another extremely interesting example of historical reclamation, Ahsan, Malik, and Manzoor all contain chapters on the Sikhs. Ramey reclaims Bhagat Singh – a Sikh who revolted against the British and was hanged – as a Punjabi hero. Ahsan groups the emergence of Sikhism in Punjab along with Sufism and Bhakti devotionalism, noting in particular that (in the cases of Sikhism and Sufism) "the two most energetic and lasting movements to fuse the two subcontinental civilizations into one [i.e., Indus and India] were initiated, with passion and dynamism, in those very areas where the two cultures intermingled."[15] Such an interpretation, though primordialist in its own way as Ahsan clearly constructs a trans-epochal "Indus" person, is a far cry from the Two Nations Theory, in which matters of faith were said to underwrite incompatible nationalities even between neighbors. Sang-e-Meel publishers chose to reprint, in 1996, the *tazkirah* of Punjabi history, *Tārikh-e-Makhzan-e-Panjāb*, by Mufti Ghulam Sarwar Zahib Qureshi Lahorvi (b.1828), written some time presumably in the middle of the nineteenth century – during or immediately following the height of Ranjeet Singh's rule in Punjab.

The *tazkirah* is a genre of history or literary history in Urdu inherited from Persian traditions. It is profoundly non-narrative and non-chronological: the form itself resembles a Western encyclopedia, or anthology, though perhaps of more limited scope. The word derives from an Arabic root meaning "to mention, remember."[16] "*Tazkirah*" in Urdu is

---

the ancient history of Pakistan stands out as an exception, with his early work in the 1960s on the Indus Valley and the Kushans continued through his more recent work on the Northern Areas, Central Asia, and Taxila.

[14] Manzoor, *The Pakistan Problem*, 202.
[15] Ahsan, *Indus Saga*, 140.
[16] The Arabic trilateral root is thal-kaf-re.

defined as "Memory, remembrance; any aid to the memory; a memorandum, note; a biographical memoir, biography."[17] The *tazkirah* is thus a long list, a sort of written recitation. In its classic form, it represents the author's vision of a literary canon, with poets' names accompanied by brief descriptions of their œuvre, perhaps inclusive of a few noteworthy lines of their poetry.[18]

Tārikh-e-Makhzan-e-Panjāb, said in the introduction to be of even greater use today to understanding the history of Punjab, is an enormously long list of short descriptions: of rivers, of cities, of towns, of rulers, and of religions. All the descriptions appear very matter-of-fact, without the veneer of the Ideology of Pakistan, and thus are inclusive of Hindus, Sikhs, and Muslims alike. (Interestingly, in the same way this *tazkirah* lists different kinds of Hindus, it also lists different "kinds" of Muslims: Sunni, Shia, "Tafzaniliya," Sufi, and Firqa Wahabiya.) It indeed suggests a slice of life in the Punjab of more than 150 years ago, when many different kinds of people lived side-by-side, and to describe that life required a full panorama.[19]

If the Sikhs can become necessary to a full understanding of the history of the territory, Sikh literature in the Punjabi language's Gurmukhi form, cannot be ignored: a 1,000-page volume, *Kalām-e-Nānak* ("Writings of Guru Nanak") was published in Pakistan in 2002.[20] This fascinating book is the product of painstaking transliteration of the Sikh scriptures, written in Gurmukhi script, into "Shahmukhi," or Arabic-script Punjabi. That this book exists at all marks a reversal from earlier decades when attempts by the Punjabi Studies department of the University of Punjab to engage with Sikh studies or Sikh literature were deemed by the state to be anti-national and forbidden.

Having looked at the return of the non- and pre-Islamic pasts to regional ways of thinking about Pakistani history – history through the region, not the nation – we now come to the issue of the Pakistan Movement and its actors. To have played a part in the political agitations which resulted in the largest partition in human history, the largest mass migration of all time, and the creation of the first modern nation-state formed on the basis of religion, is to have changed the path of history

---

[17] See Platts, *Dictionary of Urdu*, 314.
[18] For an excellent and highly approachable explanation of the *tazkirah* tradition in Urdu literature, see Chapter 5, "Tazkirahs" Frances W. Pritchett, *Nets of Awareness* (Berkeley: University of California Press, 1994); available from ark.cdlib.org/ark:/13030/ft10000326/.
[19] See Mufti Ghulam Sarwar Zahib Qureshi, *Tārikh-e-Makhzan-e-Panjāb* (Lahore: Dost Associates, 1996), 574–6.
[20] See Guru Nanak, *Kalām-e-Nānak*, trans. Jeet Singh Sital (Lahore: APNA and Punjabi Heritage Foundation, 2002).

Bringing back the local past 145

itself, and new histories written in the 1990s want to carve space for their own regions in the stories of that struggle. Perhaps nothing is as important as the Pakistan Movement to an understanding of today's Pakistan – for it is both the beginning as well as endpoint for the national narrative.

Who made Pakistan? Seeking recognition

The number of books rewriting the Pakistan Movement from "regional" perspectives overwhelmingly evidence a desire for recognition. Each one of these books opens with some sort of statement of anguish that the great contributions of their people, their region, their *history*, have been summarily overlooked. Every one of the writers expresses a palpable sense of injustice:

> Punjab was a vast and spacious country in which several cultures were mixed. In 1891 Jammu and Kashmir were contained within its borders. Its borders ran from Ambala Division in western India to the Attock river; and north-south it spread as far as Bhawalpur. That India was called a Golden Bird was solely because of the abundance of Punjab's production.
>
> But look at the clever tyranny of the circumstances: in the lesson books we are usually taught that in the war of independence of 1857, Punjab played no role whatsoever and neither did it take any important actions in the struggle for Indian independence. This is only on the basis of discrimination. In this book the circumstances and events from the war of independence (1857) to 1947 (90 years) are given in summary, from which an ordinary reader will be able to guess what resulted from the spectacular feats of the people of Punjab, whom the history of the world will never forget.[21]

The above introductory passage, from M. J. Awan's *Tahrīk-e-āzādī men Panjāb kā Kirdār,* is representative of the genre. Every book opens with similar statements delimiting the importance of their region's history: "Without understanding the geographical and political importance of NWFP and its culture and history, it is difficult, in fact impossible, to understand Pakistani political and human history."[22] And having established the importance of the region, how could each region have been so unjustly left out of national history:

> The people of Sindh kept claiming that the title "Gateway of Islam" in the subcontinent had been given to their nation. From the very first day they struggled against the foreigners, meaning that in order to obtain the fortress of Islam, "Pakistan," they sacrificed far more – body, mind, and wealth – in comparison

---

[21] M. J. Awan, *Tahrīk-e-āzādī men Panjāb kā Kirdār* (Islamabad: Modern Book Depot, 1993), 5–6.
[22] Sabir, *Tahrīk-e-Pākistān men Subah-e-Sarhad kā Hissah* [NWFP's Part in the Pakistan Movement], 20.

with others, and held their heads high, but when history was apportioned, justice was not done to them.²³

One historian of Punjab's contributions to the Pakistan Movement states his region's importance in the bluntest possible terms:

Because of its geographical place of occurrence and its being a Muslim majority province, Punjab held the status of "Foundation Stone" in the Pakistan Scheme. Had the Muslim population in India been scattered – meaning, were it not in a particular area or centralized areas – then the demand for a separate country could not have been made. But because the eastern and the western areas were obviously majority Muslim, the Pakistan demand was made on this basis. It would be difficult to assess or estimate which part was proportionately more important; nevertheless, it can be said that the western part bore greater importance in terms of war (*harbī*) and livelihood. In the same manner, within the west the Punjab stands before us as a place worthy of pride. If the motherland of the five rivers had not been obtained, then in terms of geography, it would have been impossible to establish Pakistan. Despite this importance of Punjab, to date no research pulling together the Pakistan Movement with reference to Punjab has appeared.²⁴

Each of these passages makes a similar case: that the idea of, the struggle for, and the actualization of Pakistan was manifestly impossible without the participation of Punjabis, Sindhis, and Sarhadis – yet having made those sacrifices, these groups found themselves and their experiences missing from the national presentation of that struggle. Indeed, these authors make a critically important point: how can the state present a national history that is truly *national* without including the contributions and sacrifices made by people of and in the regions that comprise Pakistan? Taking just one example from the perspective of Punjab, the standard story of the birth of Pakistan – with its narrative of political action, opposition by the Indian National Congress, an almost-agreement to a federal scheme with the Cabinet Mission Plan, failure when the Congress refuses to agree, and then the birth of Pakistan as a grand achievement, a glorious moment ushering in freedom – fails to confront the extensive human tragedies which attended Partition. For Punjab, this meant physical bloodshed and violence on an unimaginable scale. In the words of one historian, "along with the happiness of freedom came as well countless complications and battles."²⁵ How can the

---

²³ Dr. Abdul Jabbar Abid Leghari, *Tahrīk-e-āzādī men Sindh kā Kirdār*, 2 vols. (Hyderabad (Pakistan): Rahbar United Publications, 1992), Vol. 1, 2.
²⁴ Dr. Muhammad Azam Chaudhry, *Tahrīk-e-Pākistān men Panjāb kā Kirdār* (Karachi: Royal Book Company, 1996), 9.
²⁵ "Panjāb ke lie 1947 kā sāl āzādī kī khushī ke sāth sāth beshumār uljhanen aur shadīd khāna jangī ke imkānāt le kar āya." See Chapter 5, "panjāb aur qayām-e-pākistān, 1947" in *ibid.*, 193–229.

national past, with its *telos* of freedom realized on August 14, 1947, be reconciled with the regional past that cannot so easily forget the trauma incurred at that same moment?

One methodological way the new histories craft a new Pakistani past from the "margins" lies in their use of the *tazkirah* form. Most of these present first a series of short chapters covering either chronological episodes or particular subjects – like the Unionist Party, for example – within a larger chronological framework that culminates in the birth of Pakistan. In this way the new histories of the Pakistan Movement are just like any other narrative historiography we might encounter anywhere in the world: there is indeed a plot, though these works differ from the state-created version of Pakistan's past by offering different perspectives on that narrative, and different actors in the drama. Yet there is a second part to many of the revisionist histories, one that draws upon another kind of historiography which links these works inextricably into another kind of representative discourse. If the *tazkirah* of the eighteenth and nineteenth centuries was a form created expressly for semi-public gatherings for oral poetry recitation (the *musha`ira*), the *tazkirah* histories here – printed for public, literate consumption – represent an appropriate updating of the form, used not in the service of furthering great verse but to preserve and disseminate the exemplars of regional value. These histories are thus also anthologies of historical figures the authors want inserted in the public record, new entrants to the roster of public memory.

The question is analytically related to that of including the history of the regions comprising the current state of Pakistan regardless of religion or ideological position on the merits of Partition. This is one of the most important intellectual debates facing Pakistan today because it hits the core dilemma of how the state seeks to represent itself, its past, and its cultural conditions for full citizenship.

Conclusion: language, history, territory, and belonging

Pakistan's experience in the production of a national past that required significant processes of forgetting – in this case, of regional value and regional history – offers some ways to think about territory, history, and ethnic belonging. If this seems like abstract theorizing, it is not: not only is it the core question of historical representation in Pakistan, but one with implications for many other postcolonial states facing dilemmas of ethnic heterogeneity.

The early years of Pakistan's existence were marked by a profound concern on the part of state policy planners for the construction of an overarching national identity, a national past which would transcend the "merely" and narrowly regional. That the solution would be a focus on producing the people within the straightjacket of an Islamic nation divested of its rich and composite subcontinental heritage rather than a focused effort to emphasize this historical richness *as* the national points to a very interesting disjuncture between territory and belonging. The new, *national* past sought to produce affect located in a deterritorialized idea of an Islamic nation, an Islamic *ummah*, yet acknowledging its subcontinental and non-Arab genealogical provenance through the privileging of the grandeur of the recent South Asian Islamic past, much of which was in fact located outside of Pakistan and inside north India. Urdu "culture" thus became the synecdoche for the larger imaginative leap of anchoring the entire historical narrative, which every citizen already knows must culminate in the Two Nations Theory and the creation of Pakistan, in the land which was left behind.

The emergence of efforts to reinscribe regional value on that national past by drawing upon regional literatures and regional heroes – whatever their religion – thus represents a return to a profoundly Westphalian model of sovereignty. In the Westphalian model, political and historical space occupies territory with cleanly demarcated boundaries, separating nations as well as respective national pasts. International relations theorist John G. Ruggie has remarked in a provocative essay on territoriality on the remarkable similarity between the transition in spatial orientation characteristic of the visual arts as well as of political space in the transition from the medieval to the early modern era. This transition, Ruggie notes, can be best understood as the emergence of the single-point perspective. No longer would the visual arts represent their subjects through "different sides and angles" – and no longer would political territory retain characteristics of undefined, indeterminate boundaries.[26] In Ruggie's terms, we can see how the Pakistani state offered a program of national history which diverged from that of the single-point territorial perspective through aligning its cultural center with lands in Arabia and left behind in India. The new efforts seek to "shift" the single-point perspective back to the lands comprising the contemporary nation-state.

While on the one hand, these historical projects of reclamation overtly essentialize the ethnic rubric instead of the Islamic national rubric – for what else are we to make of the claim that Shiva was Punjabi, an ethnic category hardly in existence during the Indus Valley, let alone applicable to a deity? – on the other hand, these historiographical efforts at the same time open space for the idea of a nation as a composite project,

---

[26] See especially "Social Epistemes" in John Gerard Ruggie, "Territoriality and Beyond," *International Organization* 47 (1993): 157–60.

a quality more permissive of a liberal-democratic agenda than that of the totalizing state. We can see this in the statements of their political agendas, which do not call for an invigoration of Punjabi consciousness in the name of secessionist agendas, but rather in the name of building a Pakistan based on greater pluralism. In Ahsan's words, "fundamentalist obscurantism displaced liberal modernism in this country. And thus the dire and pressing need to go back to our roots, to go back to our origins, and to trace our own steps from pre-history to the establishment of Pakistan."

This phenomenon marks the historiographical analogue to the value hierarchies of national language/national culture analyzed in Chapters 4 and 5. The presence of demands from Punjab, along with NWFP and Sindh, for inclusion in national history underscores how political and economic dominance in a polity do not obviate desire for recognition in national historical narratives. As with the question of the national language, so too does the national past represent an arena in which participants are keenly aware of the "own" presence or absence of symbolic capital. Further, the phenomenon once again suggests limits on the constructed-ness of national historiography, showing how difficult it is to craft a fully new national past without incorporating reference to local territories and their narrative pasts.

And this question indeed is the crux of the history–nation linkage. The recognition of local *absence* from national narratives structures a need for revisionism to give the local past value, symbolic capital, in the national story. What remain unanswered here, however, are the larger implications of these lessons for the linkages between cultural patrimony, symbolic capital, and a modern polity. While on the one hand, the emergence of regional emphases against a backdrop of national erasure can be understood as a sort of counter-consciousness, a move for recognition, the picture becomes much more complicated if we place this national story in comparative context. If, for example, we compare the resurgence of regional histories and emphases on regional cultures in Pakistan with those of the states of the former Soviet Union, we find that in the first case the state aggressively offered a national culture and history dismissive of the regional, yet in the second, the state aggressively courted the idea of "national states" constitutive of the larger federation. Is it possible to draw out formal lessons on what elements create a "successful" national culture, one that wins acceptance among all? To answer these questions, we will need to look comparatively.

8 Speaking like a state: language planning

> When the United Nations was established in 1945, 750 million people – almost a third of the world's population – lived in territories that were non-self-governing, dependent on colonial powers. Today, fewer than 2 million people live in such territories.
>
> United Nations, "The United Nations and Decolonization"

From its founding in 1945 through today, the number of "member states" of the United Nations ballooned from the original fifty-one to its current membership of 192 states.[1] This one measure illustrates the dramatic reshaping of the world's political geography, ushering out the era of empire and inaugurating a true globalization of the nation-form in just fifty-some years. The new nation-states each declared new national languages and undertook new programs of language modernization and development to effect their national usage. If the age of empire, as Bernard Cohn astutely reminded us, required the command of language and the language of command to effect dominance of a very few over the very many,[2] a different understanding of the relationship between language and polity emerged from the decolonization wave – namely, the necessity of an entire population sharing a national language in order to demonstrate national unity. Doubtless, the age of empire produced certain types of official languages: in British India and the Dutch East Indies, for example, Hindustani and brabbel-Maleisch were clearly products of the colonial encounter, languages which accommodated a certain kind of transregional communication, nearly entirely urban, not entirely possible through Bengali, Tamil, or Javanese. But at the same time, the abrupt epistemic break with decolonization resulted in nationalists themselves declaring emphatically that a single language would be the way forward to forge a real nation, even with the knowledge that to create such a situation would require enormous work. This would

---

A brief history of the United Nations' trusteeship role on decolonization is available on the UN website, www.un.org/Depts/dpi/decolonization/history.htm.

[1] See www.un.org/Overview/growth.htm.
[2] See Cohn, "Command of Language."

initiate a brand-new industry, that of language planning, to mediate that relationship, and mark a transition to new epistemologies as well. Gone would be the prominent role of core disciplines linked to empire, such as privileged philological traditions and the study of classical cosmopolitan languages – Sanskrit and Persian, for example. The twentieth-century world of nation-states thus coincided with new epistemologies of science and progress: modernization theory, "political development," the discourse of nation-building, and the new hybrid policy science of language planning that nestled within all three.

This chapter links two central claims. In continuation with the arguments presented earlier, focused on the processes and impact of the Pakistani state's national language and national history creation, I argue that the national language in the largest "new states" to have emerged from colonial rule (India, Indonesia, and Pakistan), emerged as the post-facto result of state-instantiated logics of language standardization and educational regimentation rather than as the natural environmentally-determined fertile soil that launched nationalist enthusiasm. Though this may appear obvious, this reversal of the logical order in popular understandings of nationalism permits us to focus instead on the efforts necessary to produce national linguistic uniformity. Of course, some scholars of nationalism have remarked on this oddity: for example, Eric Hobsbawm's work on nationalism and language in Europe, and the trenchant observation of Geoff Ely and Ronald Grigor Suny in their introduction to *Becoming National*:

creative political action is required to transform a segmented and disunited population into a coherent nationality ... One of the best examples of such creativity, because in the past it provided the commonest "objective" rationale for the existence of a nation, has been the adoption of national languages, which were very far from simply choosing themselves as the natural expression of majority usage ... Language is less a prior determinant of nationality than part of a complex process of cultural innovation, involving hard ideological labor, careful propaganda, and a creative imagination.[3]

By acknowledging the *produced* nature of the national language, this claim allows us to better explain the otherwise puzzling persistence of attachment to more regional or local languages that one might have expected to fall into desuetude if nationalist enthusiasm were in fact the result of (rather than the precondition for) widespread monolingualism, print-capitalism, industrialization, the Mamlukization of society, and the emergence of a stable national space–time subscribed to by

---

[3] Geoff Eley and Ronald Grigor Suny, ed., *Becoming National* (Oxford: Oxford University Press, 1996), 7; Hobsbawm, *Nations and Nationalism Since 1780*.

citizen-subjects. If these historical experiences of India, Indonesia, and Pakistan alone (one-quarter of the world's population) do not offer a sufficiently convincing rationale for reconsidering the theoretical linkage of language and nationalism, consider this: even a cursory look at the history of France points to a much weaker causal link between language and national consciousness than has been presupposed by key theories of nationalism. As Eugene Weber noted with reference to France, "The Third Republic found a France in which French was a foreign language for half the citizens."[4]

If we accept the contention, then, that some kind of national consciousness is a precondition for forging a national language rather than the other way around, the processes through which this language-propagation takes place come into sharper relief. Thus this chapter makes a second argument: the spread (or "success") of a national language in countries seeking to forge one is intimately related to the symbolic ideologies with which it is invested. This is no mere symbol manipulation, however; it is linked to emphases on literary and religious traditions, oral as well as written, traditions with histories and internal narratives of their own. To explore this claim, I look here at the assumptions inherent to the language planning exercises of the mid-twentieth century, then examine how the best-laid plans for national language unification in India ultimately gave way to an explicitly multilingual national framework. India's eighteen national languages are perhaps an extreme case, but a case that proves that cultural and linguistic diversity does not de facto cause national disintegration.

New states, national languages, and language planning

At the moment of decolonization, a desire to collapse regions of intense multilinguality into a new national zone of monolingualism became politically exigent. This shift appears to be an automatic and inevitable outcome in nationalism, regardless of empirical realities and historical evidence of deep multilinguality. In South Asia, for example, it had been possible under precolonial and colonial regimes – however undemocratic those may have been – for various languages to coexist in an unremarkable way. If the Mughals, for example, chose to employ Persian as the language of state, it was also true that the early rulers spoke Turkish and enjoyed its poetry; Hindvi was a regional language with appreciated merits and semi-official state recognition; and though illiterate, Akbar maintained a library of texts to be read out to him in Arabic, Persian,

---

[4] See Weber, *Peasants into Frenchmen*, 70.

Hindi, Greek, and Kashmiri.⁵ With British colonization in the Indian subcontinent (and more or less the same in the case of Dutch colonization of the East Indies), the age of empire did not coincide with a notion that mass populations should be re-engineered to speak in one tongue. Certainly some Indians acquired an education in English and the regional-specific Indian language deemed necessary by the British Raj: Bengali, Hindustani, and Tamil. And surely the colonial encounter with Indian languages – as we saw in Chapter 1 – would produce new forms of those languages, resulting in the case of Hindustani in the idea that Hindus and Muslims had different languages; this same colonial encounter produced a new kind of Bengali language as well.⁶ Yet surely this form of presenting a language-menu for the purposes of administrative gain suggests a far different effort than an initiative to propagate a single language throughout a region of millions in order to fully achieve becoming national. This represents a transformative break in ideas about the uses of language. Borrowing the method of juxtaposition used by Kittler in *Discourse Networks*, I want to briefly contrast practices of language and administration first under empire and then in the postcolonial state to highlight how they differ.⁷

Expanding further on Bernard Cohn's observations about the language of command, we find a lesson – one he likely did not intend – to be learned from the methodological preoccupations of administrators of the British Empire in India. In short, some of the most important early administrators were literary scholar-statesmen, practicing philologists, men who perceived as necessary for a "command of language" the thorough exploration of literatures. Cohn presents an illustrative list of "leading texts" of the period 1770–85, a perusal of which underscores their preoccupation with language-learning and translation of literatures:

Alexander Dow, The History of Hindostan, 1770; Sir William Jones, A Grammar of the Persian Language, 1771; George Hadley, The Practical and Vulgar Dialect of the Indostan Language Commonly Called Moors, 1772; N.B. Halhed, A Code of Gentoo Laws, or, Ordinations of the Pundits, 1776, and A Grammar of the Bengal Language, 1778; John Richardson, A Dictionary of English, Persian and Arabic, 1780; William Davy, Institutes Political and Military of Tmour, 1783; Francis Balfour, The Forms of the Herkern, 1781; Charles Wilkins, The Bhagvat Geeta, 1785; William Kirkpatrick, A Vocabulary, Persian, Arabic and

---

⁵ See Alam, "Pursuit of Persian," 317–19, 323.
⁶ See Sudipta Kaviraj, "The Two Histories of Literary Culture in Bengal," in *Literary Cultures in History*, ed. Pollock (2003). Kaviraj notes the "peculiar relation of transaction with both Sanskrit and English" that determined the shape of modern Bengali (542); and also early efforts to develop a "Muslim Bangla," (541).
⁷ Friedrich A. Kittler, *Discourse Networks 1800/1900*, trans. Metteer with Cullens (Stanford: Stanford University Press, 1990).

English; Containing Such words as have been Adopted from the Two Former Languages and Incorporated into the Hindvi, 1785; Francis Gladwin, Ayeen I Akberry or the Institutes of the Emperor Akbar, 1783–6; John A. Gilchrist, A Dictionary English and Hindustani, Part I, 1787.[8]

We might only add to Cohn's list that the emphasis on language and literary *study* as a necessary dimension of knowledge for administering this imperial polity did not end in 1785. Sir William Jones (1746–94), to take a prominent example, was sent to India as a judge in 1783, and supplemented his study of the "classical languages" (Arabic, Hebrew, Persian) with Sanskrit. In addition to his Persian dictionary listed above, he published an English translation of Kalidasa's Sanskrit drama *Shakuntala* in 1789,[9] so successful throughout Europe it ran through four reprints and astounded both Herder and Goethe with its beauty.[10] Jones became a prominent advocate for the study of "Asiatic" literatures as part of a global cultural heritage. He founded the Asiatick Society (now the Asiatic Society) in 1784; his writings on the remarkable similarity between Greek, Latin, and Sanskrit changed the era's scientific wisdom about the origins and relationship between languages – and indeed, of peoples.

Fort William College, founded in 1800 in Calcutta, trained functionaries of the British Raj in various contemporary as well as classical languages – Persian, Arabic, Sanskrit, Bengali, and Hindustani – and its analogue in the south, the Company's College at Fort St. George (in today's Chennai), provided training in South Indian languages as well as Hindu and Muslim law.[11] Some sixty-four years later, after the British acquisition of the Punjab from the Sikhs, the founding of Government College in Lahore provided a similar training for administrative elite; its first principal, G. W. Leitner, founded the Anjuman-e-Punjab a year later, and presided over readings and translations.[12] An analogue in the Dutch East Indies was the colonial creation of Balai Pustaka, a publishing house,[13] which brought out "educational" stories in Javanese,

---

[8] Cohn, "Command of Language," 282. Note that the first title, Alexander Dow's *History of Hindostan*, is the very same history cited in the previous chapter as the translation of Farishta's Persian-language history of the Indian subcontinent.

[9] Sir William Jones, *Sacontalá; or, The Fatal Ring: an Indian Drama. By Cálidás. Translated from the original Sanscrit and Prácrit*. (London: Printed for Edwards by J. Cooper, 1790).

[10] William Crawley, "Sir William Jones: A Vision of Orientalism," *Asian Affairs* 27, no. 2 (1996): 172–3.

[11] Cohn, "Command of Language," 324.

[12] See Frances W. Pritchett, "Introduction to Excerpts from Ab-e-Hayat," *Annual of Urdu Studies* 13 (1998): 39.

[13] Balai Pustaka remains alive today as the primary national sales/distribution outlet for state-produced publications relating to language, culture, dictionaries for various

Sundanese, and of course Bahasa Melayu – indeed a Dutch colonial language project itself.

Whatever else we might say about these early practices of translation and language-learning – for it is certainly true that these were an effort to repackage Asian knowledge as European products, in service to European power – the fact remains that the intellectual climate was one that placed enormous emphasis on literature and the wisdom contained within it, as well as an engagement with contemporary spoken language traditions. Even this brief sketch shows an ethos in which the concept of knowledge was heavily informed by an idea that administering a polity requires familiarity with those traditions, conceptualized as multilingual, and that the present was a product of the heritage of the past. In fact, to take a closer look at the heritage of the past, specifically in the South Asian region, we find a history of participation in multiple language communities. This is no small feature. Rather, it marks an ongoing social-communicative relationship with language and literature entirely different from what we now understand as the reductive or "nationalist" Herderian philosophy of language-nations.

Herderianism and language-as-nation

In sharp contrast, the twentieth-century world of the nation-state brings along with it a valorization of the national language as a vehicle of national unification as well as the evidentiary basis for national existence. If the nation-form spread modularly, so too did a near-religious belief in the singularity of language as proof of nationality. Recall Jinnah's proclamations that Urdu and only Urdu was the language of the Muslim nation of the Indian subcontinent; Gandhi's idea that a national language of Hindustani must be cultivated for the soon-to-be independent India. These two stances mark a very different understanding of polity and language than the "fuzzy boundaries" of colonial and precolonial (indeed, premodern) evidence suggests.[14]

This ethos shows a radical break from an approach to knowledge as something to be gleaned from older texts, thus necessitating sustained textual study, to an idea that the challenges of modernity can best be answered through greater regimentation and emphasis on technologies of modernization – including policy approaches to national ideology institutionalization and national language creation through social engineering, a sort of production line model of shaping citizens. Max Weber's

---

Indonesian regional languages, and translation projects which would not likely find a large market otherwise.

[14] Kaviraj, "Writing, Speaking, Being."

notion of "rationalization" fits within this spirit of modernization; particularly with respect to language, the new economies of prestige and legitimacy create what Bourdieu describes as the "production and reproduction of legitimate language."[15] As Bourdieu explains,

> only when the making of the "nation," an entirely abstract group based on law, creates new usages and functions does it become indispensable to forge a *standard* language, impersonal and anonymous like the official uses it has to serve, and by the same token to undertake the work of normalizing the products of the linguistic habitus.[16]

Of course, this new infatuation with modernization was not unique to Pakistan; in fact, it exemplifies what James Scott refers to as a worldwide high-modernist vision of "thin simplifications," the precise opposite of mētis, or practical knowledge.[17] If mētis implies an intuitive sense of knowledge acquired through direct familiarity, the "thin simplification" approach posits ideal-type social reforms, reforms to better the world through increasing uniformity and legibility. Scott presents these state simplifications in the realms of architecture, urban planning, forest management, and Soviet collective farming, providing rich detail and specific case studies. He briefly engages the question of the standardized official language, suggesting that it "may be the most powerful" of all state simplifications, the "precondition of many other[s]." In particular, Scott briefly outlines two phases of national or official language propagation: first, the desire for "legibility of local practice" (a notion of increasing administrative ease, and doing so by replacing local forms with those of the center); and second, the rise of a "cultural project," the "implicit logic" of which will "define a hierarchy of cultures, relegating local languages and their regional cultural to, at best, a quaint provincialism."[18] Though Scott spends only two pages on the question of language, and does not further develop the thought beyond what I have cited here, his intuition is correct. What this implies for our purposes is a super-functionalist approach to education planning, an approach in which the state bears down upon the irremediably teeming Tower of Babel in the hopes of transforming it into a sleek Eiffel Tower instead.

This, then, is the difference between approaches to knowledge exemplified by the science of philology versus the science of language

---

[15] See Bourdieu, *Language and Symbolic Power*.
[16] See *ibid.*, 48.
[17] While this process of standardizing and regimenting language clearly can be seen as a bureacratic rationalization in Weberian terms, I find Scott's oppositions to be a better analytic lens on the question. See especially "Thin Simplifications and Practical Knowledge: Mētis" in Scott, *Seeing Like a State*, 309–41.
[18] *Ibid.*, 72–3.

planning. One seeks answers in understanding what already exists; the other seeks to shape what exists to better suit administrative convenience. This context of privileging administrative convenience appears so widespread by the middle of the twentieth century that it would have been extremely difficult for the new states to have somehow resisted the homogenizing tendency of the nation-form and the idea of a singular language as necessary to evidence national unity. This scientific "rationalization" approach places a heavy burden on the acquiescence of national citizen-subjects if it is to succeed. That such an exercise in large-scale social engineering has not worked smoothly in many salient cases – *but has in others* – is the perplexing query underlying this chapter and the following.

The emergence of language planning as an administrative science and an applied discipline in the middle of the twentieth century parallels the massive increase in new nation-states emerging from decolonization. Where political science formed the disciplinary site of knowledge-production concerning democratization – what was then (and perhaps still is) conceptualized as the natural telos of "political development"[19] for these new states – the political dimensions of language choices were taken up by the science of language planning. This science, as with most prescriptive social sciences of the era, was confident that its recommendations would produce national unity and a better way of life for the states in which its advice was deployed. Note, for instance, this under-historicized assertion from perhaps the most widely-cited edited volume in the entire field:

The more intensive communication in modernizing societies puts a premium on linguistic unity and distinctiveness: nation-states have been most securely founded where all nationals speak the same language, and preferably a language all their own.[20]

This uncritical belief in the necessity of forging a unified, singular national language as the sign of national arrival was so widespread by 1970 that Indian political scientist Jyotirindra Das Gupta was writing *against* this received wisdom when he argued that a top-down notion of implemented national unity appeared to be inconsistent with the high rhetoric of democratization; he proposed instead, looking at the

---

[19] On "political development" as a concept, see Fred W. Riggs, "The Rise and Fall of 'Political Development'," in *The Handbook of Political Behavior, Vol. 4*, ed. Long (New York: Plenum Press, 1989). Riggs concludes that the term is best thought of as an "autonym" – a word which generates its own meaning.
[20] See Dankwart A. Rustow, "Language, Modernization, and Nationhood – An Attempt at Typology," in *Language Problems of Developing Nations*, ed. Fishman, Ferguson, and Das Gupta (New York: John Wiley & Sons, 1968), 87.

experience of India, that greater linguistic pluralism should not be seen to imply a lesser commitment to the nation.[21]

Where the previous chapters of this book have explored the politics of language policy, literature, and national history curricula decisions in Pakistan, the following examines in comparative fashion the results of language policy decisions in two other national contexts: India and Indonesia. Each case provides a different sort of counterpoint for Pakistan's experience with language planning, highlighting divergent outcomes. India illustrates an eventual abandonment of the Herderian reverse, the language paradox of nation-building. In acquiescing to the local demands that regional languages be given explicitly *political* roles, language conflict has virtually disappeared.

India

As Pakistan's national twin, separated at birth, the kinds of decisions India made about language policy seem a natural point of historical comparison, though India's size makes that comparison more than asymmetric. Still, in the sense that India dwarfs Pakistan not just in population but as well in number of languages, the lessons can be useful, for the challenges were always more numerous and on a larger scale. Yet by the end of the twentieth century, language conflict had for the most part ceased in India, though to be sure some areas of conflagration remain, notably Assam.[22] For a country that was wracked by language riots in its early decades, this outcome marks a significant reversal of affairs.

The sheer scale of linguistic diversity in India, in terms of both spoken language and established literary traditions as well, had long worried politicians and policymakers in independent India. The worries encompassed two significant policy dilemmas: one, the question of what could be the national language; and two, whether language should serve as the primary criterion of differentiation in redesigning administrative boundaries at the state level.[23]

---

[21] See especially Jyotirindra Das Gupta, *Language Conflict and National Development* (Berkeley: University of California Press, 1970), 1–30.

[22] See particularly "Cultural Politics of Language, Subnationalism, and Pan-Indianism," in Sanjib Baruah, *India Against Itself* (Philadelphia: University of Pennsylvania Press, 1999), 69–90.

[23] For the best overviews on the nation and language policy, see Das Gupta, *Language Conflict and National Development*; Hans Raj Dua, *Language Planning in India* (New Delhi: Harnam Publications, 1985). For a game-theoretic explanation of India's stable language equilibrium of 3±1, see David D. Laitin, "Language Policy and Political Strategy in India," *Policy Sciences* 22, no. 4 (1989).

Speaking like a state: language planning

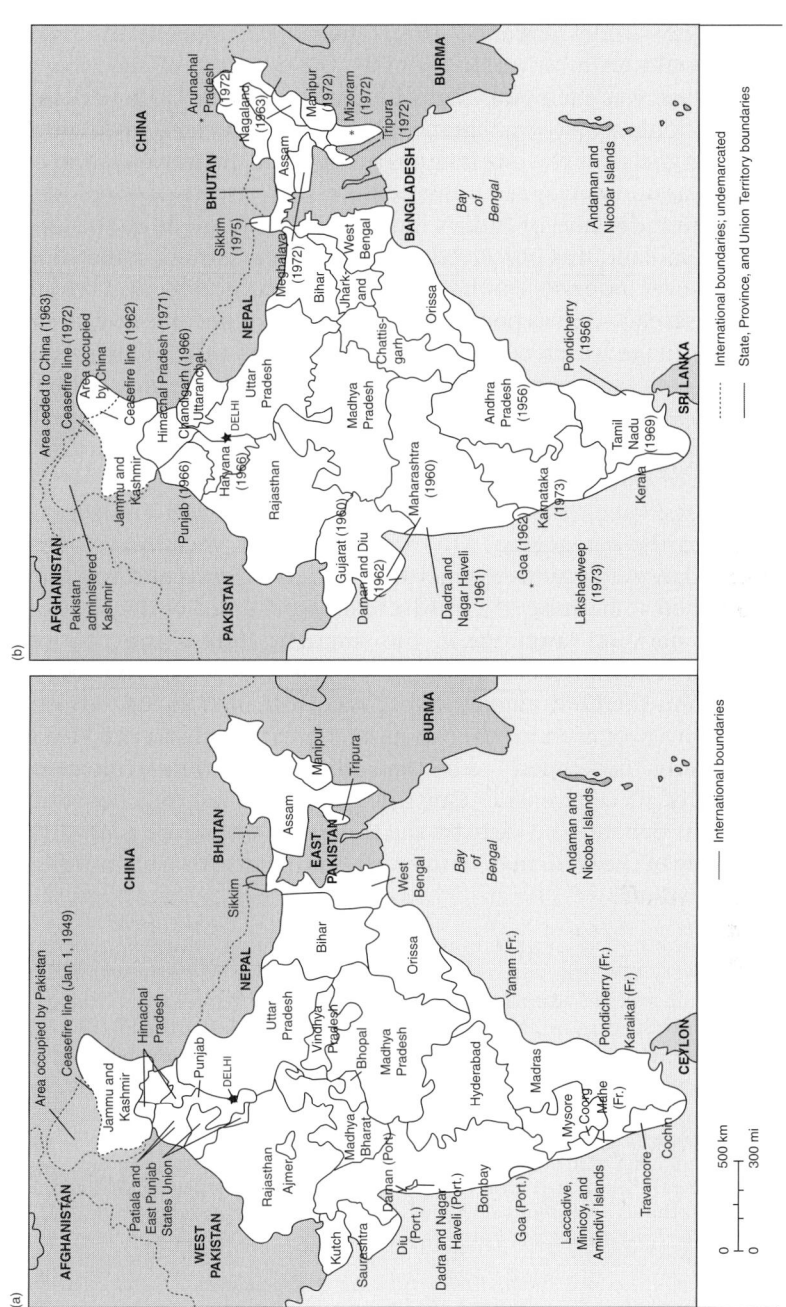

Map 4 (a) India – before the linguistic states reorganization (state boundaries of 1950), (b) India – after the linguistic states reorganization (states as of 2008). Names and boundary representation are approximate, and not necessarily authoritative.

160   Speaking Like a State

Given that no single language group (according to contemporary census data) could claim a simple majority, the question of choosing a national language was the point of most vigorous debate. Despite being the language of only a very small percentage of elite educated in colonial institutions, English was the one language that could claim some kind of pan-Indian cosmopolitan spread. But could it serve as the national language? In the first decades of India's independence, English, as the language of the colonizer, was perceived as a foreign imposition, something which could never nourish the national genius of Indians and which should be expelled as soon as possible. The quest then became one for an indigenous language which could serve as a national, official language. While census data on Hindi speakers showed it to be the most widely spoken language in India, it could never claim more than 40 percent of the population, and even this claim might well have been an artifact of the practice of census-taking and language-nominalization – for the process collapsed speakers of many different speech-forms (dialects or languages) into the category of Hindi.[24] In addition to Hindi, twelve other modern languages with extensive literary traditions and millions of speakers posed something of a hurdle to any presumptive declaration of Hindi as a national language in the singular. India's constitution makers chose a compromise formulation with a three-tier arrangement: legally, "Hindi in the Devanagari script" was enshrined as the "official language," with a provision for the concurrent use of English until Hindi could be properly "developed" to assume all official and link functions after a period of fifteen years.[25] But this was a decision reached only after significant debate, and only by the thinnest of margins according to the testimony of the chairman of the constitution drafting committee, Dr. B. R. Ambedkar:

It may now not be a breach of a secret if I reveal to the public what happened in the Congress Party meeting when the Draft Constitution of India was being considered, on the issue of adopting Hindi as the national language. There was no article which proved more controversial than Article 115 which deals with the question. No article produced more opposition. No article, more heat. After a prolonged discussion when the question was put, the vote was 78 against 78.

[24] The 1961 census, with a narrow definition of Hindi, reported 30 percent of the population as speakers – but with a broader definition in later censuses, its share increased to 38–40 percent. See Jyotirindra Das Gupta, "Language Policy and National Development in India," in *Fighting Words*, ed. Brown and Ganguly (Cambridge: MIT Press, 2003), 26–7. Relatedly, see Bernard S. Cohn, "The Census, Social Structure, and Objectification in South Asia," in *An Anthropologist among the Historians and Other Essays* (New Delhi: Oxford India, 1987). Also Arjun Appadurai, "Number in the Colonial Imagination," in *Orientalism and the Postcolonial Predicament*, ed. Breckenridge and van der Veer (Philadelphia: University of Pennsylvania Press, 1993).
[25] For the Constitutional articles relating to language, see indiacode.nic.in/coiweb/coifiles/p17.htm.

The tie could not be resolved. After a long time when the question was put to the Party meeting the result was 77 against 78 for Hindi. Hindi won its place as a national language by one vote.[26]

In addition to this structure, another legal category of "national languages" was created, in which a total of fourteen languages achieved constitutional status as national. The Eighth Schedule of the Indian Constitution [Articles 344(1) and 351], finalized in 1949, originally contained the following fourteen "national languages:" Assamese, Bengali, Gujarati, Hindi, Kannada, Kashmiri, Malayalam, Marathi, Oriya, Punjabi, Sanskrit, Tamil, Telugu, Urdu. Two later amendments added first Sindhi (1967), then Konkani, Manipuri, and Nepali (1992) to this list.[27] The idea was that these national languages could be the languages of state for those states which chose them, but ideally Hindi (or English if the state did not or could not use Hindi) would be the language of communication from the states to the center and between states.

Despite the original intent of the constitution as well as the recommendations of the Official Language Commission five years later, the "phase-out" provisions for English in fact never took place.[28] First, the bureaucracy did not abandon the use of English, and it remained a prestige language in terms of social distinction, science and bureaucratic power.[29] But secondly, some regions vehemently objected to the implementation of Hindi as the sole official language. By the time the first fifteen years of constitutionally-permitted English use were about to expire, unexpectedly violent protest against Hindi took place. This resistance was strongest in Madras state, where in 1964 and 1965 several young men killed themselves in spectacularly gruesome and public ways in protest against Hindi and in devotion to Tamil.[30] Such objections were not limited to Tamil speakers alone; Bengal and Mysore states, and the then-autonomous Government of Kashmir had serious reservations about Hindi assuming sole status of official language.[31] The argument

---

[26] B. R. Ambedkar, *Thoughts on Linguistic States*, reprint edn (Aligarh: Anand Sahitya Sadan, 1989 [1955]), 20.
[27] For the Eighth Schedule, see indiacode.nic.in/coiweb/welcome.html.
[28] The report of the Official Language Commission published in 1956 offers a fascinating glimpse at the period's ideas about language, nation, and national development. See B. G. Kher, "Report of the Official Language Commission" (New Delhi: Government of India Press, 1956).
[29] In Laitin's apt phrase, "Formal compliance ... [which] hid practical subversion." Laitin, "Language Policy and Strategy," 419. On science policy and language, see Hans Raj Dua, *Science Policy, Education, and Language Planning* (Mysore: Yashoda Publications, 2001).
[30] Ramaswamy, *Passions of the Tongue*.
[31] See the dissenting notes (essays, really) to the Official Language Commission report authored by Suniti Kumar Chatterji and P. Subbarayan Kher, "Report of the Official Language Commission," 275–330.

against Hindi as the sole official language, should English be de-certified as an acceptable alternative, was that although the Hindi speakers presented the question as simply a matter of national expediency, in all cases where Hindi was closely in competition with another language (Urdu and Punjabi, notably), the Hindi lobby displayed its rampant chauvinism and attempted to impose itself as if by right.[32] Worse yet, as Das Gupta notes, many of the most active pro-Hindi organizations explicitly identified themselves as *Aryan* precisely during the decades of a growing pro-Dravidian consciousness and anti-Brahminism in the south. The Hindi language advocates such as the Arya Samaj, Arya Sanskriti, Arya Bhasha, and Arya Lipi alienated Muslims and Sikhs in the North, but for their co-religionists in the south – by virtue of the south's own growing Dravidian pride – a shared Hindu religion was not sufficient to support what they perceived as an overtly Aryan project.[33]

So the official language compromise with English perdured, conceptualized as perenially supposed-to-be-superceded-by the more "Indian" Hindi, though the hindsight of more than fifty years suggests that will never come to pass. In addition, Indian literature in English, the dramatic rise in global prominence of Indian science and global business (conducted virtually entirely in English) has very effectively established the language's national bona fides. At the same time, early planners' concern that Hindi was not yet suitably "developed" for modern life has surely been answered; the language has undergone something of a wholesale transformation since Independence, having been endowed with a highly Sanskritic vocabulary for the lexicon of modern life.[34] Rather, this compromise formulation of the official language being "Hindi in the Devanagari script" supported by English has, over time, proved to be a solution that appears to least offend – though notably not the unitary national language that had originally been imagined.

National languages and linguistic provinces reorganization

Aside from the matter of official language was the dilemma of "linguistic provinces." This was a question of political administration debated long

---

[32] See Das Gupta, *Language Conflict and National Development*, 157–8, 188–90.
[33] *Ibid.*, 191. On Dravidianizing Tamil, Dravidianism and India, and the DMK, see Ramaswamy, *Passions of the Tongue*, 62–77.
[34] The Constitution explicitly called for the development of Hindi "by drawing, wherever necessary or desirable, for its vocabulary, primarily on Sanskrit and secondarily on other languages." See Article 351, "Directive for the Development of the Hindi Language," via indiacode.nic.in/coiweb/coifiles/p17.htm. On the standardization and nationalization process of Hindi, see especially "Roads to the Present," Chapter 7 of Rai, *Hindi Nationalism*, 106–122. On literary development and Sanskritization of Hindi as the nation fostered its role of official language, see Trivedi, "Hindi and the Nation."

before Independence; the solution would in fact replicate the decision the Indian National Congress had taken to facilitate its anti-colonial struggle. Under Gandhi's leadership, the Congress had long championed Hindi-Hindustani as the emblematic all-India language, in both Devanagari and Persian script forms.[35] But the Congress as well recognized that in terms of organization and political expediency, it could better function through a regional-language architecture:

> Since 1921 the Congress has discarded British administrative provinces for its work and has created provinces, many of which are more or less linguistic ... In 1928 the Nehru Report fully endorsed the Congress view and strongly emphasised the desirability of creating these linguistic Provinces. And since then the Congress has included in its election manifesto the formation of linguistic provinces as one item of its programme.[36]

After Independence, the Constituent Assembly appointed the Linguistic Provinces Committee to study the issue. No easy compromise could be found; to be sure, the committee recognized that there was considerable demand for the redrawing of provincial boundaries, and that administering education, public life, and legislatures would be expedited if they could be organized into more homogenous linguistic units. But they were concerned above all about whether the formation of new boundaries along linguistic lines would bring new subnationalisms into existence, and further what the impact might be in terms of creating new relations of majority–minority dynamics.[37] For example, should a new Kannada-speaking state be carved out of Madras and Mysore states, a significant minority of Marathi-speakers would find themselves in a new subordinate position.

Within the south, in what was then-Madras state, agitations began for a separate state of Telugu speakers as well as a partitioning of Marathi and Kannada speakers. Gujarati speakers in Bombay state argued for a separate Gujarati-speaking state; Marathi-speakers wanted a Maharashtra. Punjabi-speakers sought to rescue themselves from a minority status in a Punjab that had suddenly become primarily Hindi-speaking as a result of Partition and the exodus of millions of Punjabi-speaking Muslims to Pakistan. The question of linguistic provinces became a serious matter of public debate, with the biggest names in Indian political life issuing reports either recommending a linguistic provinces reorganization (Ambedkar, for example) or against it (Patel, Sitaramayya, and Nehru).[38] The argument in favor of linguistic provinces ran generally

[35] See Gandhi, *Our Language Problem [Collected Writings, 1918–1948]*.
[36] Government of India Constituent Assembly of India, "Report of the Linguistic Provinces Commission" (New Delhi: Government of India Press, 1948), 1.
[37] *Ibid.*, 28.
[38] Ambedkar, *Thoughts on Linguistic States*; Sardar Vallabhbhai Patel, B. Pattabhi Sitaramayya, and Jawaharlal Nehru, *Report of the Linguistic Provinces Committee*

along Herderian lines, the benefits of life immersed in an environment of one's own national genius.[39] The argument against raised the specter of imminent Balkanization, invoking the recent trauma of Partition and the necessity for the Indian Union to foster great unity rather than further divisions, exemplified by this sentence from the Patel, Sitaramayya, and Nehru report: "The context demands, above everything, the consolidation of India and her freedom ... the promotion of unity in India ... It demands further stern discouragement of communalism, provincialism, and all other separatist and disruptive tendencies."[40]

Despite this, a massive reorganization of state boundaries did indeed take place, in shifts, absolutely along linguistic lines, and through a process of combining princely states and carving up the huge British-organized "presidencies." First, the 1953 Andhra State Act carved a Telugu-speaking state of Andhra out of Madras. Chandernagore was folded into West Bengal in 1954. Then the 1956 states reorganization produced the "new" states of Andhra Pradesh (by adding more territory to Andhra), Kerala, Madhya Pradesh, and Tamil Nadu; it also redesigned the borders of Himachal Pradesh, West Bengal, Assam, Bihar, and the various Union territories. The 1959 Rajasthan and Madhya Pradesh Transfer of Territories Act reapportioned land to each; the 1960 Bombay Reorganisation Act created Gujarat and Maharashtra; the 1962 Nagaland Act created Nagaland; the 1966 Punjab Reorganisation Act forged a new Hindi-speaking Haryana and created majority Punjabi-speaking Punjab. The 1968 Andhra Pradesh and Mysore Transfer of Territory act created Kannada-speaking Karnataka, and finally the 1971 North-eastern States Reorganisation Act produced Meghalaya, Mizoram, Tripura, Manipur, and Arunachal Pradesh.[41]

Quite obviously, the primary analytic principle for all these reorganizations was linguistic. More than fifty years after the major states reorganization of 1956, most contemporary observers judge the administrative organization to have been a policy success, for language conflict is now relatively rare (again, Assam the salient exception) and language riots practically non-existent.[42] Did the creation of more homogenous

---

appointed by the Jaipur Congress (Dec. 1948) (New Delhi: Indian National Congress, 1953 [1949]).

[39] Herder, "Reflections."

[40] Patel, Sitaramayya, and Nehru, *Report of the Linguistic Provinces Committee*, 4.

[41] The clearest way to see the chronological development of linguistic reorganization is to examine the First Schedule of the Constitution, which lists all the states of the Union and gives dates as well as the precise acts which brought them into their present forms. See parliamentofindia.nic.in/const/shed01.htm.

[42] Recent language conflict in Bangalore, for example, has involved anti-Tamil demonstrations in 1990, and protests against attempts in 1994 to broadcast Urdu-language news on local (state-operated) television, resulting in protests. See Asghar Ali

administrative territories produce new subnationalisms? From the perspective of the center, the answer appears to be broadly no. Yet if we ask this same question from another vantage point, that of speakers of a minority language within the linguistically-demarcated states, we do find that the majoritarian language hegemony Patel, Sitaramaya, and Nehru worried about has come to pass. Two points should be noted in this regard. First, for minority language speakers within states – using Dua's example of Dakkani speakers in Mysore – the required language repertoire can be as high as five languages (Dakkani, high Urdu, Kannada, Hindi, English).[43] This burden is greater than the native Hindi speaker's ability to get by with studying only Hindi and English. Yet this appears not to be a significant source of conflict, and in any event high levels of multilingualism have long characterized the South Asian region. But the second point, perhaps more apposite for our purposes, lies in the way that new relationships of linguistic categories have indeed created new minorities and new majorities with unequal relations of power.

After the major states reorganization in 1956, individual states in India passed their own state-level laws to promote and develop various official languages of state; obviously, given that each state does not "contain" a homogeneous population, some citizens will de facto be speakers of "minority" languages. The creation of these new minorities has involved "fractal recursivity," in which the oppositions at one level of linguistic salience – English and Hindi, for example – find themselves *recursively* projected onto progressively smaller levels as well.[44] So the formal symmetry of dominant::subordinate opposition of English and Hindi finds itself again projected onto pairs in the following way: English::Hindi→Hindi::Kannada→Kannada::Urdu.[45] Or English::Hindi→Hindi::Gujarati→Gujarati::Kacchhi (and/or Gujarati::Urdu::Kachhi). These iterated oppositions can be identified throughout the country; their existence is at present no cause for alarm, but observers interested in a more fine-grained analysis of language and polity certainly should be cognizant of the pattern, precisely because the recursive nature of these oppositional pairs suggests that whatever the dimensions of legal

Engineer, "Bangalore Violence: Linguistic or Communal?" *Economic and Political Weekly*, October 29, 1994; Janaki Nair, "Kannada and Politics of State Protection," *Economic and Political Weekly*, October 29, 1994.

[43] Hans Raj Dua, *Language Use, Attitudes and Identity Among Linguistic Minorities*, Vol. 8, *CIIL Sociolinguistics Series* (Mysore: Central Institute of Indian Languages, 1986). See also Laitin, "Language Policy and Strategy," 415–16, n2.

[44] See Gal, "Bartok's Funeral," 443–7; Irvine and Gal, "Language Ideology and Linguistic Difference," 62–5.

[45] See Nair, "Kannada and Politics of State Protection."

recognition for language regimes at local levels, patterns of dominance in some form or another will remain a feature.

The Indian nation, its literatures, and the state

Many overviews of language policy overlook a crucial feature: how the state creates policies that affect literary production. A great portion of Chapter 4 examined efforts to forge a Punjabi literature in Pakistan as a means of redressing longstanding state biases against the language, and this book is driven by the conviction that notions of self and community identity cannot be understood without reference to the cultural products that communities lay claim to. We have seen how the post-Independence struggles in India over administrative boundaries and national languages created small subnational states, in which a regional language could serve as the language of state. This narrative provides insights into governmentality as it affects education, electoral processes, and official institutions of the state. But what about cultural production? Given India's enormous linguistic diversity, and its many literary traditions with long histories, the question of literary and cultural production would appear important.

Intriguingly, this multilayered multilingual state project has involved literature and cultural production from the start. The electronic media were very early repositories for new governmental language propagation efforts. Radio was long a domain of communication operated and administered by the state; the trajectory of the national language project can be seen in the post-Independence death of a project begun in the pre-Independence years to codify a Hindustani vocabulary for All-India Radio.[46] The composite Hindustani effort would end, to be replaced by separate Hindi and Urdu broadcasts. Regional nodes of AIR (renamed Akashvani, or "voice from the sky" in official Hindi), would create programming in regional languages, following the pattern of the linguistic provinces. Doordarshan, India's state television, follows a similar structure: national programs are created in Hindi and English, relayed throughout the country, with additional programs created at the state level in the various regional languages.

India's unique literary heritage was considered so critical for national development that a government resolution in 1954 created the Sahitya Akademi (India's National Academy of Letters). It began operation in

---

[46] For an excellent historical account of this project's demise, see David Lelyveld, "The Fate of Hindustani: Colonial Knowledge and the Project of a National Language," in *Orientalism and the Postcolonial Predicament*, ed. Breckenridge and van der Veer (Philadelphia: University of Pennsylvania Press, 1993).

1956.[47] The Sahitya Akademi exists entirely to serve as a sort of national bureau of literary recognition, with programs to translate work from one Indian language into another, as well as into English, not to mention the annual bestowing of awards for literary merit in each of the languages recognized in the Constitution.[48] This is a self-conscious effort to establish a national sensibility of unity-in-diversity through literature:

> The Akademi has resisted the bulldozing standardisation of Indian cultures and literatures while also fighting trends of balkanisation by projecting the dialectical relationship between unity and difference and creating a culture of mutual respect and collaboration among the various languages and literatures of India. Our ideal is an imagined community where the voice of every segment will be listened to with love and understanding.[49]

Of course, the project is not without its conceptual dilemmas. As Sheldon Pollock argues, a paradox inheres in the fact that this Akademi had to be created in order to forge awareness of the national literature it assumes to already exist.[50] Yet at some level, the visibility the Sahitya Akademi programs offer surely provides a greater sense of inclusion, not to mention greater consciousness of the creative literary work that might otherwise be unable to cross language barriers. In this sense the Akademi tries to mediate the many "partial publics," some overlapping but many not, that coexist in a cultural region so diverse.[51] Indeed, the Sahitya Akademi is exceptionally active: according to its official website, it has published more than 2,000 books in translation (from twenty-four languages), and has convened more than 6,000 programs of discussion at the national and regional levels.[52] By comparison, the only measure of the Pakistan Academy of Letters' output that I have been able to locate reports the publication of 150 books.[53]

If the Sahitya Akademi represents a state-instantiated effort to develop the idea of a national literature, it does so in conjunction with active voluntary associations. Throughout the post-Independence history of Indian language and literature, collaboration between agencies of the

---

[47] See www.sahitya-akademi.org/sahitya-akademi/org1.htm.
[48] Intriguingly, the Sahitya Akademi gives annual literary awards for work in Dogri, Maithili, and Rajasthani – none of which have a place in the Eighth Schedule. See www.sahitya-akademi.org/sahitya-akademi/org3.htm.
[49] See www.sahitya-akademi.org/sahitya-akademi/ach.htm.
[50] Pollock, "Literary Cultures in History," 10.
[51] On the notion of "partial publics," see Miriam Hansen, "Forward," in *Public Sphere and Experience*, ed. Negt and Kluge (Minneapolis: University of Minnesota Press, 1993), xxxvii.
[52] See www.sahitya-akademi.org/sahitya-akademi/ach.htm.
[53] See the note accompanying this Pakistan government commemorative stamp honoring the Academy of Letters: www.pakpost.gov.pk/philately/stamps2003/pakistan_academy_of_letters.html.

state and the multitude of language associations so active in Indian literary life appears to have been a central organizational model for "language development." Particularly with respect to Hindi, this may have come at a very high cost: as Jyotirindra Das Gupta notes, the "Hindi literati" played a significant role in the creation of modern standard Hindi – picking up from where the Hindi language movement left off in the late nineteenth century – coining an extensive array of new terms for modern life from Sanskrit, and promoting a brand new form of the language that aimed to create a veneer of a different kind of linguistic geneology, i.e., the modern inheritor of the great Sanskrit tradition.[54] By implication as well as overt claim, this new genealogy served to sever official Hindi from the Persianized vocabulary of its conjoined twin, Urdu.

The preceding narrative should elucidate the extent to which India the country speaks in many tongues, apart from question of whether the speakers of those tongues imagine themselves as constituting a nation. The way the national language policy has emerged has not been in accordance with the earlier high plans for propagating one singular national language (Hindi); in actuality, the "stable equilibrium" of multilinguality owes much more to notions of mētis than to any policy foresight – and certainly its stability suggests the wisdom of such a system for the political-cultural order.

As we saw above, the early organizing efforts of the Indian National Congress provided a template for what has become the current language policy – with certain slippages – but the central lesson was this: a mass, grassroots anti-colonial nationalism took place in India, the enormity of which remains unparalleled in human history, and this took place through a congeries of different languages, including English. The post-Independence efforts to make a national language in the singular fell on the sword of its own diversity, producing a multilingual national policy that effectively mirrors the sort of multilingual existence deep-rooted in the region. In this sense practices with much longer precedents rode roughshod over the bureaucratic imagined idea of a national language.

The ideological "content" carried by the national language project and its proponents, namely organizations seeking to fuse the national language and thereby the nation with an Aryan overlay, was the most important feature of the conflict with India's southern states, particularly Tamil Nadu. The Dravidian anti-Brahmin populism which

---

[54] See "Official Language: Policy and Implementation" and "Language Associations: Organizational Pattern" in Das Gupta, *Language Conflict and National Development*, 159–224. Chapter 1 briefly covered the Hindi–Urdu controversy of the nineteenth century and references the literature on this subject; perhaps the single most comprehensive study is Dalmia, *Nationalization of Hindu Traditions*.

characterized the state's politics of the 1950s and 1960s could hardly have welcomed the introduction of a language explicitly presented as some high-water mark of Aryan cultural achievement. This demonstrates how the social-ideological context trumped the program for forging national linguistic unanimity. Secondly, the case of India shows how and why literature and its histories matter. Long senses of literary traditions inscribe the history of regions with cultural exemplars, a narrative biography of a language's past. These ideas are difficult to undo.

But because of its size, the decision to administer a federal system with states drawn along lines of language communities, and considerable efforts to incorporate the work of the many language associations as effective arms of language policy, perhaps India cannot offer the most appropriate comparison for the language policy decisions taken by Pakistan. For that, we should look instead at the historical experience of Indonesia, the emergence of its national language and the role it has played, and the language ideology that has produced the opposite effects from those we have seen in Pakistan.

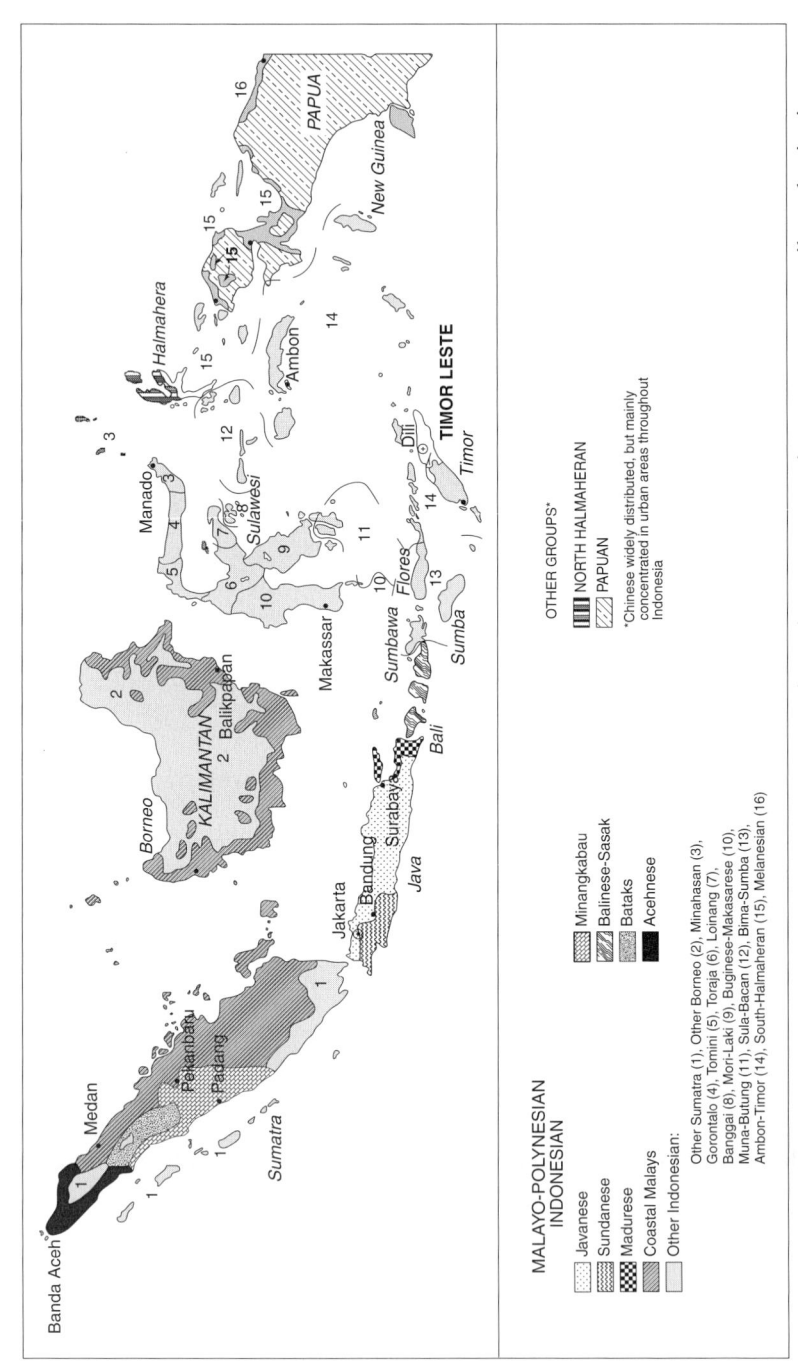

Map 5 Ethnolinguistic map of Indonesia. Names and boundary representation are not necessarily authoritative.

9 Religion, nation, language

> We the sons and daughters of Indonesia uphold as the language of unity the Indonesian language.
>
> Part three of the 1928 Sumpah Pemuda, the "Youth Pledge" of Indonesia's young nationalists

What makes a language national, beloved, and a force for unity? This question has been answered most typically with long disquisitions on civilizational history and the unique role of language and culture in evidencing a people's force on earth. In 1928, the youth nationalists at the vanguard of the early independence movement for the Dutch East Indies chose to invoke the "Indonesian language" as a central tenet of their movement. Yet by the time of Independence in 1945 – seventeen years *after* the youth pledge had identified Bahasa Indonesia as a core unifier of the country's nationalism – a mere 4.9 percent of the population spoke it as a first language. In truth, the language identified as the language of national unity would have to be "developed" and propagated as a language, and with national reach, much after the moment at which it was held up as a national force. Through language planning, the modern Indonesian state created a language of unity that has indeed fulfilled the aspirations of the country's early advocates for freedom, and the story of independent Indonesia's efforts to make this language truly national stands as one of the most remarkable successes of modern nation-building in history.

The experience of the Indonesian language could not differ more from Pakistan's experience with Urdu, although both countries share a remarkable number of structural similarities. Where the previous chapter looked at language planning in India, and the results of the eventual decision to craft states along linguistic lines and abandon plans for Hindi to replace English, this chapter looks at the social successes of the Indonesian language as a force for unity in independent Indonesia. Despite a limited presence in the Dutch East Indies, Bahasa Indonesia indeed played a unifying role in the nationalist movement, and later, in knitting together the bewildering cultural diversity of this archipelago.

Indonesia has experienced separatist movements, notably in Aceh, Papua, and East Timor, but at no point has language ever been a focal point of complaint in the agitations. This case thus stands as an opportunity to compare effects of language policy decisions on national identity and citizens' acquiescence to the identity projected by the state, with virtually all other conditions similar to Pakistan.

This chapter builds in a more focused way at the politics of national language development in Indonesia, then returns to Pakistan by way of comparison. In conjunction with the previous case examining India, we can see how these three cases highlight how language ideology – at the very highest levels – plays a crucial role in determining whether a national language will spread easily, without protest, and how strongly it helps forge the national bond it is intended to create. Language ideology refers in its emphasis on the social construction of language to "the cultural system of ideas about social and linguistic relationship, together with their loading of moral and political interests."[1] This formulation, one predicated on belief rather than industrialization or print-capitalism, better captures the disjuncture we need to explain the "ardent populism" of "linguistic European nationalism" as it spread modularly, alongside the peculiar "Russifying policy-orientation" necessary to effect "official nationalism."[2]

The cases of Pakistan and Indonesia are particularly revealing when read alongside each other. Indonesia illustrates the most successful national language project perhaps in human history, and against demographic challenges very similar to those facing Pakistan. The explicit language ideological assumptions made by policymakers in both countries account for why Indonesia has experienced such great success with language propagation, in sharp contrast with Pakistan. The emblematic role of Urdu as a formal mark of Muslim-ness during the Pakistan movement was one important way the Muslim League could press their case against what appeared to be a quickly emerging popular Hindi-language public sphere with great majority support, and political demands of its own.[3] But this was true only in the Gangetic plain regions. As we saw in the first three chapters, when the Pakistani nation-state sought to present Urdu as the natural and exclusive emblem of the Muslim nation of the Indian subcontinent, investing the idea of the language with a peculiar religious sacredness, this claim would pragmatically dissociate

---

[1] Quote from Judith Irvine, "When Talk Isn't Cheap: Language and Political Economy," in *American Ethnologist* 16, 255. Cited in Woolard, "Introduction: Language Ideology as a Field of Inquiry," 4. For more on language ideology see Chapter 1.
[2] Anderson, *Imagined Communities*, 113.
[3] See Rai, *Hindi Nationalism*; Rai, *A House Divided*; Robinson, *Separatism among Indian Muslims*.

the literary traditions central to Pakistan's regional languages from the realm of faith. In sharp contrast, Indonesia's national language planners explicitly crafted Bahasa Indonesia as a uniquely modern instrument of expression, one without a deep past, literally "constructed" (*pembangun*) as one might build a gleaming skyscraper to signal an ascendant national modernization. One was a religion, the other a science. That the former policy contributed substantially to East Bengal's 1971 secession, one effect of which was genocide,[4] whereas the latter policy produced a language widely described as a sort of national glue against which protests have been "surprisingly rare"[5] should demonstrate the relevance as well as urgency of this chapter's focus.

Indonesia

The similarities between Pakistan and Indonesia are so striking that one wonders why the two rarely received sustained attention in a comparative fashion. Born within two years of each other – Pakistan in 1947 and Indonesia in 1945/49[6] – the two countries share a number of common features. Prior to 1971, both countries were nearly the same size in population terms: Pakistan had seventy-five million people in 1951, compared to Indonesia's eighty-four million in the same year.[7] Since Pakistan's truncation in 1971, Indonesia has been much more populous, home to the largest Muslim population in the world, and Pakistan is now the second; recent population figures are 238 million for Indonesia (July 2008 estimate) and 172 million for Pakistan (July 2008 estimate). Both countries are overwhelmingly Muslim, 95 percent for Pakistan and 86 percent for Indonesia.[8] Both have been ruled by authoritarian regimes for the better part of their independent existence, and have long had highly centralized polities. The military has and continues to play a disproportionate role in politics, industry, and society in both countries.

---

[4] Estimates of those killed in 1971 range from one to three million.
[5] Webb Keane, "Public Speaking: On Indonesian as the Language of the Nation," *Public Culture* 15, no. 3 (Fall 2003): 505.
[6] Indonesia received independence from Japanese occupation in 1945, but formally attained sovereignty in 1949 after a four-year tussle for regional power between the British and the Dutch. Indonesians consider 1945 their year of independence.
[7] Earliest figures for Pakistan are from the 1951 census: Central Statistical Office Government of Pakistan, *25 Years of Pakistan in Statistics* (Karachi: Government of Pakistan, 1972), 4. For Indonesia at independence, see Table 1 of Peter O. Way, *Detailed Statistics on the Urban and Rural Population of Indonesia: 1950–2010* (Washington, DC: US Bureau of the Census (Center for International Research), 1984), 13.
[8] Statistics from US Central Intelligence Agency. "The World Factbook 2007." (CIA, 2007), www.cia.gov/cia/publications/factbook/index.html. Pakistan's Muslims are approximately 75 percent Sunni, 20 percent Shi`a – a schism which has its own ongoing conflict.

Up until the mid 1970s, both countries had similar human development indicators in terms of per capita income, although they would diverge from that point forward. Indonesia's economic miracle began to take off with the discovery of oil in the early 1970s, but really took flight in the 1980s. Indeed, it was not until 1986 that President Suharto would make primary education universal in the country – and by now a vast gulf of literacy and education separates Indonesia from Pakistan. Both countries are home to bewildering ethnolinguistic diversity, yet within that diverse mosaic both have a dominant ethnic group comprising approximately half of the population: Punjab's 56 percent of Pakistan,[9] and the Javanese 40 percent of Indonesia. And despite this, both chose national languages which were the first languages of only a tiny percentage of the population: at independence, native Bahasa Indonesia speakers comprised only 4.9 percent of Indonesia's population;[10] native Urdu speakers comprised no more than 3 percent of Pakistan (East and West wings) at the same moment.[11] Most importantly for the argument here, Indonesia sought to use Bahasa Indonesia to create a cohesive Indonesian identity, envisioned as secular – whereas Pakistan sought to use Urdu to forge a cohesive identity envisioned as Islamic. Indonesia's efforts to propagate its national language have by all accounts achieved successes that make Pakistan's troubled experience with Urdu all the more striking, given the two countries' broad similarities. Thus Indonesia's experience with national language formation is the most obvious counterfactual comparison to Pakistan.

Bahasa Indonesia

Bahasa Indonesia is the state-developed form of a lingua franca, Malay, which had developed across the sea trade routes in Southeast Asia. Malay is widely used in southeast Asia, for in another national version (Bahasa Melayu) it is the national language of Malaysia, Brunei Darussalam, Singapore (where it is one of the four national languages), and it is in use though without official patronage in two southern provinces of Thailand.[12] Malay is a member of the Austronesian language

---

[9] We should recall here that at Partition, East Bengal comprised the numeric majority of Pakistan's population, with 56 percent, and Punjab at that time accounted for 22 percent. See Chapter 2.
[10] Anton Moeliono, *Language Development and Cultivation: Alternative Approaches in Language Planning*, trans. Kay Ikranagara, Pacific Linguistics, Series D, No.68, *Materials in Languages of Indonesia (No.30)* (Canberra: Department of Linguistics, Research School of Pacific Studies, The Australian National University, 1986), 27.
[11] Slade, "Census of Pakistan, 1951," 68.
[12] "Bahasa" of course means "language," so the respective names are "Indonesian language" and "Malaysian language." Readers familiar with many of the modern

family, as are many of the other major Indonesian languages, such as Javanese, Sundanese, Balinese, Batak. The region was deeply influenced by contact with Hinduism and Buddhism, reflected in the fact that up until the fifteenth century, Malay was written with a Sanskrit-derived script. Malay developed in a context in which Tamil, Arabic, Javanese, Chinese, Bengali, and Gujarati all interacted.[13] Islam came relatively late to the region, via traders in the fourteenth century, but its influence was quickly felt on the written language: between the fourteenth and nineteenth centuries, an Arabic-derived script called "Jawi" superceded the Sanskritic script.[14] With colonization by the Dutch (Dutch East Indies) as well as the British (British Malaya, now Malaysia and Singapore), in the eighteenth and nineteenth centuries a roman alphabet ("Romi") as well as the first dictionaries were developed for this lingua franca, a preoccupation in particular of Dutch philologist-colonizers.[15] The roman script is now the official script in use today for Malay/Indonesian.

As a lingua franca, Malay was used by traders and those who encountered them in the region. Its minimalist grammatical features (in its lingua franca form) bear witness to this: for example, verbs have no tense conjugation, there is no gender nor plural forms of nouns (plurals are indicated by reduplication), word order is variable, and there are no honorific forms. This sets Malay apart from Javanese, which has very highly structured hierarchy embedded in the language itself.[16] In Javanese, it is not simply that one adds honorific titles or particles to words; rather, there are distinct modes of speaking that depend on the speaker's place in relation to the addressee.

While Malay was a commerical language which spread – again, in a lingua franca form – due to merchant travels, we should also note that Old Malay was the language of state of the great Sriwijaya Empire, centered in southern Sumatra. The much more populous island of Java, however, was the site of the region's literary giant, Javanese. Javanese

languages of South Asia or Sanskrit will recognize the word's origins in Sanskrit "bhāṣā."

[13] For example, the colonial scholar Sir Richard Winstedt's conclusion with respect to the many divergent versions of the Ramayana in the region that "the source was itself an oral version and that into it had flowed the flotsam and jetsam from the east, the west and the south-west of continental India." Sir Richard Winstedt, *A History of Classical Malay Literature* (Petaling Jaya: Malaysian Branch of the Royal Asiatic Society, 1991[1940]), 27.

[14] On Indonesian scripts see Ann Kumar and John McGlynn, *Illuminations: the Writing Traditions of Indonesia* (Jakarta; New York: Lontar Foundation and Weatherhill, 1996).

[15] John Hoffman, "A Foreign Investment: Indies Malay to 1901," *Indonesia* 27 (1979): 77–92.

[16] See Joseph Errington, *Structure and Style in Javanese* (Philadelphia: University of Pennsylvania Press, 1988); Siegel, *Solo in the New Order*.

was an important language of the Majapahit kingdoms, and it includes extensive poetic traditions, performing arts, and written epics. Javanese managed to survive and indeed flourish from the impact of Sanskrit and Pali influence (early Hindu and Buddhist periods) as well as the sacred language of Arabic when Islam gradually became the dominant religion of the archipelago from the fourteenth century onwards. The famed Javanese epics, *Ramayana* and *Mahabharata*, are of course drawn from the eponymous Indian Sanskrit literary works, the performance of which comprises the primary form of popular theater in its puppet-theater forms in Java.

Given the rich cultural heritage of Javanese, and particularly the fact that a plurality of Indonesians were and are Javanese, it is perhaps surprising that this lingua franca, Malay, would become the national language. But it was a purposeful choice, one made by those challenging colonial authority. Nearly all narratives – oral or written – of Indonesia's independence struggle and the development of Bahasa Indonesia as the national language invoke the *Sumpah Pemuda*, the 1928 Youth Pledge, as a moment that crystallized the fusion of the anti-colonial nationalist movement with a vision of civic national belonging and a singular language:

Firstly: We the sons and daughters of Indonesia declare that we belong to one fatherland, Indonesia.

Secondly: We the sons and daughters of Indonesia declare that we belong to one nation, the Indonesian nation.

Thirdly: We the sons and daughters of Indonesia uphold as the language of unity the Indonesian language.[17]

This Youth Pledge, taken by a group of nationalists at the second Youth Congress on October 28, 1928, forms the commemorative basis for the Indonesian nation, now celebrated annually. This Congress – in the same way that *Ekushe* functions for Bangladesh – marks the beginning of the historical narrative of the Indonesian nation that culminates with its independence. Its significance is widely accepted, and the story of the Second Youth Congress is told and re-told today as the national point of origin. For our purposes, its significance lies in the fact that it instantiated an allegiance to a very new idea of a homeland, defined in national terms, and articulated as national through a single language. This pledge also gave the Malay language a new national name, Bahasa Indonesia, which served to inaugurate the twin trajectories of the nation and its language with one stroke. Most importantly, the Youth Congress

---

[17] Translated as given by Khaidir Anwar, *Indonesian: The Development and Use of a National Language* (Yogyakarta: Gadjah Mada University Press, 1980), 15.

chose a language for this national exercise that they knew had only shallow, but far more geographically widespread, roots in the region. It was the language of no one for all intents and purposes – but the young nationalists felt (with great foresight) that it offered the best opportunity to unify a disparate region into one with a larger sense of cohesion. The Indonesian nation and its national language were literally willed into being.[18]

But the Youth Pledge could hardly by invocation alone transform what was not yet an independent country into a nation-state with an Indonesian-language speaking population. In a remarkable example of nation-building and language development, both recursively fortifying the other, key intellectuals undertook the project of language modernization to *develop the Indonesian language such that it could become a vehicle of expression for a modern nation-state*. There is no better example of the language paradox than this.

Of course, two moments in the pre-Independence history had lain some of the groundwork for Indonesian to emerge with the possibility of becoming a national language. First, the Dutch had patronized Malay and their work in developing dictionaries and basic readers resulted in the systematization of bazaar Malay, or *brabbel-Maleisch*, into "school Malay," which then became the language of educated Indonesian elite.[19] It was, however, only used by those fortunate enough to attend the limited number of colonial schools (the number of Indonesians educated in Dutch was fewer still). Balai Pustaka, the colonial publishing house, offered short literary works in this emergent school Malay, while also publishing in Javanese and Sundanese. The nationalist intellectuals,

[18] See of course Anderson, *Imagined Communities*. But also: Benedict Anderson, "Language, Fantasy, Revolution," in *Making Indonesia: Essays on Modern Indonesia in Honor of George McT. Kahin*, ed. Lev and McVey (Ithaca: Southeast Asia Program, Cornell University, 1996); Benedict Anderson, *Language and Power* (Ithaca: Cornell University Press, 1990); Joseph Errington, "Indonesian('s) Authority," in *Regimes of Language*, ed. Kroskrity (Santa Fe: School of American Research Press, 2000); Joseph Errington, *Shifting Languages* (Cambridge: Cambridge University Press, 1998), 51–64; Ariel Heryanto, *Language of Development and Development of Language: the Case of Indonesia*, No. 86, Pacific Linguistics, Series D (Canberra: Department of Linguistics, Research School of Pacific Studies, The Australia National University, 1995); Webb Keane, "Knowing One's Place: National Language and the Idea of the Local in Eastern Indonesia," *Cultural Anthropology* 12, no. 1 (1997); Keane, "Public Speaking"; James T. Siegel, *Fetish, Recognition, Revolution* (Princeton: Princeton University Press, 1997).
[19] See Hoffman, "A Foreign Investment: Indies Malay to 1901." Professor Anton Moeliono, the former head of Indonesia's Pusat Bahasa (Language Center) and the intellectual inheritor of Alisjahbana's role as steward of the national language, believes that modern Indonesian grew out of school Malay, not from bazaar Malay. Interview, December 11, 2002. Also see Moeliono, *Language Development and Cultivation: Alternative Approaches in Language Planning*, 97–8n4.

however, sought something different than a school-gibberish, and began to create new reading materials in Indonesian that would "satisfy the demands for a more nationalistic literature."[20] Sutan Takdir Alisjahbana was the towering figure among these nationalists. His prolific writings – in English as well as in Indonesian – exemplify the spirit of modernist enthusiasm for the great project of new language-making as nation-making. High modernist ideals of systemization led to spelling reforms, the development of new vocabularies for new fields, and the emergence of literary magazines written in this new language. A mere glance at the titles of some of his many English-language writings readily illustrates his focus on the nexus of language, nation, and becoming modern: *The Concept of Culture and Civilization*; *Indonesia in the Modern World*; and "The Indonesian Language: By-product of Nationalism," to name a few.[21] In Indonesian, Alisjahbana would go on to found a new literary magazine in 1933, *Pujangga Baru* ("New Poet"), as well as take part in the writings which became known as the "cultural polemics," or *Polemik Kebudayaan*.

Secondly, the three years of Japanese occupation of Indonesia (1942–5), eliminated what had been the prestige relationship of Dutch to the archipelago by eliminating its use entirely and inaugurated a far greater rationalization of the Indonesian language than had previously been the case.[22] Since no one spoke or read Japanese, the most expedient language for the Japanese authority's administrative exercises – census, labor conscription, not to mention propaganda – was Indonesian.[23] These three short but apparently highly efficient years made deep inroads for Indonesian's spread.

[20] Anwar, *Indonesian: The Development and Use of a National Language*, 24.
[21] Sutan Takdir Alisjahbana, *The Concept of Culture and Civilization: Problems of National Identity and the Emerging World in Anthropology and Sociology*, published version of speech given at Symposium on New Social Thought, Cordova (April 18, 1985), organized by UN University, Tokyo edn (Jakarta: Dian Rakyat, 1989); Sutan Takdir Alisjahbana, *Indonesia in the Modern World*, trans. Benedict R. Anderson, English edn, *Basic Books – Congress for Cultural Freedom* (New Delhi: Prabhakar Padhya for the Congress for Cultural Freedom, 1961); Sutan Takdir Alisjahbana, *Indonesia: Social and Cultural Revolution*, 2nd edn, first published in English as "Indonesia in the Modern World," trans. Anderson, 1961 edn (London: Oxford University Press, 1966); Sutan Takdir Alisjahbana, *Indonesian Language and Literature: Two Essays*, *Cultural Report Series No. 11* (New Haven: Yale University Southeast Asia Studies, 1962); Sutan Takdir Alisjahbana, "The Indonesian Language: By-product of Nationalism," *Pacific Affairs* 22, no. 4 (December 1949); Sutan Takdir Alisjahbana, *Values as Integrating Forces in Personality, Society and Culture* (Kuala Lumpur: University of Malaya Press, 1966); Sutan Takdir Alisjahbana, ed., *The Modernization of Languages in Asia* (Kuala Lumpur: The Malaysian Society of Asian Studies, 1967).
[22] For example, see Alisjahbana, "By-product of Nationalism," 390.
[23] See Aiko Kurasawa, "Propaganda Media on Java Under the Japanese 1942–1945," *Indonesia* 44 (October 1987).

By the time of Indonesia's national independence, there appeared to be little contest or even question as to the language of the new nation-state, despite the fact that this country comprised of thousands of islands had nine languages with millions of speakers and hundreds of lesser-spoken languages. Sukarno's invented national ideology of *Pancasila* ("Five Principles"), the adoption of which was required by law for all institutions and associations in the country, counted among them the "unity of Indonesia," the elaboration of which invoked the 1928 Youth Pledge.[24] The entire month of October would become a nationally recognized month of commemoration, culminating in the annual celebration of the Youth Pledge each 28th of October. It was a confirmation of a situation yet to be realized, but apparently unobjectionably so. By comparison with India and Pakistan, Indonesian's uncontested emergence as a national language is something of a marvel and extraordinary in its impact. It was not an issue of protest, and throughout Indonesia's independent existence, language issues have been neither politicized nor the focus of violent conflict.[25]

That this new national language, known by all to be in fact in the process of "development" and contributing to the development of the nation at the same time, has met with widespread acceptance requires a closer look. How did this language, forged first as an informal lingua franca by traders, then shaped into a "school Malay" by the Dutch, later literally propagated throughout the country by the Japanese, finally become a language of state, science, and modern commerce? The answer to this question appears to lie in the purposeful creation and development of Indonesian as a language explicitly allied with modernity, and the vehicle for national as well as individual progress.

If Alisjahbana was representative of his time as well as the unique circumstances of the formation of modern Indonesia(n), we should take seriously the preoccupations his work embodied. Like Pakistan's intellectual Jamil Jalibi, and indeed mirroring the concerns voiced by Nehru, Patel, and Sitaramayya in India, Alisjahbana similarly saw deep-rooted regional languages as forces of division. Historian of language Khaidir Anwar writes that Alisjahbana's contributions to the "Cultural Polemics" showed his conviction that the region's old cultures would "promote divisive regionalism and hinder the growth of the spirit of national unity." Further, Alisjahbana would define the idea of Indonesian-ness as "the will which emerges in the twentieth century among these millions of

---

[24] On Pancasila and its deployment by the major institutions of the Indonesian state, see Douglas E. Ramage, *Politics in Indonesia* (New York: Routledge, 1995).
[25] Jacques Bertrand, "Language Policy and the Promotion of National Identity in Indonesia," in *Fighting Words*, ed. Brown and Ganguly (2003), 264.

population to unite into a single nation, and through that create unity to strive together to secure a rightful position beside other nations."[26]

In another passage from an early essay of the "Cultural Polemics," Alisjahbana fully spelled out a vision of cultural and linguistic rupture which he envisioned as the key to forging a new Indonesia:

> Indonesia, being the ideal of the young generation, is not a continuation of [the] Mataram [kingdom], not a continuation of the Banten kingdom, not the kingdoms of Minangkabau or Banjarmasin. Likewise, in the perspective of this [young Indonesia], Indonesian culture cannot possibly be a continuation of the Javanese culture, the continuation of the Malay culture, the continuation of the Sundanese culture, or any other cultures.[27]

This idea of a new nation, with its new language conceptualized as part of the process of becoming modern/young, a discontinuity from the traditional/old, infused the nationalist movement. Of course, embedded in such an idea is the acknowledgment that the traditional/old is the situation actually in existence and that becoming modern/young would require some re-engineering. The challenges, then, would be to "develop" the language into one suitable for modern life, while simultaneously promulgating the language nationally so that it could be understood. Indeed, in 1949 Alisjahbana acknowledged this challenge: "the Indonesian people must learn as quickly as possible to think and to express themselves fluently in their national tongue, so that there may shortly appear in Indonesian a great variety of books and magazines dealing with all aspects of modern life."[28] And of course, success in such a venture depends upon acceptance of the language for this role by millions of the new country's citizens.

National language development, regional languages, and propagation

Actual language policy was not as dismissive of regional languages and cultural traditions as Alijshabana may have wished; the "bahasa daerah" or "regional languages" have had limited but present patronage. While Indonesian has constitutional status as the language of state, article thirty-six of the constitution also contains a clause mandating that regional languages be "respected and preserved." The Ministry of Education and Culture in 1952 issued a directive "To foster and develop Indonesian

---

[26] Anwar, *Indonesian: The Development and Use of a National Language*, 24. Alisjahbana quote cited from Sutan Takdir Alisjahbana, *Polemik Kebudajaan* in A. Kartahadimadja, ed. Djakarta, 1954, 26.
[27] Translated by Ariel Heryanto; cited in Heryanto, *Language of Development*, 14.
[28] Alisjahbana, "By-product of Nationalism," 392.

language and literature, including regional languages and literatures."²⁹ In the education system, regional languages can be used as the medium of instruction up to the third grade, though this is only possible for regions in which there is a local homogeneity of language. South Sulawesi, for example, a multilingual region, must use Indonesian instead of any of the regional languages. Given the hundreds of languages in use in Indonesia, many of which have few speakers, the compromise formula produced supports a mere few regional languages for these early years of primary education: Javanese, Sundanese, Madurese, Batak, Balinese, Acehnese, and/or Buginese, Minang, Banjarese, and Sasak.³⁰

Over the course of decades, the Indonesian state has put its full moral and financial muscle behind developing the Indonesian language. It now has a huge scientific and technical vocabulary, fully systematized grammar explicated in grammar books, and comprehensive dictionaries. This process of "developing" Indonesian has been a state project at the very highest of levels. The national language institute, Pusat Bahasa, is an important department within the Ministry of Education that carries out language development work (such as creating new words and preparing dictionaries) as well as language propagation throughout the country.³¹ The Pusat Bahasa, created in 1975, is the organizational successor to a number of different language institutions, including Balai Pustaka, Balai Bahasa, and Lembaga Bahasa Nasional, all of which had been actively creating and furthering this language for decades.

Most fascinating is how this exemplary language project has actually managed to produce not only a national language now widely spoken and written throughout the country, animating new kinds of literature (Chairil Anwar's modernist free verse in the 1950s, or the current Sastri Wangi writers, for example) but marking successes not seen in comparable situations such as India or Pakistan. The Indonesian language has not been the site of protest – in fact, Indonesian remains (unironically) the language utilized even by restive areas such as West Papua.³² The remarkable and widespread adoption of Indonesian over the course

---

²⁹ Anwar, *Indonesian: The Development and Use of a National Language*, 80.
³⁰ See Bertrand, "Language Policy and the Promotion of National Identity in Indonesia," 279; Moeliono, *Language Development and Cultivation*, 37, 100n19. The census data breaks out population counts for Javanese, Sundanese, Madurese, Batak, Minang, Balinese, Buginese, and Banjarese.
³¹ Pakistan's Muqtadira Qaumi Zaban, or National Language Authority, is a department of the Cabinet Division; in this regard it should be noted that it was founded only in 1979. Interview with MQZ Chairman Fateh Mohammad Malik, October 15, 2002.
³² Danilyn Rutherford, *Raiding the Land of the Foreigners: The Limits of the Nation on an Indonesian Frontier* (Princeton: Princeton University Press, 2002).See also Danilyn Rutherford, "Frontiers of the lingua franca: Malay, Meeforsch, and the Papuan Soul" (Unpublished manuscript, n.d.).

Table 1 *The reach of Indonesian in Indonesia.*

Year	% as first language	% able to speak it
1971	–	40
1980	12	48 (61 including native speakers)
1990	12/15*	68 (80–3 including native speakers)
1995	14/18†	68 (82–6 including native speakers)

Sources: Table 14 in Sensus Penduduk 1971; "A Brief Note on 1980 Population Census" in Sensus Penduduk 1980 p. 24; Table 59 in Peter O. Way, *Detailed Statistics on the Urban and Rural Population of Indonesia*; Tables 15.9 and 19.3 in Sensus Penduduk 1990; Tables 15.9 and 19.3 in Survei Penduduk Antar Sensus 1995 (Supas95).

Notes
* A discrepancy regarding the 1991 figures: two separate tables enumerate population by mother tongue. One lists 19m as native Indonesian speakers, versus another which gives 24m as speaking Indonesian in the home.
† The same discrepancy appears in the 1995 figures, as shown above.

of the country's independence can be partly gauged through census statistics which assess both the percentages of Indonesians speaking Indonesian as a mother tongue as well as those able to speak it as an additional language.

As the figures above show, statistics about citizens' ability to speak Indonesian bears out the narrative that Indonesia's national language has made significant strides throughout the country, literally becoming the language of a nation and thus the national language. That this has taken place without conflict is all the more remarkable. Many observers rightly point to the Indonesian government's public policy emphasis on primary education from the 1970s forward as the key to this success; this strikes me as a necessary yet not sufficient explanation. We should recall here that language conflicts in our two comparative cases, India and Pakistan, were already underway from independence until around 1965, in the case of India, and continuing further in the case of Pakistan. Indonesians simply did not protest the new national language during this same period, even prior to the advent of Suharto's universal primary education program. How can we understand this divergence?

That the Indonesian language has been crafted by the Indonesian state as a tool of modernity has been explicated at length by Ariel Heryanto.[33]

[33] James Siegel's remarkable book, *Fetish, Recognition, Revolution*, explores at length the idea of Indonesian as a fetish of modernity; his analysis is focused on new literatures and the imagination of the nation through this new language.

Table 2 *Number of terms coined by subject area in Indonesian.*

Sciences	148,593
Economic activities	69,203
Life sciences	61,598
"Exact" sciences	49,068
Human sciences	37,927
State (administration)	35,295
Technical	27,293
Arts	14,054
Daily life	12,281
Economy	9,366
Phil/religion	5,625

Source: Adapted from Table 9 *bis*, "Les Termes de la Komisi Istilah. Production Par Domaine (Masses Principales)" in Jérôme Samuel, "Modernisation Lexicale et Politique Terminologique: Le Cas de l'Indonesien" (PhD thesis, Institut National des Langues et Civilisations Orientales, 2000), 191C.

In an insightful essay linking the "language of development" and the "development of language," Heryanto demonstrates how in the case of Indonesia, the ethos of modernization theory aimed quite literally to erect the new nation a new language, just like any other project of development. Heryanto's keywords approach, drawing upon Raymond Williams, illustrates the technocratic overlay, the sense of engineering involved in the creation of whole new vocabularies and Indonesian-language terms for the bureaucratic demands of modern life.[34]

But it is not just a few words: thoroughly supporting Heryanto's work in a quantitative way is the recent dissertation by Jérôme Samuel on the lexical and political terminology modernization of the Indonesian language. His data provides an astonishing lens into how, precisely, a language could bear the idea of modernity. In the early work of the "Komisi Istilah," or "Term Commission," they quite literally coined an arsenal of new words for technological spheres of life, far outweighing new coinages for the realm of the humanities.

In a non-trivial sense, it is as if the act of speaking in Indonesian came to inscribe modernity directly on the speaker as the terminology and vocabulary expanded. The heavy unfamiliarity of the new language as

---

[34] Heryanto, *Language of Development*. Relatedly, see also Ariel Heryanto, "The Development of 'Development'," *Indonesia* 46 (October 1988).

it was developed has of course been remarked upon elsewhere – notably Benedict Anderson's observation that the new Indonesian began taking on the structural role of high Javanese with its formal qualities and complicated vocabulary.[35] But I think it is important to note here that it was through Indonesian that Indonesian citizens gained access to the machineries of modernity. This is a large point of difference with India and Pakistan, where the technical spheres of life remain English-language even today.

So we have the remarkable creation of a utopian language project, one which goes hand-in-hand with the creation of a new nation that arguably had little else to hold it together. Through the creation of a new national utopia, Indonesian could allow citizens to participate in the national public sphere. Notably, the fact that Indonesian was forged, constructed, with a biography as modern as the state itself, permitted the language to coexist ideologically alongside the languages and cultural traditions indigenous to the country, and without threatening either their claims to historical truth or their aesthetic pleasures. In Anderson's words, "Indonesian is a language without extensive historical memories and connotations to it. It looks to the future." Indigenous literary traditions were not displaced by a new national canon, for there was no such thing. The country has continued to feature indigenous aesthetic traditions as national culture: Javanese shadow puppetry, the primary performance of the Indic epics, has remained an important art form signifying Indonesia's composite literary and cultural history, broadcast on state television.[36] Most importantly, the Indonesian language as a language of a resolutely statist secular project furthermore offered no symbolic competition to indigenous cultures as a sine qua non of regional faith.[37] I locate this point of divergence with Pakistan's national language project as the single most important, for it is here – at the level of ideology – we can best understand why millions of people would accept a new language as "national" in Indonesia, but in Pakistan, the very same exercise produced conflict. Speaking Indonesian never required Indonesian

---

[35] Benedict Anderson has remarked on the parallel opposition of Jakarta slang versus formal, developed Indonesian as mirroring the relationship of Javanese *ngoko* (low) and *krama* (high). Benedict Anderson, "The Languages of Indonesian Politics," *Indonesia*, no. 1 (April 1966): 107. At the time of his writing, 1966, Indonesian's spread throughout the country was still limited; Anderson noted that it was "by no means the everyday language of more than a tiny segment of the population."

[36] In the past decade it has become a matter of public discussion that Indonesians increasingly cannot understand the language of this tradition. See, for example, the cartoon in Errington, "Indonesian('s) Authority," 223.

[37] Anderson, "The Languages of Indonesian Politics," 105.

citizens to abjure their cultural history, nor their sense of faith – while speaking Urdu ideologically reminded Bengali, Punjabi, Sindhi, Siraiki, Pashto, and Balochi speakers (among others) that the national language implicitly displaced their cultural and regionally-specific Islamic pasts. To speak Indonesian and speak the nation was like adding a veneer; what lay beneath remained unharmed. To speak Urdu and speak the nation, in marked contrast, required an unmooring of the ethnic self from the past.

Becoming national

There is, however, no getting around two interrelated facts: first, the language which animated the *idea* of Indonesian national unity was clearly not actually a national language in the sense of one spoken and understood by the majority of citizens, at least not for several decades. In Herderian terms, the paradox of the situation was that the national genius existed without the language to evidence it. Second, those who agitated for this twin package of the nation and its language were clearly the educated elite – in the case of Indonesia, a far more rarified segment of society than in India. Thinking comparatively, we can see how this curious disjuncture was true as well for Pakistan as it was for India. The disjuncture forces us to acknowledge the prominent role of intellectuals in the "articulation of the nation," to follow Ronald Grigor Suny and Michael Kennedy.[38]

And the corollary to this acknowledgment reinforces the observations resulting from the case of Punjab. In an important and undeniable way, the "national language" could not possibly have been the vehicle for mobilizing the masses or even creating a widespread simultaneous national imagination. The imagined communities of Indonesians, Indians, Pakistanis, and indeed Punjabis, can be seen as a series of translated negotiations not necessarily unified through print capitalism. In the three cases we have seen here – not outliers, or anomalous cases but rather the most important postcolonial movements of the twentieth century – the fact is unavoidable that literacy levels were low, and the mass public was comprised of many different language speakers. (We might, in fact, be better off positing a series of "partial publics" rather than any mass public.)

While print capitalism as a new form of communication allowed greater connection and a sense of simultaneity to emerge – there

---

[38] See Suny and Kennedy, *Intellectuals and the Articulation of the Nation*.

is no disputing this point – we must acknowledge that these three independence movements, movements that envisioned nations that had never before existed, were able to convert the masses who did not actually read. This suggests that the "meme" of national consciousness can indeed coalesce through oral communication, public addresses, and other forms of non-print communication that can take place in multiple, even mixed, language forms.

Though this is a negative inference from the available evidence, we do find traces of the past that point to this very conclusion. Iqbal's 1930 address to the All-India Muslim League – the address in which he presented the idea of autonomous Muslims regions – was delivered in English, and translated afterwards for those who did not understand. Documentary eyewitness reports of Jinnah's address in Lahore during the 1940 annual meeting of the Muslim League records him speaking to the crowd in English, then followed by someone to translate his speech, the Lahore Resolution, into Urdu. So too does there appear to have been an always-already process of translation mediating the early nationalist movement in Indonesia. Indeed, in Pramoedya Ananta Toer's magnificent "Buru Quartet" of historical novels, one senses a constant interplay of languages throughout.[39] Dutch, Malay, Javanese, even Chinese – the foregrounding of language's many levels and many arenas of use in the biography of the nation, personified in the central character of Raden Mas Minke, points to complicated interrelationships that, if we cannot ascertain exactly what they were, certainly undermine any idea of a mass public sphere able to tap into nationalist enthusiasm and a simultaneous political space–time achieved through print-capitalism.

We need here to acknowledge that it has been historically possible to create a sense of national belonging – through the work of the imagination to be sure, but through vectors not limited to the printed world of the national language. Crucial to the acceptance of this imagination is the ability of the national language project to achieve acceptance, for only then can such a great experiment fulfill its national writ. As we saw with Pakistan, the ideological interference of the national language project with the deeply felt values of regional language traditions halted this process in the case of Bengal, and in fact led to conflict in nearly every other province of the truncated state. But with Indonesia, the complementary language ideology offered by Bahasa Indonesia did not conflict with regional language cultures. India, on the other hand, solved

---

[39] The language play would obviously be more apparent in the Indonesian original. See Pramoedya Ananta Toer, *This Earth of Mankind*; *Child of All Nations*; *Footsteps*; and *House of Glass*, all trans. Max Lane (New York: Penguin, 1996).

this problem by giving regional languages greater internal authority, and prescribing a nationwide multilinguality that ensured recognition for all. Indeed, in these three critical cases examined here, we can see how the national language emerged only as the product of official programs crafted to make national citizens learn to speak – like a state – and achieved national acceptance only when not in conflict with the local past.

10 Conclusion

> Pākistān kā matlab kyā? Lā ilāhā illallāh.
> What is the meaning of Pakistan? There is but one God, Allah.
> Qudratullah Shahab, "Pākistān kā matlab kyā?" *Shahābnāma* (1987)

The foregoing chapters have offered a set of interlocking discussions concerning the cultural logic of the nation and its language(s) in a paradigmatic country, Pakistan. We first examined, in Chapter 1, the impact of British colonization on this region of multilinguality, and saw how British assumptions about the isomorphic relationship of race and language led to the differentiation of an Indian lingua franca, Hindustani, into Hindi/Hindu and Urdu/Muslim languages. This process fed into religious reform movements in the latter part of the nineteenth century which sought to purify and in fact codify the practices of Hindu and Muslim Indians, creating firmer boundaries of religion as well as language from a previous sociology of boundaries that had been far "fuzzier."[1] This schismogenesis grew to such an extent that by the 1930s it became possible to advance a new idea about nationality, the "Two Nations Theory," which posited that Hindus and Muslims were separate nations which could not coexist in a single polity.

Regardless of the historical and empirical problems with that argument, the Two Nations Theory succeeded politically. With the departure of the British, India achieved independence but at a huge price: the carving of a two-winged nation-state to be a home for the Muslims of the Indian subcontinent, amidst a catastrophic loss of life and the displacement of millions. The territories which became Pakistan were the Muslim-majority regions of British India (East Bengal, Punjab, NWFP, Sindh, Baluchistan) and the princely states in the contiguous territories, excepting Kashmir. But Pakistan's emergence into the world of nation-states took place against an assumption of cultural and linguistic national consciousness which located this new nation's historical narrative primarily in lands which remained in India. This historical narrative

---

[1] Kaviraj, "Writing, Speaking, Being."

privileged the literary traditions of the Urdu language as the exemplar and indeed repository of Muslim consciousness.

As Chapters 2 and 3 explored, right from the very start, the assumption that Urdu by right should be the national language of this new country resulted in conflict, often of a violent nature. National education and language policies were designed explicitly to shape this new country into one of cultural and linguistic uniformity in the face of all evidence to the contrary. Early policymakers were very concerned that their bid to create a new nation would be invalid, indeed illegitimate, without a national culture and a national language to evidence its own existence. This circuitous logic resulted in, on the one hand a national narrative which asserted the age-old nature of this unitary nation, while on the other simultaneously took steps to carve it out of a reality of heterogeneity. Pakistan's leaders declared Urdu the national language, a primary marker of this civilizational heritage, despite the fact that it was the first language of no more than three percent of the country's overall population.

But effecting the reality of the national language required un-making regional language practices, in an important sense. Because the national language was twinned with the idea of the Muslim nation, regional languages were pragmatically demoted to a status of somehow less than Islamic, at least as authorized by the state. Language-based disputes, even conflicts, took place in East Bengal, Sindh, and the Northwest Frontier Province. Later a Siraiki movement in southern Punjab stated its case within the nation. Each of these conflicts represented groups at the periphery of power and national consciousness arguing for greater inclusion. In the case of East Bengal, despite comprising the numerical majority of the country, strongly held prejudices against the Bengali language prevented it from attaining effective national language status alongside Urdu. Language was not the only grievance East Bengal had against the center, to be sure – and by the time of East Bengal's secession and formation of Bangladesh in 1971, Bengalis could enumerate economic, defense, legislative, and political disparities between their East Wing and the West. But the way Bangladesh commemorates its national history is by celebrating the martyrdom of Bengali language activists. The memory of that conflict now circulates language as its primary marker.

Alongside these tears in the fabric of the national narrative from the margins, we also found the slow emergence of a Punjabi language movement, one which makes no arguments about secession or political dispensation, but instead makes many arguments about the primacy of Pakistan's regional languages, including Punjabi, to a sense of "national subjectivity." Chapters 4 and 5 looked in detail at the Punjabiyat movement in its elite and popular forms. This language movement, unfolding from within the very heart of the region long portrayed as the ethnic chauvinist, the cultural and political hegemon of the country, cannot be easily dismissed as the instrumental front for a bid to gain greater political power. Though this movement appears formally like an ethnonationalism, it makes no political claims other than a desire to "restore" Punjabi to its rightful place in the nation.

One of the most intriguing, and puzzling, aspects of the Punjabiyat movement is its emphasis on forging a literary culture and writing new histories from the perspective of Punjab. This effort explicitly draws upon Punjabi language sources – historical, literary, and folk forms – to reclaim an ethnic biography of heroism from what they assert has been an unjust depiction of Punjab as a land of subservience. Strangely, the very fact that this movement takes as a primary goal the expansion of a Punjabi-language literary sphere serves to underscore the fact that the circulation of such ideas about the necessity of the Punjabi language to the ethnic self has not been taking place through a textual corpus primarily in the Punjabi language – they seek to *develop* the Punjabi language in order to demonstrate its civilizational greatness. Once again, we find a pattern of circularity.

In addition, the fact that this effort has emerged from the province widely regarded as that commanding economic and political power, not to mention the largest population, inverts the generally-held assumption that language politics are instrumental proxies for the pursuit of formal *power* – typically political and economic. The Punjab case demonstrates that a language nationalism can be motivated by the pursuit of symbolic capital accumulation as an end in itself.

Given the emphasis on the past, and the politics of history that characterize these movements, Chapter 6 traced the state policy planning process that crafted a history disconnected from the territory of the new country through Pakistani state documents. The chapter showed how efforts to "Islamize" the national past were not instituted during the Zia era alone, contrary to now-received wisdom, but rather were an ongoing process beginning with the country's birth. As a result, the unmooring of regional pasts from their territory precipitated the growth of new regional histories, the emerging phenomenon studied in Chapter 7. Just as the Punjabiyat literary corpus crafted new literary forms to excavate figures from the Punjabi past as heroes for the present era, a corollary effort to revise national history from the regions is underway. In a sharp break with the state-projected national historical form, new region-focused revisionist histories seek the reincorporation of pre-Islamic eras of their land as a source of their cultural particularity – and of pride. Efforts focused on Punjab were examined in greater detail. If Choudhary Rahmat Ali's national narrative presented "The Dawn of History" as the moment of Arab invasion of Sindh in 712 CE, for example, a Punjabiyat counter-narrative reclaimed the Indus Valley civilizations from the murky depths of pre-history and even claimed the Hindu god Shiva as a son of the Punjabi soil. We saw how Punjabiyat heroes included the great Raja Poras, the warrior-king who, in 327 BCE, fought Alexander the Great and never lost his sense of dignity. Or Dulla Bhatti, the Punjabi who defied Mughal authority and as a result was portrayed in official narratives as a criminal, a traitor.

Each of these instances represents a case of literarily rescuing history from the nation, restoring a past deemed outside the history of faith, a past that has been marginal, even inimical to national consciousness. To "rescue history from the nation," the alternative narratives were drawn from literary traditions indigenous to Punjab and in the Punjabi language. That these literary traditions – whether oral or written – have over centuries maintained a particular consciousness of some kind of identity, the Punjabi identity, shows us why language matters. Though one of the most pliable aspects of human interaction, language also in an important way participates in cultural reproduction through literary traditions. The canon debates in Punjab – recalling the assertion that the Urdu poets are all officially taught, while a long roster of Punjabi poets are not "allowed admission" into schools in Pakistan's Punjab – show how a sense of self and history is linked to literary canons forged through language traditions over time. One corollary of this observation is that a narrow focus on language rationalization without taking into account deeper cultural memories, the product of cultural reproduction through literary canons, will miss aspects of why concerns about relative value and one's own symbolic capital matter at all.

Chapter 8 moved to examine the epochal differences in treatment of language and culture in colonization versus in the modern age of decolonization. The former, for all its faults, was informed by an idea that governance required familiarity with cultural traditions, conceptualized as multilingual. The latter sought to bring into being a uniformity to evidence political parity in the new world of nation-states – a modern world of science and practice in which state simplifications were the solution for the unruliness of contemporary existence. How the world's largest democracy resolved these issues was illustrative. As originally planned, Hindi was to assume the mantle of national language, to replace English, by 1965. Nehru objected to early proposals that India should delineate states with boundaries determined by language, which he argued would lead to the end of Indian national unity. But these plans were overturned by the country's realities. India's national language project ambitions were modified in the recognition that the ideological baggage of Hindi led to outright rejection, particularly in the south. India chose to abandon the project in favor of giving linguistic autonomy to its various regions through the Linguistic Provinces Reorganization. Contrary to early fears, the reorganization did not lead to the collapse of India's union but rather made it stronger.

Chapter 9 then offered a comparative analysis that highlighted the peculiar paradox of Indonesia's highly successful national language project under arguably the very same structural conditions obtaining in Pakistan. Though by now Indonesia has far and away provided much greater opportunities for primary education to its citizens with its universal primary education push, the two decades of independence prior to that education policy – one which made great strides in propagating Indonesian throughout the country, and perhaps could have been the site of conflict – were still remarkably free of language conflict. If we were to follow Gellner's thinking on industrialization and rising literacy creating greater awareness of difference, leading to nationalism, we still find no evidence of language protests against Indonesian over the course of the country's more literate and more industrialized past three decades. Language conflict has been absent, regardless of varying social conditions.

In sharp contrast, Pakistan's linguistic national biography has exhibited many instances of conflict in nearly all its regions, at many different points in the nation's history. Indonesians accepted the Indonesian language as the one which would be national, while in Pakistan Urdu has faced a variety of challenges. These divergent histories can be explained by looking more carefully at the language ideologies governing the national language projects in each country. Pakistan's effort chose to valorize one language as the bearer of religion, the nationally authorized conduit of the nation's Islamic past – a move which unhinged regional language traditions from their own practices of faith. Indonesia's language project, by contrast, explicitly framed the language as the bearer of modernity and the ideological or aesthetic competitor to no regional language. Just as ideology can create difference, it can also create the conditions for consociational existence.

Chapter 9 finally linked the national language biographies of India, Indonesia, and Pakistan back to an observation of a fundamental paradox in our theories of nationalism: by the very fact of their existence, these countries' national language projects underscored the reality that their reading publics were extremely limited, small in percentage terms, and always-already partial in the sense that there were multiple linguistic communities. Yet somehow, in some mysterious way, it had been possible prior to the creation of a mass national language to mobilize and establish mass nationalist independence movements. Ideas about nationalism and social belonging can travel, and quickly, via communicative modes of constant translation and oral/electronic means. This implies that national consciousness exists, in a sense, *beyond* language – even as it requires language, whether oral or written, to serve as a vector for its transmission.

While a unifying theory to understand this paradox of national consciousness remains elusive, I want to close with part of a biographical memoir from a noted Pakistani writer and civil servant to suggest some ways to think around the problem. This last portion of an essay by Qudratullah Shahab (1920–86) provides not only a glimpse into the language of nationalism in 1947, but as well a self-conscious questioning of what the mobilized idea of the nation, in this case Pakistan, had actually come to mean in a widespread form. Shahab was a member of the Indian Civil Service, who would later migrate to Pakistan, and his Urdu masterpiece, *Shahāb Nāma*, offered reflections on the experiences of his life. In one of his best-known essays in the memoir, "Pākistān kā Matlab Kyā?" ("What Is the Meaning of Pakistan?"), Shahab gives insight into what this new country meant for the masses. The essay opens with Shahab in Orissa, listening to the All-India Radio broadcast announcements of the Partition Plan on June 3, 1947, joined by his Kashmiri cook Ramzan and Bengali driver Roz Mohammad, who were "sitting glued to the radio." When it came time for Jinnah's speech, "Ramzan caressed the radio set with great love and devotion."

When the speeches had ended, Ramzan thanked Allah in all sincerity that such exalted English, Hindu, and Sikh people of such high positions together were making a Pakistan for the Muslims. "Ramzan, do you even know what the meaning of Pakistan is?" I asked. "Yes, Sir, absolutely. What does Pakistan mean? La ilaha illallah"[2] Ramzan rejoiced gleefully. "Do you know how it has been made?" I tried to prod him further. "Yes, Sir. I know. Absolutely. Simply this: la ilaha illallah. La ilaha illallah." Ramzan replied steadfastly.[3]

Ramzan's inability to connect political events unfolding before him with human actions, and indeed, his near-simpleton belief that the English, Hindus, and Sikhs were responsible, along with the grace of God, for Pakistan's birth, spurs Shahab into staying up half the night. He revisits

---

[2] "La ilaha illallah" is the first half of the *kalima*, the confession of faith in Islam. This phrase means "There is but one God, Allah."
[3] All translated from "Pākistān kā Matlab Kyā?" in Qudratullah Shahab, *Shahābnāma* (Lahore: Sang-e-Meel, 1987), 289–93.

dozens of events documented in his scrapbook clippings, as he thinks about the path that had led to Pakistan's emergence. His clippings take him through significant events in British India, from the 1857 war of independence, to Sir Sayyid's Aligarh movement, to Allama Iqbal's Allahabad address of 1930, to "An identity rising up in the form of a separate Muslim nation on religious, social, economic, cultural, civilizational and political bases." At that point Shahab's clippings turn to the perceived incompatibility of Hindus and Muslims – the Two Nations Theory – and what he sees as Congress's unwillingness to share power, and a "plan to keep Muslims, like an insignificant minority dependent on the compassion and mercy of the majority, forever under Hindu control." Shahab's reflections on these historic moments, all given as a call-and-response prompted by the phrase "Pākistān kā Matlab Kyā?" then ends with "The Muslim nation's unity, faith, and discipline during the time of the Pakistan Movement."

With half the night over, Shahab realizes that many more clippings remain in his scrapbook, but he has become tired. He begins humming the line of poetry from Asghar "Saudai" of Sialkot, the same line Ramzan the cook had been reciting gleefully earlier: *Pākistān kā matlab kyā? Lā ilāha illallah*. It leads him into a trance, a peaceful sleep, in which:

Even in my sleep, the emotional echo of "*Pākistān kā matlab kyā? Lā ilāha illallah*" kept swirling in my ears, and even for a moment my consciousness was not clouded with the worry that:

So what if your Mind proclaims "There is but one God"?
It matters little if your Heart and Soul are not Muslim.[4]

Shahab's essay presents us with his memory of the night of the "Partition Plan" announcement given over All-India Radio on June 3, 1947. This broadcast was one in which Lord Mountbatten announced that Congress and the Muslim League had not been able to come to an agreement on the Cabinet Mission Plan, and that the British had agreed to the transfer of power, and the partition of the country. With the publication of the multi-volume Jinnah Papers, it is possible to read Shahab's memoir against the actual text of the broadcasts made that evening, giving us the tools for a better historical anthropology of that moment of epistemic change. Most importantly, *the broadcasts were in English*.[5] As with

---

[4] The last couplet is a line from Iqbal. See *ibid*. Complete text translated from Shahab, *Shahābnāma*, 289–93.

[5] For the complete texts of the speeches given by Lord Mountbatten, Jawaharlal Nehru, and Mohammad Ali Jinnah, see *Pakistan in the Making: 3 June – 30 June 1947*, ed. Z. H. Zaidi, 7 vols., vol. II, *Quaid-i-Azam Mohammad Ali Jinnah Papers* (Islamabad: National Archives of Pakistan, 1994), 13–22.

all Jinnah's speeches, and as with Iqbal's 1930 address to the All-India Muslim League, so too was this one in English. It emanated from a small box, a radio, one which the Kashmiri cook Ramzan "caressed" as if it were invested with some special powers or significance – and in fact perhaps it was. A disembodied voice announced that the British would quit India and that a Pakistan would come into being, its shape dependent upon the outcome of votes cast by the Bengal and Punjab assemblies and a referendum in the NWFP – surely such an announcement, even if completely incomprehensible to someone like Ramzan, must have appeared to contain some special truth; his loving caress of the radio suggests a sort of recognition of the box's sacred message. But as Shahab describes, Ramzan's actual understanding of what Pakistan was going to mean hinged not on any appreciation for recent political struggles or ideas about power-sharing in an ethnically diverse confederation, but instead on a blunt notion of religious exclusivism divested of all other meaning. Worse yet, it had been reduced down to a slogan, a recitation of faith. Was that all the Pakistan Movement meant in a mass way? Shahab's ambivalent conclusion, his trance undisturbed by complicating thoughts, suggests that in fact the answer was yes, and with grave consequences to come.

Bibliography

Qaumī Zabān, February 16, 1961, 21.
"6 Points." *Pakistan Forum* **1**, no. 4 (1971): 8–9.
Abbas, Hassan. *Pakistan's Drift into Extremism: Allah, the Army, and America's War on Terror.* Armonk, NY: M.E. Sharpe, 2004.
Addleton, Jonathan S. "The Importance of Regional Languages in Pakistan." In *The Rise and Development of Urdu and the Importance of Regional Languages in Pakistan*, edited by M. Geijbels and Jonathan S. Addleton, 34–60. Murree: Christian Study Centre, 198–?.
Ahmad, Aijaz. "Some Reflections on Urdu." *Seminar* **359** (1989): 23–29.
―― "In the Mirror of Urdu: Recompositions of Nation and Community, 1947–65." In *Lineages of the Present: Political Essays*. Delhi: Tulika Press, 1993 [1996].
Ahmed, Akbar S. "The Politics of Ethnicity in Pakistani Society." *Asian Affairs* **21**, no. 1 (1990): 20–35.
Ahsan, Aitzaz. *The Indus Saga and the Making of Pakistan*. 3rd edn. Lahore: Nehr Ghar Publications, 2001 [1996].
Alam, Muzaffar. "The Culture and Politics of Persian in Pre-Colonial Hindustan." In *Literary Cultures in History: Reconstructions from South Asia*, edited by Sheldon Pollock. Berkeley and London: University of California Press, 2003.
―― *The Languages of Political Islam in India*. Indian edn, Permanent Black; US edn, Chicago: The University of Chicago Press, 2004.
―― "The Pursuit of Persian: Language in Mughal Politics." *Modern Asian Studies* **32**, no. 2 (1998): 317–49.
Ali, Choudhary Rahmat. "What Does the Pakistan National Movement Stand For?" Cambridge: Pakistan National Movement, 1942 [1933].
―― *Pakistan: The Fatherland of the Pak Nation*. 3rd edn. Cambridge: Pakistan National Liberation Movement, 1946 [1935].
Ali, Imran. *The Punjab under Imperialism, 1885–1947*. Princeton: Princeton University Press, 1988.
Ali, K. *A New History of Indo-Pakistan*. 2nd edn. Dacca: Ali Publications, 1968.
―― *A New History of Indo-Pakistan: Since 1526*. 3rd edn. Lahore: Aziz Publishers, 1977.
―― *A Study of Muslim Rule in Indo-Pakistan*. 3rd edn. Dacca: The Famous Publishers, 1963.

Alisjahbana, Sutan Takdir. *The Concept of Culture and Civilization: Problems of National Identity and the Emerging World in Anthropology and Sociology*. Published version of speech given at Symposium on New Social Thought, Cordova (April 18, 1985), organized by UN University, Tokyo edn. Jakarta: Dian Rakyat, 1989.

Indonesia in the Modern World. Translated by Benedict R. Anderson. English edn, *Basic Books – Congress for Cultural Freedom*. New Delhi: Prabhakar Padhya for the Congress for Cultural Freedom, 1961.

Indonesia: Social and Cultural Revolution. 2nd edn, first published in English as "Indonesia in the Modern World," translated by Benedict Anderson for Basic Books series of the Congress for Cultural Freedom, 1961 edn. London: Oxford University Press, 1966.

Indonesian Language and Literature: Two Essays, Cultural Report Series No. 11. New Haven: Yale University Southeast Asia Studies, 1962.

"The Indonesian Language: By-Product of Nationalism." *Pacific Affairs* **22**, no. 4 (1949): 388–92.

Values as Integrating Forces in Personality, Society and Culture. Kuala Lumpur: University of Malaya Press, 1966.

Alisjahbana, Sutan Takdir. ed. *The Modernization of Languages in Asia*. Kuala Lumpur: The Malaysian Society of Asian Studies, 1967.

Ambedkar, B. R. *Thoughts on Linguistic States*. Reprint edn. Aligarh: Anand Sahitya Sadan, 1989 [1955].

Amjad, Yahya. *Tārīkh-e-Pākistān: Qadīm Daur*. Lahore: Sang-e-Meel Publications, 1989.

Anderson, Benedict. *Imagined Communities*. 2nd edn. London and New York: Verso, 1991.

"Language, Fantasy, Revolution." In *Making Indonesia: Essays on Modern Indonesia in Honor of George Mct. Kahin*, edited by Daniel S. Lev and Ruth McVey, 26–40. Ithaca: Southeast Asia Program, Cornell University, 1996.

Language and Power: Exploring Political Cultures in Indonesia. Ithaca: Cornell University Press, 1990.

"The Languages of Indonesian Politics." *Indonesia*, no. 1 (1966): 89–116.

Anwar, Khaidir. *Indonesian: The Development and Use of a National Language*. Yogyakarta: Gadjah Mada University Press, 1980.

Appadurai, Arjun. "Number in the Colonial Imagination." In *Orientalism and the Postcolonial Predicament*, edited by Carol A. Breckenridge and Peter van der Veer, 314–39. Philadelphia: University of Pennsylvania Press, 1993.

Asani, Ali. "At the Crossroads of Indic and Iranian Civilizations: Sindhi Literary Culture." In *Literary Cultures in History: Reconstructions from South Asia*, edited by Sheldon Pollock. Berkeley: University of California Press, 2003.

Awan, M. J. *Tahrīk-e-Āzādī men Panjāb Kā Kirdār*. Islamabad: Modern Book Depot, 1993.

Ayres, Alyssa. "Language, the Nation, and Symbolic Capital: The Case of Punjab." *Journal of Asian Studies* **67**, no. 3 (August 2008): 917–46.

"Two Punjabs: A Cultural Path to Peace in South Asia?" *World Policy Journal* **22**, no. 4 (Winter 2006): 63–8.

Aziz, K. K. *The Murder of History in Pakistan.* Lahore: Vanguard, 1993.
Aziz, K. K. ed. *Complete Works of Rahmat Ali.* Vol. 1. Islamabad: National Commission on Historical and Cultural Research, 1978.
Balibar, Etienne. "The Nation Form: History and Ideology." In *Race, Nation, Class: Ambiguous Identities*, edited by Etienne Balibar and Immanuel Wallerstein, 86–106. London, New York: Verso, 1991 [1988].
Barth, Fredrik. *Ethnic Groups and Boundaries.* Boston: Little, Brown, 1969.
Baruah, Sanjib. *India Against Itself: Assam and the Politics of Nationality.* Philadelphia: University of Pennsylvania Press, 1999.
Bateson, Gregory. *Steps to an Ecology of Mind.* 2nd edn. New York: Ballentine Books, 1972.
Bauman, Richard, and Charles L. Briggs. "Language Philosophy as Language Ideology: John Locke and Johann Gottfried Herder." In *Regimes of Language: Ideologies, Polities, and Identities*, edited by Paul Kroskrity, 139–204. Santa Fe: School of American Research, 2000.
Bayly, C. A. *The Local Roots of Indian Politics: Allahabad 1880–1920.* Oxford: Clarendon Press, 1975.
Bennett Jones, Owen. *Pakistan: Eye of the Storm.* New Haven: Yale University Press, 2002.
Bertrand, Jacques. "Language Policy and the Promotion of National Identity in Indonesia." In *Fighting Words: Language Policy and Ethnic Relations in Asia*, edited by Michael E. Brown and Sumit Ganguly, 263–90. Cambridge: BCSIA and MIT Press, 2003.
Bourdieu, Pierre. *Language and Symbolic Power.* Translated by Gino Raymond and Matthew Adamson. Cambridge: Harvard University Press, 1991.
Brass, Paul R. "Elite Groups, Symbol Manipulation and Ethnic Identity among the Muslims of South Asia." In *Political Identity in South Asia*, edited by David Taylor and Malcom Yapp, 35–77. London: Curzon Press, 1979.
  Language, Religion and Politics in North India. Cambridge: Cambridge University Press, 1974.
Bregman, Jacob, and Nadeem Mohammad. "Primary and Secondary Education – Structural Issues." In *Education and the State: Fifty Years of Pakistan*, edited by Pervez Hoodbhoy, 68–91. Karachi: Oxford University Press, 1998.
Chatterjee, Partha. *The Nation and Its Fragments.* Princeton: Princeton University Press, 1993.
  "The Social Sciences in India." In *The Cambridge History of Science*, edited by Theodore Porter and Dorothy Ross, 482–97. Cambridge: Cambridge University Press, 2003.
Chaudhry, Dr. Muhammad Azam. *Tahrīk-e-Pākistān men̠ Panjāb Kā Kirdār.* Karachi: Royal Book Company, 1996.
Chaudhry, Nazir Ahmad. *Development of Urdu as Official Language in the Punjab (1849–1974), Punjab Government Record Office Publications.* Lahore: Government of Punjab (Directorate of Archives), 1977.
Cohen, Stephen P. *The Idea of Pakistan.* Washington, DC: Brookings Institution Press, 2004.

Cohn, Bernard S. "The Census, Social Structure, and Objectification in South Asia." In *An Anthropologist Among the Historians and Other Essays*, 224–54. New Delhi: Oxford India, 1987.
"The Command of Language and the Language of Command." In *Subaltern Studies IV*, edited by Ranajit Guha. Delhi: Oxford University Press, 1985.
Coll, Steve. *Ghost Wars: The Secret History of the CIA, Afghanistan, and Bin Laden, from the Soviet Invasion to September 10, 2001*. New York: Penguin, 2004.
Connor, Walker. *Ethnonationalism: The Quest for Understanding*. Princeton: Princeton University Press, 1994.
Constituent Assembly of India, Government of India. "Report of the Linguistic Provinces Commission." New Delhi: Government of India Press, 1948.
Crawley, William. "Sir William Jones: A Vision of Orientalism." *Asian Affairs* 27, no. 2 (1996): 163–76.
Dalmia, Vasudha. *The Nationalization of Hindu Traditions: Bharatendu Harischandra and Nineteenth-Century Banaras*. New Delhi: Oxford University Press, 1997.
Dani, Ahmad Hasan. "The Discovery of Pakistan." Review of Aitzaz Ahsan – The Indus Saga and the Making of Pakistan. *Dawn Magazine*, September 6, 1996, 6.
Daniel, E. Valentine. *Charred Lullabies: Chapters in an Anthropography of Violence*. Princeton: Princeton University Press, 1996.
Das Gupta, Jyotirindra. *Language Conflict and National Development*. Berkeley: University of California Press, 1970.
"Language Policy and National Development in India." In *Fighting Words: Language Policy and Ethnic Relations in Asia*, edited by Michael E. Brown and Sumit Ganguly, 21–50. Cambridge, MA: MIT Press, 2003.
Dave, Bhavna. "Politics of Language Revival: National Identity and State Building in Kazakhstan." Doctoral dissertation, Syracuse University, 1996.
Deshpande, Satish. "Imagined Economies: Styles of Nation-Building in Twentieth-Century India." *Journal of Arts and Ideas* 25–6 (1993): 5–36.
Dow, Alexander. *The History of Hindostan; Second Revised, Corrected and Enlarged Edition with a Prefix on Ancient India Based on Sanskrit Writings; Translated from Persian*. Reprint edn. 3 vols. New Delhi: Today and Tomorrow's Printers & Publishers, 1973 [1770].
Dua, Hans Raj. *Language Planning in India*. New Delhi: Harnam Publications, 1985.
Language Use, Attitudes and Identity among Linguistic Minorities (A Case Study of Dakkhini Urdu Speakers in Mysore). Edited by D. P. Pattanayak. Vol. 8, CIIL Sociolinguistics Series. Mysore: Central Institute of Indian Languages (CIIL), 1986.
Science Policy, Education, and Language Planning. Mysore: Yashoda Publications, 2001.
Duara, Prasenjit. *Rescuing History from the Nation*. Chicago: University of Chicago Press, 1995.
Eley, Geoff, and Ronald Grigor Suny, eds. *Becoming National*. Oxford: Oxford University Press, 1996.

Engineer, Asghar Ali. "Bangalore Violence: Linguistic or Communal?" *Economic and Political Weekly*, October 29, 1994, 2854–8.
Errington, Joseph. "Indonesian('s) Authority." In *Regimes of Language*, edited by Paul Kroskrity. Santa Fe: School of American Research Press, 2000.
Shifting Languages: Interaction and Identity in Javanese Indonesia. Cambridge: Cambridge University Press, 1998.
Structure and Style in Javanese: A Semiotic View of Linguistic Etiquette. Philadelphia: University of Pennsylvania Press, 1988.
Farani, Saeed Ahmad. *Panjābī Zabān Nahīn Maregī; Panjābī Kā Muqaddamah Panjāb Men [The Punjabi Language Will Never Die: The Case of Punjabi in Punjab]*. Jhelum: Punjabi Esperanto Academy, 1988.
Farishta, Mohammad Qasim. *Tārikh-e-Farishta*. Translated by Abdul Hai Khwaja. Urdu edn. 2 vols. Lahore and Karachi: Shaikh Ghulam Ali and Sons, 1962 [c.1607].
Faruqi, Shamsur Rahman. *Early Urdu Literary Culture and History*. Delhi: Oxford University Press, 2001.
Ferguson, Charles A. "South Asia as a Sociolinguistic Area." In *Dimensions of Sociolinguistics in South Asia. Papers in Memory of Gerald B. Kelley*, edited by Edward C. Dimock, Braj B. Kachru, and Bhadriraju Krishnamurti, 25–36. New Delhi, Bombay, and Calcutta: Oxford & IBH Publishing Co., 1992.
Fishman, Joshua A. *In Praise of the Beloved Language: A Comparative View of Positive Ethnolinguistic Consciousness*. Berlin and New York: Mouton de Gruyter, 1997.
Gal, Susan. "Bartok's Funeral: Representations of Europe in Hungarian Political Rhetoric." *American Ethnologist* **18**, no. 3 (1991): 440–58.
"Language and Political Economy." *Annual Review of Anthropology* **18** (1989): 345–67.
Gal, Susan, and Judith T. Irvine. "The Boundaries of Languages and Disciplines: How Ideologies Construct Difference." *Social Research* **62**, no. 1 (1995): 967–1001.
Gandhi, M. K. *Our Language Problem [Collected Writings, 1918–1948]*. Edited by Anand T. Hingorani. Pocket Gandhi Series, No. 13. Bombay: Bharatiya Vidya Bhavan, 1965.
Gankovskiy, Yu. V. "Ethnic Composition of the Population of West Pakistan." In *Pakistan: History and Economy*, edited by A. M. D'Yakov. Washington, DC: U.S. Joint Publications Research Service, 1961 [1959].
Gazdar, Mushtaq. *Pakistan Cinema 1947–1997*. Karachi: Oxford University Press, 1997.
Geertz, Clifford. "The Integrative Revolution: Primordial Sentiments and Civil Politics in the New States." In *The Interpretation of Cultures: Selected Essays by Clifford Geertz*, 255–310. New York: Basic Books, 1973.
Geijbels, M. "Urdu and the Pakistani National Language Issue." In *The Rise and Development of Urdu and the Importance of Regional Languages in Pakistan*, edited by M. Geijbels and Jonathan S. Addleton, 17–33. Murree: Christian Study Centre, 198–?.
Geijbels, M. and Jonathan S. Addleton, ed. *The Rise and Development of Urdu and, the Importance of Regional Languages in Pakistan*. Murree: Christian Study Centre, 198–?.
Gellner, Ernest. *Nations and Nationalism*. Ithaca: Cornell University Press, 1983.

Goindi, Farrukh Suhail. *Panjāb Kā Maslah: Depoliticization Aur Awāmī Tahrīk Kā Na Calnā*. Lahore: Jamhuri Publications, 1988.
Government of Indonesia, Biro Pusat Statistik. *Sensus Penduduk 1971*. Jakarta: Government of Indonesia, 1975.
Sensus Penduduk Indonesia 1980. Jakarta: Biro Pusat Statistik, 1982.
Sensus Penduduk Indonesia 1990. Jakarta: Biro Pusat Statistik, 1992.
Survei Penduduk Antar Sensus 1995 (Supas 95). Jakarta: Biro Pusat Statistik, 1996.
Government of Pakistan. 2007. Average Circulation of Newspapers and Periodicals by Language/Type, 1996–2006. In *Federal Bureau of Statistics*, Federal Bureau of Statistics, www.statpak.gov.pk/depts/fbs/statistics/social_statistics/periodicals_by_language.pdf.
Pakistan 2000 Agricultural Census. Islamabad: Federal Bureau of Statistics, Government of Pakistan, 2000.
Population and Housing Census of Pakistan 1998, Vols. 1–5. 127 vols. Islamabad: Population Census Organisation (Pakistan), 1998.
Population and Housing Census; Advance Tabluation on Sex, Age Group, Marital Status, Literacy and Educational Attainment (Figures Provisional). 127 vols. Vol. VI. Islamabad: Population Census Organisation, Statistics Division, 1998.
Government of Pakistan, Central Statistical Office. *25 Years of Pakistan in Statistics*. Karachi: Government of Pakistan, 1972.
Government of Pakistan, Education Division. *Six-Year National Plan of Educational Development for Pakistan*. 2 vols. Karachi: Government of Pakistan Press, 1952.
Government of Pakistan, Ministry of Education. *Development of Education in Pakistan (1978–80): Country Report for the 38th Session of International Conference on Education, Geneva, 10–19 November 1981*. Islamabad: Government of Pakistan, Ministry of Education, 1981.
The Education Policy, 1972–1980. Islamabad: Government of Pakistan, 1972.
Report of the Commission on National Education, January-August 1959. Karachi: Government of Pakistan Press, 1960.
Government of Pakistan, Ministry of Education (Bureau of Educational Planning and Management). *Major Trends in Education: Report Presented at the 36th Session of the International Conference on Education, Ibe/Unesco Geneva, September 1977*. Islamabad: Printing Corporation of Pakistan Press, 1977.
Government of Pakistan, Ministry of Education (Curriculum Wing). *Development of Education in Pakistan, 1973/75*. Islamabad: Government of Pakistan, Ministry of Education (Curriculum Wing), Examination Reforms and Research Sector, 1975.
Gramsci, Antonio. *Selections from Cultural Writings*. Translated by William Boelhower. Edited by David Forgacs and Geoffrey Nowell-Smith. Cambridge: Harvard University Press, 1985.
Hanaway, William L., and Mumtaz Nasir. "Chapbook Publishing in Pakistan." In *Studies in Pakistani Popular Culture*, edited by William L. Hanaway and Wilma Heston, 339–614. Lahore: Lok Virsa Publications and Sang-e-Meel Publications, 1996.
Hansen, Miriam. "Forward." In *Public Sphere and Experience: Toward an Analysis of the Bourgeois and Proletarian Public Sphere*, edited by Oskar Negt

and Alexander Kluge, ix–xlix. Minneapolis: University of Minnesota Press, 1993.
Haqqani, Husain. *Pakistan: Between Mosque and Military*. Washington, DC: Carnegie Endowment for International Peace, 2005.
Hasan, Khalid. Telephone interview, March 19, 2003.
Hastings, Adi. "Signifying Sanskrit in Hindu Revivalist and Nationalist Discourse." Paper presented at the Semiotics: Culture in Context workshop, University of Chicago, 2002.
Herder, Johann Gottfried. "National Genius and the Environment." In *Reflections on the Philosophy of the History of Mankind*, 3–78. Chicago: University of Chicago Press, 1968 [1784].
Heryanto, Ariel. "The Development Of 'Development'." *Indonesia* **46** (1988): 1–24.
  Language of Development and Development of Language: The Case of Indonesia. No. 86, Pacific Linguistics, Series D. Canberra: Department of Linguistics, Research School of Pacific Studies, The Australia National University, 1995.
Hobsbawm, E.J. *Nations and Nationalism since 1780*. Cambridge: Cambridge University Press, 1992 [1990].
Hobsbawm, E.J., and Terence Ranger, eds. *The Invention of Tradition*. Cambridge: Cambridge University Press, 1983.
Hoffman, John. "A Foreign Investment: Indies Malay to 1901." *Indonesia* **27** (1979): 65–92.
Hoodbhoy, Pervez. "Preface: Out of Pakistan's Education Morass: Possible? How?" In *Education and the State: Fifty Years of Pakistan*, edited by Pervez Hoodbhoy, 1–22. Karachi: Oxford University Press, 1998.
Hoodbhoy, Pervez Amirali, and Abdul Hameed Nayyar. "Rewriting the History of Pakistan." In *Islam, Politics and the State: The Pakistan Experience*, edited by Mohammad Asghar Khan, 164–77. London: Zed Books, 1985.
Huntington, Samuel P. *Who Are We? The Challenges to America's National Identity*. New York: Simon and Schuster, 2004.
Hyder, Qurratulain. *River of Fire (Aag Ka Darya)*. Translated by Qurratulain Hyder. New Delhi: Kali for Women, 1998.
Irvine, Judith T., and Susan Gal. "Language Ideology and Linguistic Difference." In *Regimes of Language*, edited by Paul Kroskrity. Santa Fe: School of American Research Press, 2000.
Islam, Rafiqul. "The Bengali Language Movement and Emergence of Bangladesh." *Contributions to Asian Studies* **XI** (1977): 142–52.
  "The Language Movement." In *Bangladesh: Volume One, History and Culture*, edited by S.R. Chakravarty and Virendra Narain, 147–61. New Delhi: South Asian Publishers, 1986.
Jackson, Jean. "Language Identity of the Colombia Vaupes Indians." In *Explorations in the Ethnography of Speaking*, edited by Richard Bauman and Joel Sherzer, 50–64. New York: Cambridge University Press, 1974.
Jaffrelot, Christophe, ed. *Pakistan: Nationalism without a Nation?* New Delhi, London, and New York: Manohar Publishers and Zed Books Ltd., 2002.
Jahan, Rounaq. *Pakistan: Failure in National Integration*. Dhaka: Oxford University Press, 1973.

Jalal, Ayesha. "Conjuring Pakistan: History as Official Imagining." *International Journal of Middle East Studies* **27**, no. 1 (1995): 73–89.

Self and Sovereignty: Individual and Community in South Asian Islam since 1850. London and New York: Routledge, 2000.

The Sole Spokesman: Jinnah, the Muslim League, and the Demand for Pakistan. Cambridge: Cambridge University Press, 1985.

Jalibi, Jamil. *Pakistan: The Identity of Culture.* Translated by Hadi Husain. Translation of "Pākistānī Kalcar," Urdu; 1964 edn. Karachi: Royal Book Company, 1984.

Pākistānī Kalcar: Qaumī Kalcar Kī Tashkīl Kā Masla. Karachi: Mushtaq Book Depot, 1964.

Qaumī Zabān: Yak Jehatī, Nifāz, Aur Masael. Islamabad: Muqtadira Qaumi Zaban (National Language Authority), 1989.

Jinnah, Mahomed Ali. *Quaid-i-Azam Mahomed Ali Jinnah: Speeches as Governor-General of Pakistan 1947–1948.* Karachi: Pakistan Publications, 1976.

Jones, Allen Keith. "Muslim Politics and the Growth of the Muslim League in Sind, 1935–1941." Unpublished thesis. Duke University, 1977.

Jones, Sir William. *Sacontalá; or, the Fatal Ring: An Indian Drama. By Cálidás. Translated from the Original Sanscrit and Prácrit.* London: Printed for Edwards by J. Cooper, 1790.

Kahut, Chaudhry Nazir. *Āo, Panjābī Ko Qatl Karen̲ [Come, Let's Kill Punjabi].* Karachi: Waris Shah Publications, 1992.

Kamran, Gilani. *Pakistan: A Cultural Metaphor.* Lahore: Ravian English Masters Association and Nadeem Book House, 1993.

Kanjoo, Abdul Majid. Conference presentation, Sustainable Development Policy Institute (Islamabad), March 11, 2002.

Kaviraj, Sudipta. "The Imaginary Institution of India." In *Subaltern Studies VII: Writings on South Asian History and Society*, edited by Partha Chatterjee and Gyanendra Pandey, 1–39. Delhi, Oxford, and New York: Oxford University Press, 1992.

"The Two Histories of Literary Culture in Bengal." In *Literary Cultures in History*, edited by Sheldon Pollock, 503–66. Berkeley: University of California Press, 2003.

"Writing, Speaking, Being: Language and the Historical Formation of Identities in India." In *Nationalstaat Und Sprachkonflikt in Süd-Und Südostasien*, edited by Dagmar Hellmann-Rajanayagam and Dietmar Rothermund, 25–65. Stuttgart: Franz Steiner Verlag, 1992.

Keane, Webb. "Knowing One's Place: National Language and the Idea of the Local in Eastern Indonesia." *Cultural Anthropology* **12**, no. 1 (1997): 37–63.

"Public Speaking: On Indonesian as the Language of the Nation." *Public Culture* **15**, no. 3 (2003): 503–30.

Kennedy, Charles H. *Bureaucracy in Pakistan.* Karachi: Oxford University Press, 1987.

Khan, Adeel. "Pakistan's Sindhi Ethnic Nationalism: Migration, Marginalization, and the Threat of 'Indianization'." *Asian Survey* **42**, no. 2 (2002): 213–29.

Politics of Identity: Ethnic Nationalism and the State in Pakistan. New Delhi: Sage Publications India, 2005.

Kher, B.G. "Report of the Official Language Commission." New Delhi: Government of India Press, 1956.

King, Christopher R. *One Language, Two Scripts: The Hindi Movement in Nineteenth Century North India*. Bombay: Oxford University Press, 1994.

Kittler, Friedrich A. *Discourse Networks 1800/1900*. Translated by Michael Metteer with Chris Cullens. Stanford: Stanford University Press, 1990.

Kumar, Ann, and John McGlynn. *Illuminations: The Writing Traditions of Indonesia*. Jakarta and New York: Lontar Foundation and Weatherhill, 1996.

Kurasawa, Aiko. "Propaganda Media on Java under the Japanese 1942–1945." *Indonesia* **44** (1987): 59–117.

Laitin, David D. *Identity in Formation: The Russian-Speaking Populations in the Near Abroad*. Ithaca: Cornell University Press, 1998.

——— "Language Games." *Comparative Politics* **20**, no. 3 (1988): 289–302.

——— "Language Policy and Political Strategy in India." *Policy Sciences* **22**, no. 4 (1989): 415–36.

Latif, Amir. "Alarming Situation of Education in Pakistan." Review, UNESCO Education for All (2001). Online, available at: www.unesco.org/education/efa/know_sharing/grassroots_stories/pakistan_2.shtml.

Leghari, Dr. Abdul Jabbar Abid. *Tahrīk-e-Āzādī Men Sindh Kā Kirdār*. 2 vols. Hyderabad (Pakistan): Rahbar United Publications, 1992.

Lelyveld, David. "The Fate of Hindustani: Colonial Knowledge and the Project of a National Language." In *Orientalism and the Postcolonial Predicament*, edited by Carol A. Breckenridge and Peter van der Veer, 189–214. Philadelphia: University of Pennsylvania Press, 1993.

——— "Zuban-E-Urdu-E-Mu'Alla and the Idol of Linguistic Origins." *Annual of Urdu Studies* **9** (1994): 57–67.

Ludden, David. *India and South Asia: A Short History*. Oxford: Oneworld Publications, 2002.

Malik, Akram Ali. *Tārikh-e-Panjāb*. Lahore: Salman Matbu'at, 1990.

Malik, Fateh Mohammad. *Punjabi Identity*. Lahore: Sang-e-Meel, 1989.

Mansoor, Hasan. "Winners and Losers in the Great Sindh Game." *The Friday Times*, January 10–16, 2003.

Mansoor, Sabiha. *Punjabi, Urdu, English in Pakistan: A Sociolinguistic Study*. Lahore: Vanguard, 1993.

Manzoor, Manzoor Ahmed. *The Pakistan Problem: Historical Backwardness of Punjab and Consolidation of Pakistan*. Lahore: The Frontier Post Publications, 1993.

McGrath, Allen. *The Destruction of Pakistan's Democracy*. Karachi: Oxford University Press, 1998.

McGregor, Stuart. "The Progress of Hindi, Part 1: The Development of a Transregional Idiom." In *Literary Cultures in History*, edited by Sheldon Pollock, 912–57. Berkeley: University of California Press, 2003.

Midrar Naqshbandi, Midrarullah. *Khān Abdul Ghaffār Khān: siyāsat aur 'aqā'id*. Mardan: Idarah-yi Isha'at Midrarul'ulum, 1995.

Mill, James. *History of British India*. Edited by H.H. Wilson. (Wilson reissue with continuation from 1805ff.). 10 vols. London: James Madden, 1858 [1817].

Mir, Farina. "The Social Space of Language: Punjabi Popular Narrative in Colonial India, c.1850–1900." PhD dissertation, Columbia University, 2002.
Mirza, Sarfaraz Hussain. *Tasawwar-e-Pākistān Se Qarārdād-e-Pākistān Tak [From Imagining Pakistan to the Pakistan Resolution]*. Lahore: Pakistan Study Center, Punjab University, 1983.
Mirza, Shafqat Tanveer. *Resistance Themes in Punjabi Literature*. Lahore: Sang-e-Meel, 1992.
Mitchell, Jonathan. Telephone interview, March 12, 2002.
Moeliono, Anton. *Language Development and Cultivation: Alternative Approaches in Language Planning*. Translated by Kay Ikranagara. Edited by W. A. L. Stokhof. Pacific Linguistics, Series D, No.68, Materials in Languages of Indonesia (No. 30). Canberra: Department of Linguistics, Research School of Pacific Studies, The Australian National University, 1986.
Nair, Janaki. "Kannada and Politics of State Protection." *Economic and Political Weekly*, October 29, 1994, 2853–4.
Nanak, Guru. *Kalām-e-Nānak*. Translated by Jeet Singh Sital. Lahore: APNA and Punjabi Heritage Foundation, 2002.
Nandy, Ashis. *The Intimate Enemy: Loss and Recovery of Self under Colonialism*. Delhi: Oxford India, 1983.
Nasr, Seyyed Vali Reza. *Islamic Leviathan: Islam and the Making of State Power*. New York: Oxford University Press, 2001.
Nayyar, A. H., and Ahmed Salim. *The Subtle Subversion: The State of Curricula and Textbooks in Pakistan (Urdu, English, Social Studies and Civics)*. Islamabad: Sustainable Development Policy Institute, 2002.
Nehru Memorial Museum and Library. "Khan Abdul Ghaffar Khan: A Centennial Tribute." New Delhi, 1995.
Newberg, Paula R. *Judging the State: Courts and Constitutional Politics in Pakistan*. Cambridge: Cambridge University Press, 1995.
Oberoi, Harjot. *The Construction of Religious Boundaries: Culture, Identity, and Diversity in the Sikh Tradition*. Chicago: The University of Chicago Press, 1994.
Oldenburg, Philip. "'A Place Insufficiently Imagined': Language, Belief, and the Pakistan Crisis of 1971." *Journal of Asian Studies* **44**, no. 4 (1985): 711–33.
Pakistan Academy of Letters. *Ban Lifted after 18 Years from Fakhar Zaman's 4 Books: Full Text of the Writ Petition & the Judgment of Lahore High Court*. Islamabad: Pakistan Academy of Letters, 1996.
Pakistan Educational Conference. *Proceedings of the Pakistan Educational Conference, Held at Karachi, from 27th November to 1st December 1947*. Reprint edn. Islamabad: Government of Pakistan, Ministry of the Interior (Education Division), 1983 [1947].
Pandey, Gyanendra. *The Construction of Communalism in Colonial North India*. Delhi: Oxford University Press, 1990.
Patel, Sardar Vallabhbhai, B. Pattabhi Sitaramayya, and Jawaharlal Nehru. *Report of the Linguistic Provinces Committee Appointed by the Jaipur Congress (Dec. 1948)*. New Delhi: Indian National Congress, 1953 [1949].
Pirzada, Syed Sharifuddin, ed. *Foundations of Pakistan: All-India Muslim League Documents: 1906–1947*. Vol. II, 1924–1947. Karachi: Ferozesons, 1970.

Platts, John T. *A Dictionary of Urdu, Classical Hindi, and English*. Sang-e-Meel (Lahore), 1994 edn. London: Crosby Lockwood and Son, 1911.
Pollock, Sheldon. "Cosmopolitan and Vernacular in History." *Public Culture* 12, no. 3 (2000): 591–625.
"India in the Vernacular Millenium: Literary Culture and Polity, 1000–1500." *Daedalus* 127, no. 3 (1998): 41–74.
"Introduction: From Literary History to Literary Cultures in History." In *Literary Cultures in History: Reconstructions from South Asia*, edited by Sheldon Pollock, 1–38. Berkeley, London: University of California Press, 2003.
The Language of the Gods in the World of Men: Sanskrit, Culture, and Power in Premodern India. Berkeley and London: University of California Press, 2006.
Pramoedya Ananta Toer. *Child of All Nations*. Translated by Max Lane. Vol. 2, Buru Quartet. New York: Penguin USA, 1996.
Footsteps. Translated by Max Lane. Vol. 3, Buru Quartet. New York: Penguin USA, 1996.
House of Glass. Translated by Max Lane. Vol. 4, Buru Quartet. New York: Penguin USA, 1996.
This Earth of Mankind. Translated by Max Lane. Vol. 1, Buru Quartet. New York: Penguin USA, 1996.
Prasad, Bimal. *The Foundations of Muslim Nationalism*. Vol. 1, Pathway to India's Partition. New Delhi: Rajendra Prasad Academy and Manohar, 1999.
A Nation Within a Nation. Vol. 2, Pathway to India's Partition. New Delhi: Rajendra Prasad Academy and Manohar, 2000.
Pritchett, Frances W. "Introduction to Excerpts from Āb-e-Hayāt." *Annual of Urdu Studies* 13 (1998): 37–53.
Nets of Awareness: Urdu Poetry and Its Critics. Berkeley: University of California Press, 1994. Online, available at: http://ark.cdlib.org/ark:/13030/ft10000326/
Puri, Girdhari Lal. *Khan Abdul Ghaffar Khan, a True Servant of Humanity*. New Delhi: Congress Centenary (1985) Celebration Committee, AICC(I), 1985.
Qadir Yar. *Puran Bhagat / Qādir Yār*. Translated by Taufiq Rafat. Introduction by Athar Tahir edn. Lahore: Vanguard Books, 1983.
Qureshi, Mufti Ghulam Sarwar Zahib. *Tārikh-e-Makhzan-e-Panjāb*. Lahore: Dost Associates, 1996.
Qureshi, Regula. "Recorded Sound and Religious Music." In *Media and the Transformation of Religion in South Asia*, edited by Lawrence A. Babb and Susan S. Wadley. Philadelphia: University of Pennsylvania Press, 1995.
Radhakrishnan, N. *Khan Abdul Ghaffar Khan: The Apostle of Nonviolence*. New Delhi: Gandhi Smriti and Darshan Samiti, 1998.
Rahman, Tariq. *The History of the Urdu-English Controversy*. Vol. 311, Silsilah-e-Matbu'at-e-Muqtādirah-e-Qaumī Zabān. Islamabad: National Language Authority (Government of Pakistan), 1996.
Language, Education, and Culture. Islamabad: Oxford University Press and Sustainable Development Policy Institute, 1999.

Language, Ideology and Power: Language-Learning Among the Muslims of Pakistan and North India. Karachi: Oxford University Press, 2002.
"Language Policy in Pakistan." *Ethnic Studies Report* **14**, no. 1 (1996): 73–98.
Language and Politics in Pakistan. Karachi: Oxford University Press, 1996.
"Language, Politics and Power in Pakistan: The Case of Sindh and Sindhi." *Ethnic Studies Report* **17**, no. 1 (1999): 21–34.
"The Pashto Language and Identity-Formation in Pakistan." *Contemporary South Asia* **4**, no. 2 (1995): 151–70.
"The Punjabi Movement in Pakistan." *International Journal of the Sociology of Language* **122** (1996): 73–88.
"The Sindhi Language Movement and the Politics of Sind." *Ethnic Studies Report* **14**, no. 1 (1996): 99–116.
"The Siraiki Movement in Pakistan." *Language Problems and Language Planning* **19**, no. 1 (1995): 1–26.
"The Urdu-English Controversy in Pakistan." *Modern Asian Studies* **31**, no. 1 (1997): 177–207.
Rai, Alok. *Hindi Nationalism.* New Delhi: Orient Longman, 2000.
"Making a Difference: Hindi, 1880–1930." *Annual of Urdu Studies* **10** (1995): 134–49.
Rai, Amrit. *A House Divided: The Origin and Development of Hindi/Hindavi.* Delhi: Oxford University Press, 1984.
Rakisitis, C. G. P. "Centre-Province Relations in Pakistan under President Zia: The Government's and the Opposition's Approaches." *Pacific Affairs* **61**, no. 1 (1988): 78–97.
Ramage, Douglas E. *Politics in Indonesia: Democracy, Islam, and the Ideology of Tolerance.* New York: Routledge, 1995.
Ramaswamy, Sumathi. *Passions of the Tongue: Language Devotion in Tamil India, 1891–1970.* Berkeley: University of California Press, 1997.
Ramey, Mohammad Hanif. *Panjāb Kā Muqaddamah [The Case of Punjab].* Lahore: Jang Publishers, 1985.
Rao, Velcheru Narayana, David Shulman, and Sanjay Subrahmanyam. *Textures of Time: Writing History in South India, 1600–1800.* New Delhi: Permanent Black, 2001.
Rashid, Abbas, and Farida Shaheed. "Pakistan: Ethno-Politics and Contending Elites." Geneva: United Nations Research Institute on Social Development, 1993.
Rasool, Abdur. *Pāk-o-Hind Kī Islāmī Tārikh.* Lahore: M.R. Brothers, 1964.
Tārikh-e-Pāk-o-Hind, Hissa Awwal: Ta 1707. Lahore: M.R. Brothers, 1965.
Tārikh-e-Pāk-o-Hind, Hissa Duwam: 1707 Ta 'Ahd-e-Hazrah. Lahore: M.R. Brothers, 1966.
Riggs, Fred W. "The Rise and Fall of 'Political Development'." In *The Handbook of Political Behavior, Vol. 4,* edited by Samuel Long, 289–348. New York: Plenum Press, 1989.
Rittenberg, Stephen. *Ethnicity, Nationalism, and the Pakhtuns: The Independence Movement in India's North-West Frontier Province.* Durham: Carolina Academic Press, 1988.
Robinson, Francis. *Separatism Among Indian Muslims: The Politics of the United Provinces' Muslims, 1860–1923.* London: Cambridge University Press, 1974.

Separatism Among Indian Muslims: The Politics of the United Provinces' Muslims 1860–1923. 2nd edn. New Delhi: Oxford University Press, 1993.

Ruggie, John Gerard. "Territoriality and Beyond: Problematizing Modernity in International Relations." *International Organization* **47** (1993): 139–74.

Rustow, Dankwart A. "Language, Modernization, and Nationhood – an Attempt at Typology." In *Language Problems of Developing Nations*, edited by Joshua A. Fishman, Charles A. Ferguson, and Jyotirindra Das Gupta, 87–105. New York: John Wiley & Sons, 1968.

Rutherford, Danilyn. "Frontiers of the Lingua Franca: Malay, Meeforsch, and the Papuan Soul." Unpublished manuscript, n.d.

Raiding the Land of the Foreigners: The Limits of the Nation on an Indonesian Frontier. Princeton: Princeton University Press, 2002.

Sabir, Muhammad Shafi`a. *Tahrīk-e-Pākistān men Subah-e-Sarhad Kā Hissah [NWFP's Part in the Pakistan Movement]*. Peshawar: University Book Depot, 1990.

"Safdar Mir Passes Away." *Dawn*, August 10, 1998.

Salim, Ahmed. "Historical Falsehoods and Inaccuracies." In *The Subtle Subversion: The State of Curricula and Textbooks in Pakistan*, edited by A. H. Nayyar and Ahmed Salim, 65–75. Islamabad: Sustainable Development Policy Institute, 2002.

Samad, Yunus. "Pakistan or Punjabistan: Crisis of National Identity." In *Punjabi Identity: Continuity and Change*, edited by G. Singh and Ian Talbot, 61–86. Delhi: Manohar, 1996.

Samuel, Jérôme. "Modernisation Lexicale Et Politique Terminologique: Le Cas De l'Indonesien." PhD thesis, Institut National des Langues et Civilisations Orientales, 2000.

Sarkar, Sumit. "The Limits of Nationalism." *Seminar*, no. **522** (2003).

Savarkar, Vinayak Damodar. *Hindutva: Who Is a Hindu?* 4th edn. Poona: S.P. Gokhale, 1949.

Sayeed, Khalid Bin. *Pakistan: The Formative Phase, 1857–1948*. 2nd edn. London, New York, and Karachi: Oxford University Press, 1968.

Schimmel, Annemarie. *Sindhi Literature*. Vol. 8, Part 2, fasc. 4, A History of Indian Literature. Wiesbaden: Harrassowitz, 1974.

Scott, James C. *Seeing Like a State: How Certain Schemes to Improve the Human Condition Have Failed*. New Haven: Yale University Press, 1998.

Shackle, Christopher. "Punjabi in Lahore." *Modern Asian Studies* **4**, no. 3 (1970): 239–67.

"Siraiki: A Language Movement in Pakistan." *Modern Asian Studies* **11**, no. 3 (1977): 379–403.

Shackle, Christopher, and Rupert Snell. *Hindi and Urdu since 1800: A Common Reader*. London: School of Oriental and African Studies, 1990.

Shahab, Qudratullah. *Shahābnāma*. Lahore: Sang-e-Meel, 1987.

Shahjahanpuri, Abu Salman. *Khutūt, Tahrīk-e Reshmī Rumāl Aur Sindh: Tārikh-e Āzādī-i Vatan Kī Ek Azimushan Tahrīk*. Lahore: Fiction House, 1997.

Shils, Edward. "Primordial, Personal, Sacred and Civil Ties: Some Particular Observations on the Relationships of Sociological Research and Theory." *British Journal of Sociology* **8**, no. 2 (1957): 130–45.

Sibte Hasan. *The Battle of Ideas in Pakistan*. Karachi: Pakistan Publishing House, 1986.

Siddiqi, Hafeez-ur Rahman, and Ahmed Anas. *Tālimī Pālisī, 1979: Do Sālah Amaldarāmad, Jaiza Aur Tajāvīz*. Islamabad: Institute of Policy Studies, 1981.
Siegel, James T. *Fetish, Recognition, Revolution*. Princeton: Princeton University Press, 1997.
Solo in the New Order: Language and Hierarchy in an Indonesian City. Princeton: Princeton University Press, 1986.
Silverstein, Michael. "Language Structure and Linguistic Ideology." In *The Elements: A Parasession on Linguistic Units and Levels*, edited by Paul R. Clyne, 193–247. Chicago: Chicago Linguistic Society, 1979.
Slade, E. H. "Census of Pakistan, 1951." Government of Pakistan, 1951.
Suny, Ronald Grigor. "Back and Beyond: Reversing the Cultural Turn?" *The American Historical Review* **107**, no. 5 (2002): 1476–99.
"Constructing Primordialisms: Old Histories for New Nations." *Journal of Modern History* **73** (2001): 862–96.
"History." In *Encyclopedia of Nationalism*, edited by Alexander J. Motyl, 335–58. San Diego: Academic Press, 2001.
The Revenge of the Past: Nationalism, Revolution, and the Collapse of the Soviet Union. Stanford: Stanford University Press, 1993.
Suny, Ronald Grigor, and Michael D. Kennedy, eds. *Intellectuals and the Articulation of the Nation*. Ann Arbor: University of Michigan Press, 1999.
Syed, Najm Hosain. *Ik Rāt Rāvī Dī*. 2nd edn. Lahore: Rut Lekha, 2000 [1983].
Recurrent Patterns in Punjabi Poetry. Lahore: Majis Shah Hussein, 1968.
Sīdhān. 2nd edn. Lahore: Majlis Shah Hussein, 1973 [1968].
Takht-e-Lāhor: Dulla Dī Vār. Lahore: Majlis Shah Hussein, 1972.
Tahir, Athar. "A Coat of Many Colors: The Problematics of Qadiryar." Edited by Pritam Singh and Shinder Singh Thandi, 55–68. New Delhi: Oxford University Press, 1999.
Talbot, Ian. "From Pakistan to Punjabistan? Region, State and Nation Building." *International Journal of Punjabi Studies* **5**, no. 2 (1998): 179–91.
Khizr Tiwana: The Punjab Unionist Party and the Partition of India. Oxford and Karachi: Oxford University Press, 2002.
Pakistan: A Modern History. Lahore: Vanguard Books Pvt. Ltd., 1999.
"The Punjabization of Pakistan." In *Pakistan: Nationalism without a Nation?*, edited by Christophe Jaffrelot, 51–62. New Delhi, London, and New York: Manohar; Zed Books, 2002.
Tambiah, Stanley J. *Leveling Crowds: Ethnonationalist Conflicts and Collective Violence in South Asia*. Berkeley and London: University of California Press, 1996.
"The Nation-State in Crisis and the Rise of Ethnonationalism." In *The Politics of Difference: Ethnic Premises in a World of Power*, edited by Edwin N. Wilmsen and Patrick McAllister. Chicago: The University of Chicago Press, 1996.
Thapar, Romila. *Somanatha: The Many Voices of an Indian History*. New Delhi: Penguin | Viking, 2004.
Trivedi, Harish. "The Progress of Hindi, Part 2: Hindi and the Nation." In *Literary Cultures in History: Reconstructions from South Asia*, edited by Sheldon Pollock, 958–1022. Berkeley: University of California Press, 2003.

Trivedi, Lisa N. "Visually Mapping The 'Nation': Swadeshi Politics in Nationalist India, 1920–30." *Journal of Asian Studies* **62**, no. 1 (2003): 11–41.
Tufail, Khvajah Muhammad. *Tahrīk-e Pākistān men Siyālkot Kā Kirdār*. Siyalkot: Idarah-yi Matbu`at-i Tahrik-i Pakistan, 1987.
US Central Intelligence Agency. "The World Factbook 2007." CIA, 2007. Online, available at: www.cia.gov/cia/publications/factbook/index.html.
Verdery, Katherine. "Ethnicity, Nationalism, and State-Making; Ethnic Groups and Boundaries: Past and Future." In *The Anthropology of Ethnicity: Beyond 'Ethnic Groups and Boundaries,'* edited by Hans Vermeulen and Cora Govers, 33–58. Amsterdam: Het Spinhuis, 1994.
Verkaaik, Oskar. "The Captive State: Corruption, Intelligence Agencies, and Ethnicity in Pakistan." In *States of Imagination: Ethnographic Explorations of the Postcolonial State*, edited by Thomas Blom Hansen and Finn Stepputat. Durham: Duke University Press, 2001.
Migrants and Militants: "Fun" And Urban Violence in Pakistan. Princeton: Princeton University Press, 2004.
Vermeulen, Hans, and Cora Govers, eds. *The Anthropology of Ethnicity: Beyond 'Ethnic Groups and Boundaries.'* Amsterdam: Het Spinhuis, 1994.
Way, Peter O. *Detailed Statistics on the Urban and Rural Population of Indonesia: 1950–2010*. Washington, DC: US Bureau of the Census (Center for International Research), 1984.
Weaver, Mary Anne. *Pakistan: In the Shadow of Jihad and Afghanistan*. New York: Farar, Straus and Giroux, 2002.
Weber, Eugene. *Peasants into Frenchmen: The Modernization of Rural France, 1870–1914*. Stanford: Stanford University Press, 1976.
Weinbaum, Marvin, and Gautam Sen. "Pakistan Enters the Middle East." *Orbis* **22**, no. 3 (1978): 595–612.
Winstedt, Sir Richard. *A History of Classical Malay Literature*. Petaling Jaya: Malaysian Branch of the Royal Asiatic Society, 1991 [1940].
Woolard, Kathryn. "Introduction: Language Ideology as a Field of Inquiry." In *Language Ideologies: Practice and Theory*, edited by Bambi Schiefflin, Kathryn Woolard, and Paul Kroskrity. New York: Oxford University Press, 1998.
Wright, Theodore P., Jr. "Center-Periphery Relations and Ethnic Conflict in Pakistan: Sindhis, Muhajirs, and Punjabis." *Comparative Politics* **23**, no. 3 (1991): 299–312.
Yousaf, Mirza Muhammad. *A-One Textbook of Pakistan Studies*. Lahore: A-One Publisher, 1991.
Yule, Henry, and A.C. Burnell. *Hobson-Jobson: A Glossary of Colloquial Anglo-Indian Words and Phrases, and of Kindred Terms, Etymological, Historical, Geographic, and Discursive*. Reprint edn. London: Routledge & Kegan Paul, 1996 [1886].
Zahidi, Syed Masood. *Pākistān Kā Muqaddamah*. Lahore: Classic, 1988.
Zaidi, Z.H., ed. *Pakistan in the Making: 3 June–30 June 1947*. Vol. II, Quaid-i-Azam Mohammad Ali Jinnah Papers. 7 vols. Islamabad: National Archives of Pakistan, 1994.

Zaman, Fakhar. *The Alien (English Translation of Bewatna)*. Translated by Asif Javeed Mir. Lahore: Panda Books, 1995.
Bandīwān (Punjabi Original). 2nd edn first edition People's Publications, Lahore (1984) Lahore: Nigarshaat, 1987.
Bewatan (Urdu Translation). Translated by Sitar Tahir. Lahore: Classic, 1988.
Bewatna (Punjabi; Original). Lahore: People's Publications, 1987 [1984].
The Prisoner (English Translation of Bandīwān). Translated by Khalid Hasan. New Delhi, Bombay, Calcutta, and Madras: Allied Publishers Private Limited, 1984.
Qaidi (Urdu Translation of Bandīwān). Translated by Shaista Habib. Lahore: Classic, 1989.
Zaman, Mukhtar. *Thoughts on National Language Policy/Qaumī Zabān Kī Pālisī Ke Bāre men Cand Khyālāt*. Translated by Syed Faizi. Islamabad: National Language Authority/Muqtadira-e-Qaumi Zaban, 1985.
Zia, Shakil Ahmed. *Sindh Kā Muqaddamah: Hanīf Ramey Ke Muqaddamah-e-Panjāb Par Ahl-e-Sindh Kā Jawāb-e Da`va*. Karachi: Shabil Publications Limited, 1987.
Zulfaqar, Ghulam Hussain. *Jidd-o-Jahd-e-āzādī men Panjāb kā Kirdār*. Lahore: Idarah-e-Tahqiqat-e-Pakistan, 1996.

Index

Afghan war, 5, 55, 60–61
Āg kā daryā (Hyder), 31
Aga Khan III, 39
Aga Khan Rural Support Program, 39
Ahmad, Aijaz, 44
Ahmed, Ghulam, 130
Ahmedis, 130
Ahsan, Aitzaz, 138
  The Indus Saga and the Making of Pakistan, 138, 141, 142, 143
Alam, Muzaffar, 19
Ali, K., 125, 126, 141
Ali, Liaqat, 42, 43
Alisjahbana, Sutan Takdir, 178, 179–80
All-India Muslim League, 17, 18, 23, 24, 25, 27, 59, 74, 186
  importance of Urdu to, 23, 27, 28
All-India Radio, 166
Ambedkar, B.R., 160–61
Amjad, Yahya, *Tārīkh-e-Pākistān: Qadīm Daur* ("History of Pakistan: The Ancient Era"), 138, 140
Amrohvi, Rais, 53
Anderson, Benedict, 7, 9, 14, 69, 71–72, 103, 184
Anti-One Unit Front, 57, 60
Anwar, Riaz, 57
Āo, Panjābī Ko Qatl Karen ("Come, Let's Kill Punjabi", Kahut), 58, 77, 79
A-One Textbook of Pakistan Studies, 133–35
Arabic, 39–41
Awami League, 46
Awami National Party, 61
Awan, M.J., *Tahrīk-e-āzādī men Panjāb kā Kirdār* ("Punjab's Role in the Freedom Movement"), 138, 145
Ayub Khan, Muhammad, 34, 39–40, 45, 57
Azad, Maulana, 135
Aziz, K.K., 124
  The Murder of History in Pakistan, 124

Bahasa Indonesia language 15, 45, 155, 171–85
Balai Pustaka (publishing house), 154, 177
Balibar, Etienne, 9
Balochi, 62–63
Balochistan, 62–63
Balochistan Mother Tongue Use Bill, 63
Bandīwān (Zaman), 77, 82–84
Bangladesh, history, 4–5, 42–46
barrak, 96
Barth, Fredrik, *Ethnic Groups and Boundaries*, 29
Bengal
  efforts to make more "Islamic", 44
  problems with Urdu, 41–46
  replacement of Persian with Bengali, 21–22
Bengali, *see also* Bengal, problems with Urdu
  denial of official role, 41–42
  "Indic" appearance, 44
  replacing Persian as court language, 21–22
  usage in 1951, 32
Bewatna (Zaman), 79, 80–81, 83
Bhutto, Benazir, 35
Bhutto, Zulfiqar Ali, 34, 53–54, 76, 129, 130–31
birādarī networks, 96
Bizenjo, Ghaus Baksh, 62
BMM (Bhawalpur Mutaheda Mahaz), 57–58
Bombay Presidency, 49–50
Bourdieu, Pierre, 69, 156
Brahui, 62
British colonizers, assumptions made by, 20–22
Bugti, Nawab Akbar, 62

Cabinet Mission Plan, 134, 146, 194
census data (Pakistan), 32, 43, 56, 58, 70, 71, 73

India, 160
Indonesia, 182
chapbooks, 92–93
Chaudhry, Muhammad Azam, *Tahrīk-e-Pākistān Men Panjāb kā Kirdār* ("Punjab's Role in the Pakistan Movement"), 138
cinema, *see also* Hamārī Zabān (film)
  see also Maula Jaṭ (film)
  Punjabi heroes in, 93–99
cirāghān dā melā festival, 75, 82
Cohn, Bernard, 150, 153–54
"Come, Let's Kill Punjabi" (*Āo, Panjābī Ko Qatl Karen*, Kahut), 58, 77, 79
Connor, Walker, 12
Cultural Zones Scheme, 120
culture, and nation, 1–8, 11, 27, 29, 102, 105, 149, 188–92
Curriculum Wing, 123–24

Dani, Ahmed Hasan, 138
Das Gupta, Jyotirindra, 157–58, 162, 168
Dave, Bhavna, 10
Dhaka University, protests, 42, 45
dichotomizing oppositions, 28, 46, 63, 165
Doordarshan (India's state television), 166
Dow, Alexander, 127
Dulla Bhatti (historical character), 76, 85, 102, 191
Dullah Bhatti Institute, 85
Durrand Line, 59

East Bengal, Bengali language, 23, 32, 41–46
ekushe ("twenty-one," Feb. 21), 41, *see also* February 21st
Eley, Geoff, 72–73, 151
Encyclopedia of Islam (1938 edn), entry for Pakistan, 25–26
English, 36–39, 160–62
Ethnic Groups and Boundaries (Barth), 29

Farani, Saeed Ahmad, *Panjābī Zabān Nahīn Maregī* ("The Punjabi Language Will Never Die"), 87–89, 90–91
Fareed, Baba, 82, 93
Farishta, Mohammad Qasim, 127–28
Faruqi, Shamsur Rahman, 19
"Father of Urdu," 16, 17
February 21st, 41, *see also ekushe*
Fort St. George College (Chennai), 154
Fort William College (Calcutta), 20–21, 154

French language, 2–3, 152

Gal, Susan, 17, 28
gandāsā, 94, 96
Gandhi, Mohandas Karamchand "Mahatma," 155
Gazdar, Mushtaq, 31, 96
Geertz, Clifford, 11, 63
Gellner, Ernest, 14, 71–72, 103, 192
Ghaffar Khan, Khan Abdul, 24, 59, 60, 135–36
Gujarati, 163
Gurdaspur-Kathiawad Salient, 142
Gurmukhi script (Punjabi), 23, 144

Hamārī Zabān (film), 31
Hamood ur-Rahman Education report, 38
Haq, Fazlul, 24
Haq, Maulvi Abdul "Father of Urdu", 16, 17
Hasan, Khalid, 77, 83
Herder, Johann Gottfried, 7–8
Herderianism, 8–9, 64, 164
  and language-as-nation, 155–58
Heryanto, Ariel, 182–83
Hilali, Maulana Khan Mir, 27
Hindi
  association with Hinduism, 22–23
  in India, 18–22, 160–62
  relationship to Urdu, 19–20
Hindi-Urdu controversy, 17–18, 21–22
Hīr-Rānjhā (Waris Shah), 82
History of British India (Mill), 127
historiography, 4, 14, 35, 82, 102, 106–49
Hobsbawm, Eric, 69, 151
Hoodbhoy, Pervez, 124–25
Hussain, Altaf, 54
Hussain, Shah, 75, 76, 82, 93, 100
Hyder, Qurratulain, *Āg kā daryā*, 31
Hyderabad, 50, 54–55

"Ideology of Pakistan", *see* Pakistan ideology
India (post-Independence), 191–92
  choice of national language, 158–62
  linguistic provinces, 162–66
  national literatures and the state, 166–69
Indian National Congress, 24, 59, 135, 146, 163, 168
Indonesia, 171–85
  Bahasa Indonesia language, 174–80
  comparison with Pakistan, 172–74, 184, 185–87, 192

Indonesia (*cont.*)
    national language development, 180–85
Indus Saga and the Making of Pakistan, The (Ahsan), 138, 141, 142, 143
instrumentalism, 11–12
Iqbal, Mohammad, 4, 25, 194
Iqbāliat (musical genre), 31
Islamiyat, 40, 124, 129, 131, 133
Italian language, 2–3

Jalal, Ayesha, 5, 124, 125
Jalibi, Jamil, 16, 137
    Pākistānī Kalcar, 105
Javanese, 175–76
Jidd-o-Jahd-e-āzādī men Panjāb kā Kirdār ("Punjab's Role in the Independence Struggle," Zulfaqar), 139
Jidd-o-Jahd-e-āzādī men Sindh kā Kirdār ("Sindh's Role in the Independence Struggle," Leghari), 138
Jinnah, Mohammad Ali, 24, 34, 37, 41, 42–43, 186
Jones, Sir William, 154

Kahut, Chaudhry Nazir, 58
    Āo, Panjābī Ko Qatl Karen ("Come, Let's Kill Punjabi"), 58, 77, 79
Kamran, Gilani, 94–96
Karachi, 50, 54–55, *see also* University of Karachi
Khabrān (newspaper), 92
Khan Sahib, Dr., 59
Khan, Monem, 45
Khan, Wali, 59, 124
Khudai Khidmatgars, 24, 135
Krishak Praja Party, 24

Lahore Resolution, 25, 105, 136, 186
Laitin, David, 10
Language Day, 45, *see also* ekushe
language ideology, 6, 15, 17, 27, 32, 33, 44, 64, 73, 100, 101, 169, 172, 184, 186, 192
language paradox, 7, 10, 15, 158, 177, 185, 192
language planning, 150–58
Leghari, Abdul Jabbar Abid
    Jidd-o-Jahd-e-āzādī men Sindh kā Kirdār ("Sindh's Role in the Independence Struggle"), 138
    Tahrīk-e-āzādī men Sindh kā Kirdār ("Sindh's Role in the Freedom Movement"), 139
Leitner, G.W., 154
Lok Virsa, 34, 76

madāris, 39–40
madrasa, 39–40, 125, *see also madāris*
madrassah, *see madrasa* and *madāris*
Mahabharata (Javanese), 175–76
Mahabharata (Sanskrit), 126–27, 128
Majlis-e-Kabir Pakistan, 119
Malay, 174–75, 176, *see also* Bahasa Indonesia language
Malik, Akram Ali, *Tārīkh-e-Panjāb: Qadīm Daur ta Jang-e-āzādī 1857* ("History of Punjab: The Ancient Era to the War of Independence: 1857"), 139, 143
Malik, Fateh Muhammad, 140
    Punjabi Identity, 77, 139
Mansoor, Sabiha, 74, 88
Manzoor, Manzoor Ahmed,
    The Pakistan Problem, 139, 143
Marathi, 19, 161, 163
Masih, Yaqoob Ilyas, 65
Maulā Jaṭ (fictional character), 93, 96, 97–98, *see also* Rahi, Sultan
Maulā Jaṭ (film, 1979), 93–94
Mill, James, *History of British India*, 127
Mir, Safdar, 84
Mirza, Shafqat Tanveer, 76
    Resistance Themes in Punjabi Literature, 77, 84, 85
Mohajir Qaumi Movement, 49
mohajirs, 48–55
"Mohajirstan," 55
Movement for the Restoration of Democracy, 54
Mujib, Shaikh (Shaikh Mujibur Rahman), 46
Munnoo Bhai, 76
Muqtadira Qaumi Zaban (National Language Authority), 132
Murder of History in Pakistan, The (Aziz), 124
Musharraf, Pervez, 35–36
Muslim League, *see* All-India Muslim League
Muttahida Qaumi Movement, 49

Nanak, *Kalām-e-Nānak* ("The Writings of Nanak"), 139, 144
NAP (National Awami Party), 60, *see also* Awami National Party
nation
    and culture, 1–2
    and language, 2–3
    as having a single language, 7–9
    national language creation, 9–10
Nayyar, Abdul Hameed, 124–25
Nazimuddin, Khwaja, 45

North-West Provinces, replacement of Persian by Hindustani in the Arabic script, 21–22
Nur Khan, *Proposals for a New Educational Policy*, 38, 52–53
NWFP (Northwest Frontier Province)
  in Pakistan National History, 135–36
  language conflict, 5
  Pashto language, 23, 59–61, 62

Official Language Committee (*Majlis-e-Zaban-e-Daftari*), 37
Old Malay, 175
One Unit proposal, 41, 51–52
Oriya, replacement of Persian with, 21–22

Pāk, 25–26
Pakhtun (magazine), 59
"Pakhtunkhwa", 61
Pakistan, 188–89
  as ideology, 128–37
  as imagined in advance, 106–22
  creation of, 116–23, 147–49, 190–91
  necessity of, 105
  periodization, 126–28
  revisionist books, 138–47
  derivation of name, 25–26
  experience with the Urdu language, 5–6, 31–46
  implications of name, 27
  political history, 33–36
Pakistan ideology, 121–22, 125, 128, 131–34, 139, 140, 142, 144
Pakistan Movement, 4, 68, 85, 102, 106, 112, 121, 133, 134, 136, 138, 140, 144–47, 172, 194, 195
Pakistan Panjabi Adabi Board, 76
Pakistan People's Party (PPP), 46, 55, 57, 58, 60
Pakistan Problem, The (Manzoor), 139, 143
Pakistan Siraiki Party, 58
Pakistan: The Fatherland of the Pak Nation (Rahmat Ali), 106–22
Pākistānī Kalcar (Jalibi), 105, 137
Panjabi Adabi Board, 34
Panjāb kā Muqaddmah (Ramey), 77, 79–80, 84–85, 139, 140, 141–42, 143
Panjābī Zabān Nahī Maregī ("The Punjabi Language Will Never Die," Farani), 87–89, 90–91
Pashto, 23, 32, 59–61
  in Balochistan, 62
Pashtunistan, 59–61
Passions of the Tongue (Ramaswamy), 98
Pollock, Sheldon, 11, 28, 102, 167

Poras, Raja (historical character), 85, 102, 134, 191
Pramoedya Ananta Toer, 186
primordialism, 11
Proposals for a New Educational Policy (Nur Khan), 38, 52–53
Punjab, 70–73
  in Pakistan National History, 136
  lessons from, 99
  Multani language, 23
  Punjabi language, 23
  replacement of Persian by Urdu, 72
  Unionist Party in, 24
Punjabi, *see also* Punjabiyat movement
  in India, 163
  heroes, 84–86
  in cinema, 93–99
  marginalization of, 72–73
  usage in 1951, 32
Punjabi Identity (Malik), 77, 139
"Punjabi Language Will Never Die, The" (Farani), 87–89, 90–91
"Punjabistan", 70–71, 78
Punjabiyat movement, 6, 67–69, 73–74, 189–90
  cultural revival, 73–77
  literature of, 80–86
  popular culture, 87–99
  Punjabi language as "lost," 78–80
Puran Bhagat, 75, 85, 102
Pusat Bahasa, 181
Pushtu, *see* Pashto

Qadianis, 130
Qaiyum Khan, Abdul, 59–60
Qasim, Muhammad bin, 125, 126, 130, 134
Qureshi, I. H., 140
Qureshi, Mufti Ghulam Sarwar Zahib, *Tārīkh-e-Makhzan-e-Panjāb* ("History of the Treasures of Punjab"), 139, 143–44

Radio Pakistan, 31, 45, *see also* All-India Radio
Rahi, Sultan, 93, 94, 97, *see also* Maula Jat
Rahman, Fazlur, 37, 123
Rahman, Tariq, 36, 73, 124
Rahmat Ali, Choudhary, 25–26, 107–22, 140
  Pakistan: The Fatherland of the Pak Nation, 106–22
Rai, Alok, 19–20
Raja Poras, *see* Poras, Raja
Ramaswamy, Sumathi, *Passions of the Tongue*, 98

Ramayana (Javanese), 175–76
Ramayana (Sanskrit), 126–27
Ramey, Mohammad Hanif, 76, 84–85, 99
  Panjāb kā Muqaddmah, 77, 79–80, 139, 140, 141–42, 143
Rashtra Bhasa Sangram Parishad (State Language Committee of Action), 42
Rasool, Sahibzada Abdur, 126
Renan, Ernest, 1
Report of the Commission on National Education (1960), 130
Resistance Themes in Punjabi Literature (Mirza), 77, 84, 85
Roman script, proposal to use, 45
Rushdie, Salman, 33

Sabir, Muhammad Shafi`a
  Tahrīk-e-Pākistān Me Subah-e-Sarhad kā Hissa ("NWFP's Part in the Pakistan Movement"), 139
  Tārī-e-Subah-e-Sarhad ("History of NWFP"), 139
Sahitya Akademi, 167
Salim, Ahmed, 133
Samuel, Jérôme, 183
Sanskrit, 20–21, 44, 48, 151, 154, 176
  cognates, 27
  spoken, 10
Sayed, G.M., 52
school Malay, 177
Scott, James, 6–7, 156
SDPI (Sustainable Development Policy Institute) report, 123–24, 133
Shackle, Christopher, 56
Shah, Bulleh, 82
Shah, Waris, 82, 93, *Hīr-Rānjhā*, 82
Shahab, Qudratullah, 188, 193–95
Shaikh, Aftab, 65
Sharif, Nawaz, 35, 63
Shils, Edward, 11
Shiva, as Punjabi, 142
Sind Adabi Board (Sind Literary Board), 52
Sindh, 48–55
  language conflict, 5
Sindhi Adabi Sangat (Sindhi Literary Society), 52, 53
Sindhi Day, 52
Sindhi language, 23, 32, 49–50
"Sindhu Desh", 55
Siraiki, 55–59
Siraiki language, 23
Siraiki Lok Sanjh, 58
Siraiki National Party, 58
Siraiki Qaumi Movement, 58
Six-Year National Plan for Education Development in Pakistan (1952), 129–30
Slade, E.H., 32
"Sleeping Beauty" theory of the nation, 105
-*stān* (suffix), 26–27
Sumpah Pemuda, 171, 176
Suny, Ronald Grigor, 7, 11, 72–73, 105, 151
Syed, Najm Hosain, 75–76, 84
Symbolic capital, 10, 14, 37, 55, 69, 92, 100-01, 103, 149, 190–91

Tagore, Rabindranath, 45
Tahrīk-e-āzādī men Panjāb kā Kirdār ("Punjab's Role in the Freedom Movement," Awan), 138, 145
Tahrīk-e-āzādī men Sindh kā Kirdār ("Sindh's Role in the Freedom Movement," Leghari), 139
Tahrīk-e-Pākistān Men Panjāb kā Kirdār ("Punjab's Role in the Pakistan Movement," Chaudhry), 138
Tahrīk-e-Pākistān Men Subah-e-Sarhad kā Hissa ("NWFP's Part in the Pakistan Movement," Sabir), 139
Talbot, Ian, 71, 136
Tamil, 98, 127, 150, 153, 161, 175, Tamilttay, 98
Tārīkh-e-Makhzan-e-Panjāb ("History of the Treasures of Punjab," Qureshi), 139, 143–44
Tārīkh-e-Pākistān: Qadīm Daur ("History of Pakistan: The Ancient Era," Amjad), 138, 140
Tārīkh-e-Panjāb: Qadīm Daur ta Jang-e-āzādī 1857 ("History of Punjab: The Ancient Era to the War of Independence: 1857," Malik), 139, 143
Tārīkh-e-Subah-e-Sarhad ("History of NWFP," Sabir), 139
tazkirah form, 147
television, *see* Doordarshan
Thapar, Romila, 127–28
thin simplifications, 156
Tiwana, Sir Khizr Hayat, 136
Two Nations Theory, 13, 16, 24, 108, 130, 134, 143, 148, 188, 194

Unionist Party, 24, 74, 136, 147, *see also* Tiwana, Sir Khizr Hayat
United Nations, 150
University of Karachi, 51
University of Sindh, 51, 53

Urdu, *see also* Hindi–Urdu controversy
  as national language, 31–33, 44, 189
  association with Islam, 22–23, 23–27
  comparison with planning Bahasa Indonesia, 171–174, 186
  emergence as national language of Pakistan, 16–17
  origins, 18–19
  privileging of, in Punjab, 72–73
  relationship to Hindi, 19–20
  usage in 1951, 32

Vali (poet), 20
vār verse form, 75
Vaupes Indians, 8
Verdery, Katherine, 29

Waris Shah Publications, 82

Weber, Eugene, 2, 152
Weber, Max, 155–56
World Punjabi Congress, 77
World Sindhi Congress, 49

Yahya Khan, Agha Mohammad, 34, 52–53
Yusuf, Kaniz Fatima, 140

Zulfaqar, *Jidd-o-Jahd-e-āzādī men Panjāb kā Kirdār* ("Punjab's Role in the Independence Struggle"), 139
Zaman, Fakhar, 67, 76, 77
  Bandīwān, 77, 82–84
  Bewatna, 79, 80–81, 83
Zia, Shakil Ahmed, 142
Zia-ul-Haq, Muhammad, 34–35, 40–41, 139–40